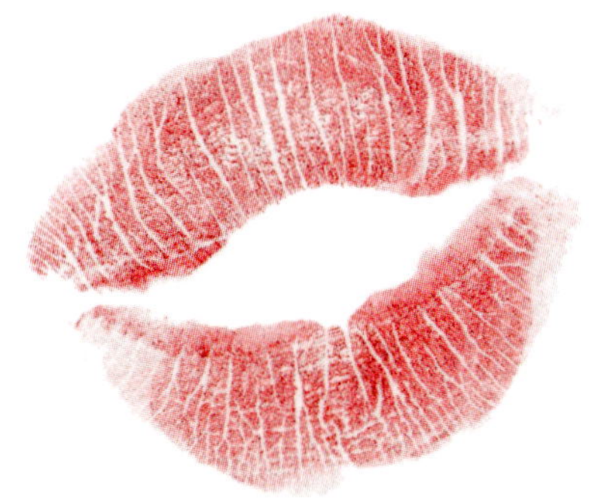

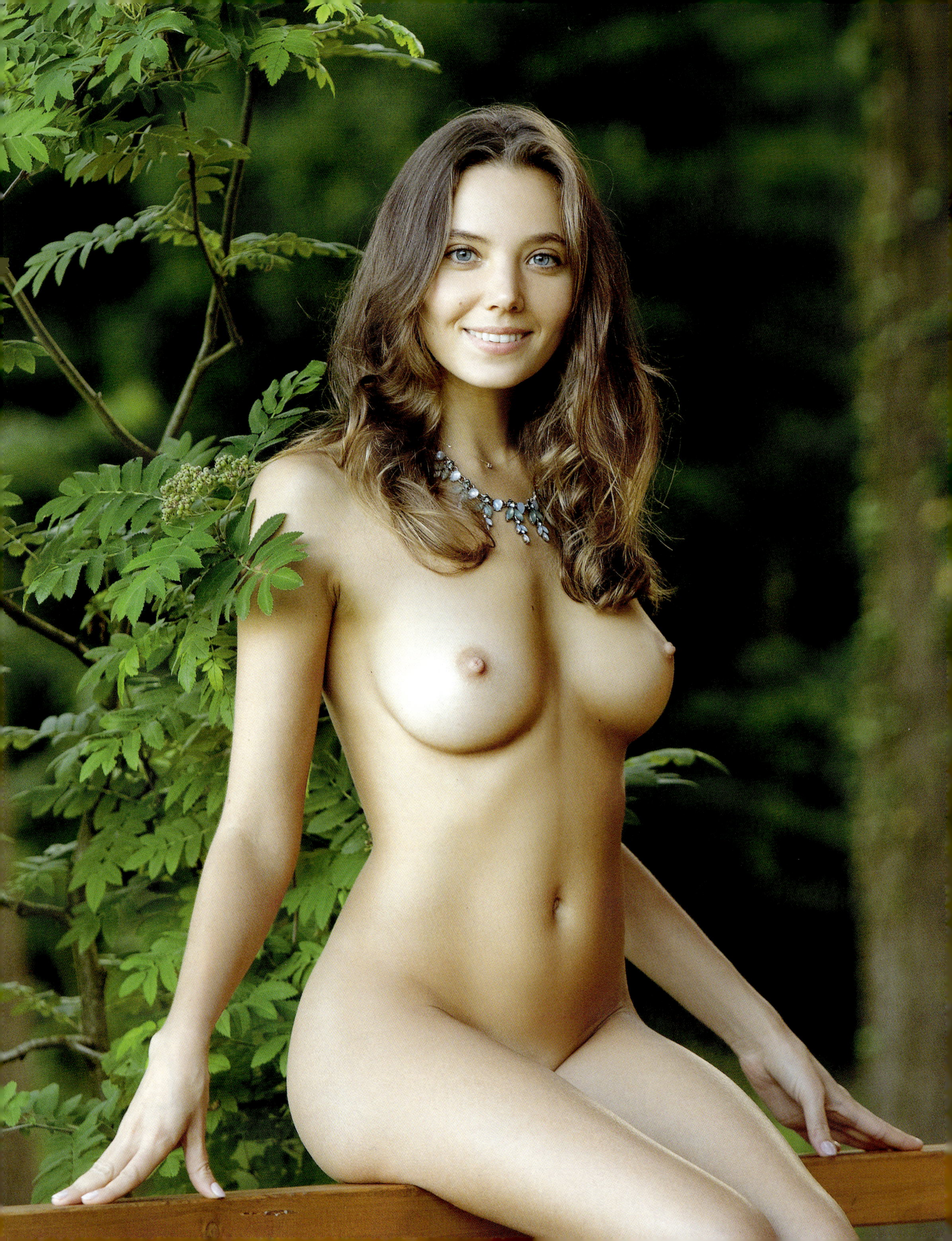

STEFAN SOELL

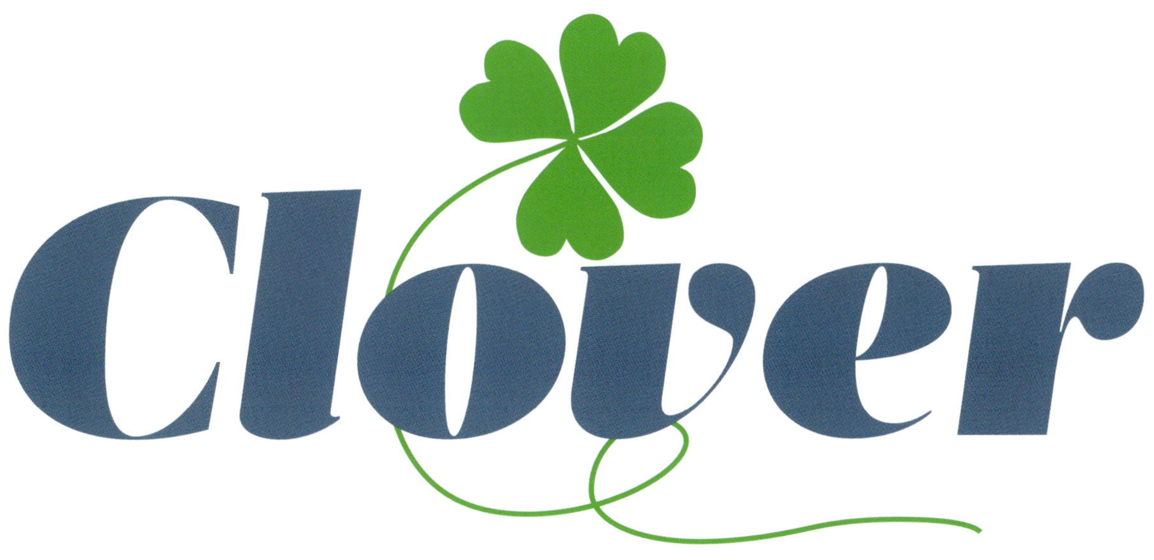

Clover

EDITION Skylight

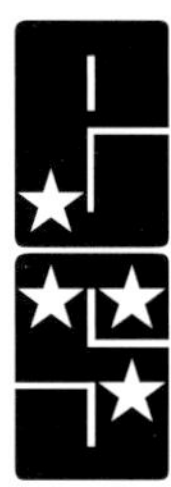

Second Edition 2025
First Edition 2023
Copyright © 2023 by Edition Skylight

EDITION SKYLIGHT
Rosengartenstr. 13B
CH-8608 Bubikon/Zürich
Switzerland
info@edition-skylight.com
www.edition-skylight.com

ISBN 978-3-03766-690-6

Bibliographic information published by Die Deutsche Bibliothek
Die Deutsche Bibliothek lists this publication in the
Deutsche Nationalbibliografie; detailed bibliographic data
are available in the Internet at http://dnb.ddb.de.

www.stefansoell.de
English text editing: Eugene Edwards

Printed in Bosnia and Herzegovina

Clover

Ich wurde im November 1989 auf Sachalin, Russlands grösster Insel, geboren. Die Insel ist ungefähr so gross wie die Schweiz und die Niederlande zusammen. Wie in so vielen Gegenden Russlands leben dort verschiedene Nationalitäten zusammen, Russen, Koreaner, Japaner u.v.a. Ich habe an einer englischsprachigen Schule studiert, bei verschiedenen Lehrern aus England und den U.S.A., was für Russland recht ungewöhnlich war. Erst heute realisiere ich, was für eine grossartige Grundlage mir die Englischkenntnisse für meinen internationalen Lebensstil mitgegeben haben. So viele Russen versäumen die internationalen Möglichkeiten, weil sie kein fliessendes Englisch sprechen können.

Nach dem Realschulabschluss setzte ich meine Ausbildung an der Sachalin State University für Orientalistik fort und studierte für 5 Jahre Koreanische Sprache und Kultur. Ausserdem verbrachte ich ein fünfmonatiges Praktikum in Süd-Korea. Während des Studiums verdiente ich Geld in Teilzeit als Buchhalterin in der Öl-Industrie bei einer russisch-holländischen Firma. Ich arbeitete dort bis zu meinem Abschluss mit 23. Auf Sachalin ist einem Asien viel näher als Moskau, der Flug dorthin dauert 10 Stunden. Meine Mutter hatte sich entschlossen, mir die Welt zu zeigen und so reisten wir jedes Jahr in Asien herum. In Europa war ich bis zum 23. Lebensjahr nur in der Türkei, dafür aber in so vielen asiatischen Ländern. Diese frühen Kontakte zu vielen verschiedenen Ländern, Kulturen und Klimazonen liessen mich realisieren wie unterschiedlich und wunderschön die Welt und die menschliche Rasse ist. Rückblickend glaube ich, es war ein grosser Vorteil in einer so vielfältigen Kultur wie auf Sachalin aufzuwachsen, da man andere Perspektiven einnehmen kann als das in «monogamen» Kulturen der Fall ist, wo einfach zwischen «uns» und «denen» und «falsch» und «richtig» unterschieden wird. Als Kind zeigte mir meine Mutter viele Aktivitäten, z.B. Musik, Tanzen und Schauspielerei, aber nur das Tanzen habe ich wirklich geliebt. Ich habe halb-professionell für 10 Jahre getanzt, bis zum 20. Lebensjahr. Danach hatte ich keine Zeit mehr alles gleichzeitig auszuüben; studieren, arbeiten und professionell zu tanzen. Heutzutage tanze ich nur noch selten. Dafür habe ich eine

I was born in November, 1989 on Sakhalin, Russian's largest island, which is the size of Switzerland and the Netherlands combined. As with many places in Russia, Sakhalin is a place of mixed nationalities, with Russian, Korean, Japanese and many others living happily together. I studied at an English-speaking school where most of the subjects were taught in that language by American or British teachers, quite unusual for Russia. I now realize that English gave me a great foundation for the international lifestyle that I have now. So many Russians miss out on international opportunities by not learning to speak fluent English.

After high school, I continued my studies at Sakhalin State University's Oriental Studies programme, where I studied the Korean language and culture for the next five years. I also did a five-month internship in South Korea. During my studies, I earned money as a accountant, working part-time in a Russian-Dutch joint venture oil company. I worked there until graduating at 23. On Sakhalin, Asia feels so much closer than Moscow, which is a 10-hour flight away. My mother was determined to show me the world, and we traveled around Asia a couple of times each year. In Europe until I was 23 I had visited only Turkey, but before then I had been to many Asian countries. This exposure to different countries, cultures and climates at an early age made me realize how diverse and beautiful the world and the human race is. I think it was a huge advantage later in life to have grown up in a diverse culture like on Sakhalin, as it gives one a very different perspective than living in monogamous cultures, where there are clear lines separating "us" from "them", and "wrong" from "right". As a child, my mother made me try many activities, for example music, dancing and acting, but it was only dancing that I really fell in love with. I danced semi-professionally for more than 10 years until I was 20, and I simply did not have enough time to study, work and dance professionally. I don't dance very often nowadays, but I have developed another passion which is cooking. I love it and I think I'm pretty good at it! I have even seriously considered becoming a chef once I stop modeling. When I was in my early teens I was very con-

andere Leidenschaft entwickelt: das Kochen. Ich liebe es und ich glaube, darin bin ich ziemlich gut! Ich habe sogar im Sinn ein richtiger Chefkoch zu werden, wenn ich mit dem Modeln aufhöre. Als Teenager hatte ich Zweifel mit meinem Körper. Mich ärgerten die Jungs und Mädchen, ich sei zu dünn. So beneidete ich all die kurvigen Mädchen und dachte übergewichtig sei weitaus besser als dünn zu sein. Ich entwickelte volle Brüste erst mit 15, während andere Mädchen schon Jahre vorher dicke Brüste und runde Hinterteile hatten. Die bekamen all die Aufmerksamkeit der Jungs. Als ich jedoch in meiner Entwicklung aufgeholt hatte, begann ich meinen Körper zu mögen. Ich realisierte, dass mein Schlanksein für jede Art von Sport vorteilhaft ist, dazu gehörte der Tanz und ich konnte mich in einem weiblichen sexy Stil kleiden, ohne dabei vulgär zu wirken. Ich erkannte auch, wie sehr es mir gefiel nackt zu sein, speziell draussen in der Natur. Ich liebte die Schönheit des menschlichen Körpers und entwickelte ein Interesse am Nudismus. Ich finde, Menschen sollten sich Ihrer Nacktheit nicht schämen. Bis heute besuche ich jedes Jahr FKK-Bereiche. Als ich nach meiner Universitätszeit anfing, nach einem richtigen Job zu suchen, entdeckte ich zufällig über das Internet das Modeln.

Mein damaliger Freund war Fotograf und wir machten eine Menge Aktfotos von mir, nur so aus Spass. Wir stellten fest, dass man damit leicht Geld verdienen konnte und wir verkauften jede Menge Fotos an eine Website-Agentur, spezialisiert auf Amateur-Aktfotos. Ein halber Tag mit Fotografieren und Filmen brachte ungefähr doppelt so viel ein wie meine Arbeit bei der Öl-Firma. Es ging jedoch nicht nur ums Geld: wir hatten eine Menge Spass und sammelten neue Erfahrungen. Wir entschlossen uns, eigene Fotos und Filme zu produzieren, nach heutigem Standard war das amateurhaft. Darüber hatten wir ja nicht gross nachgedacht, aber bald nachdem wir damit begonnen hatten, kontaktierte uns Petter Hegre, der uns nach Barcelona für eine dreitägige Foto- und Videosession einlud. Das war die erste richtige Fotosession mit einem professionellen Fotografen. Ich liebte die sexuelle Aufgeladenheit und das Posieren und in diesen drei Tagen probierte ich alle möglichen Sachen vor der Kamera aus. Es fühlte sich an wie ein Trainingslager für erotische Video- und Fotoproduktion. Das war wirklich intensiv, wir arbeiteten die ganzen Tage durch, experimentierten mit verschiedenen Einstellungen und Aktivitäten bis ich realisierte, was ich mochte und was nicht.

Die gute Sache an dieser gesammelten Erfahrung: ich merkte mit welchen Leuten ich professionell arbeiten wollte und welche Qualität und künstlerische Um-

scious about my body. I was teased by both boys and girls about being too thin, and I really envied curvy girls, often thinking that being overweight was far better than being thin. I didn't develop full breasts until I was 15, while other girls had big boobs and round butts a couple of years before me. They were the ones getting all the boys' attention. However, when I did catch up and matured sexually, I started to love my body. I realized that my slimness allowed me to practice any kind of sport, including dancing, and that dressing in a feminine, sexy way should not be perceived as vulgar. I also realized I loved being nude, and specially being nude outdoors. I fell in love with the beauty of the human body, and I developed an interest in nudism. I don't think people should feel ashamed of being seen in the nude. To this day, I try to visit a couple of areas reserved for nudists each year. When I was about to start searching for my first real job after University, I accidentally discovered internet modeling.

My then boyfriend was a photographer, and we used to do lots of nude pictures of me just for us, just for fun. We discovered that we could make easy money by taking and selling those pictures to a website specializing in amateur nudes. For a half day of shooting and filming we could get double the money I earned working part-time at the oil company. However, it was not all about money, but a lot of fun and a new experience. We decided to try and produce a few photos and videos by ourselves, but by today's standards they remain home-movie quality. We didn't think much about it, but very soon after we'd started, we were contacted by Peter Hegre, who wanted us to come and do a three-day photo and video session for him in Barcelona. This was the first time I had done a professional shoot with someone other than my boyfriend, and I liked the sense of sexual drive from being nude and acting. In those three days I tried out lots of things for the camera. It was like a bootcamp in erotic video and photo production! It was very intense, we worked all day long, experimenting with different set-ups and activities until I understood what I liked and what I didn't.

The good thing from all this experience is that I realized what kind of people I wanted to work with professionally, and what level of quality and artistic ideas I wanted to support. I realized that it is very important to have a personal ideology when working in this industry. Call it "moral standards", "ideology" or "agenda", but you have to have some philosophy that helps you to make the right choices. People will want you to do anything and everything, and there's enough money to pay for that, but I think that, as

setzung ich bevorzugte. Ich realisierte, wie wichtig es ist, eine eigene Art Ideologie in diesem Geschäft zu haben. Nennen wir es «Moralische Massstäbe», «Ideologie» oder «Agenda», aber man muss eine Philosophie verfolgen, um die richtigen Entscheidungen zu treffen. Die Leute wollen, dass Du Alles und Jedes tust, Geld ist für so etwas sicher genug zu ergattern. Aber ich glaube, als Model ist meine Arbeit ein Stempel der Qualität, mein Siegel des Einverständnisses. Wenn ich mich mit etwas nicht anfreunden kann, ich den Fotografen nicht mag, seine Arbeitsweise oder Website, dann sage ich «Nein». Es ist wichtig, starke persönliche Gründe neben dem Honorar und Mitwirkungsmöglichkeit, nicht nur im Modeln sondern auch auf persönlicher Ebene einzubringen. Wie man so schön sagt, eine Person, die für Nichts steht, wird für alles fallen. Ich glaube, das ist in diesem Business ein grosses Problem. Seit diesem ersten Shooting mit Hegre habe ich zahlreiche Produktionen realisiert, mit Masturbation, Dildo-Videos, Massage, Handjob- und Fussjob-Videos, auch lesbische und gemischtrassige. Aber was auch immer ich tat, ich hatte immer meine eigenen Gründe, auf das Geld zu verzichten, und lehnte ab, sobald es um Hardcore-Pornographie ging. Ich finde einfach keine guten Gründe so etwas zu tun. Dafür mache ich mehr Mode und arbeite für Kataloge, Lingerie und künstlerische Shootings. Das mag ich, es gibt einen schönen Gegensatz zur erotischen Fotografie, die Leute und die Arbeit sind unterschiedlich.
Inzwischen kooperiere ich mit einem ausgesuchten Zirkel an Fotografen und Produktions-Firmen, alles Leute, denen ich vertraue und die ich wertschätze.

www.katya-clover.com

Geboren: 1989
Sternzeichen: Skorpion
Grösse: 164 cm
Gewicht: 46 kg
BH-Grösse: B
Augen: blau
Haare: hellbraun
Tattoos: ein Kleeblatt an meinem linken Fuss
Piercings: keine
Sprachen: Russisch, Koreanisch, Englisch

a model, my work is my stamp of quality, my seal of approval. If I don't support something, or don't like a photographer or his approach, or his website, I say no. It's important to have strong personal reasons besides the money and the sense of empowerment, not only in modeling but also in relationships. As the saying goes, a person who stands for nothing will fall for anything. I think this is a huge problem in the industry. Since that first shooting with Hegre, I've done lots of productions featuring masturbation and dildo videos, massage, hand-job and foot-job videos, lesbian and interracial, but whatever I've done, I had my own, strong reasons why, regardless of the money. I think my open-mindedness, but also my strong ideology are what kept me away from doing hard-core commercial porn. I just don't find strong enough reasons to do it. On the other hand, I do more fashion and catalogue shoots, lingerie and artistic work now. I like it because it is a nice counterbalance to erotic photography, where the people and the type of work are very different.
I now have a very close circle of photographers and production companies that I work with, and these are the people that I trust and value.

www.katya-clover.com

Born: 1989
Zodiac Sign: scorpio
Height: 164 cm
Weight: 46 kg
Bra Size: B cup
Eyes: blue
Hair: light brown
Tattoos: a clover on my left foot
Piercings: none
Languages: Russian, Korean, English

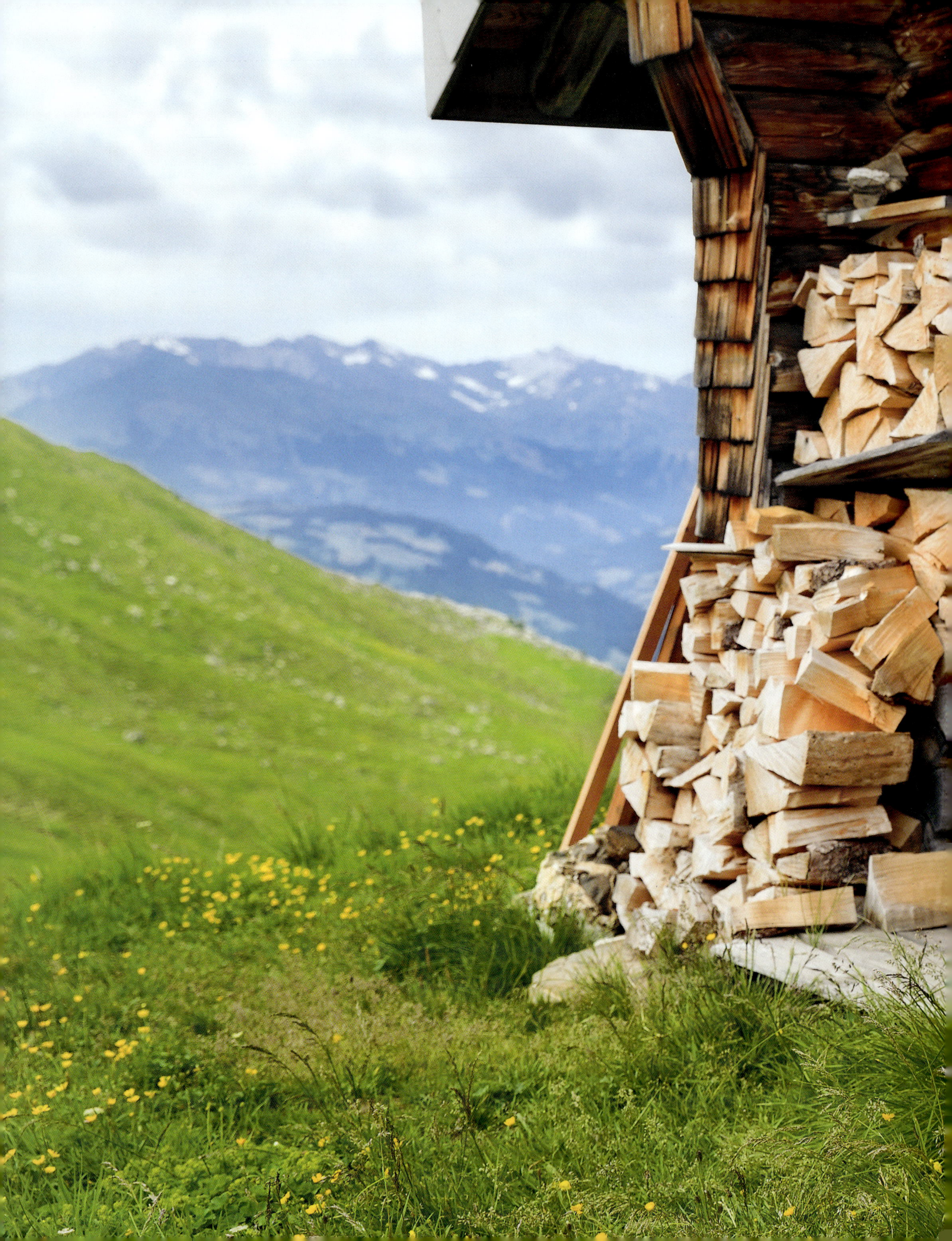

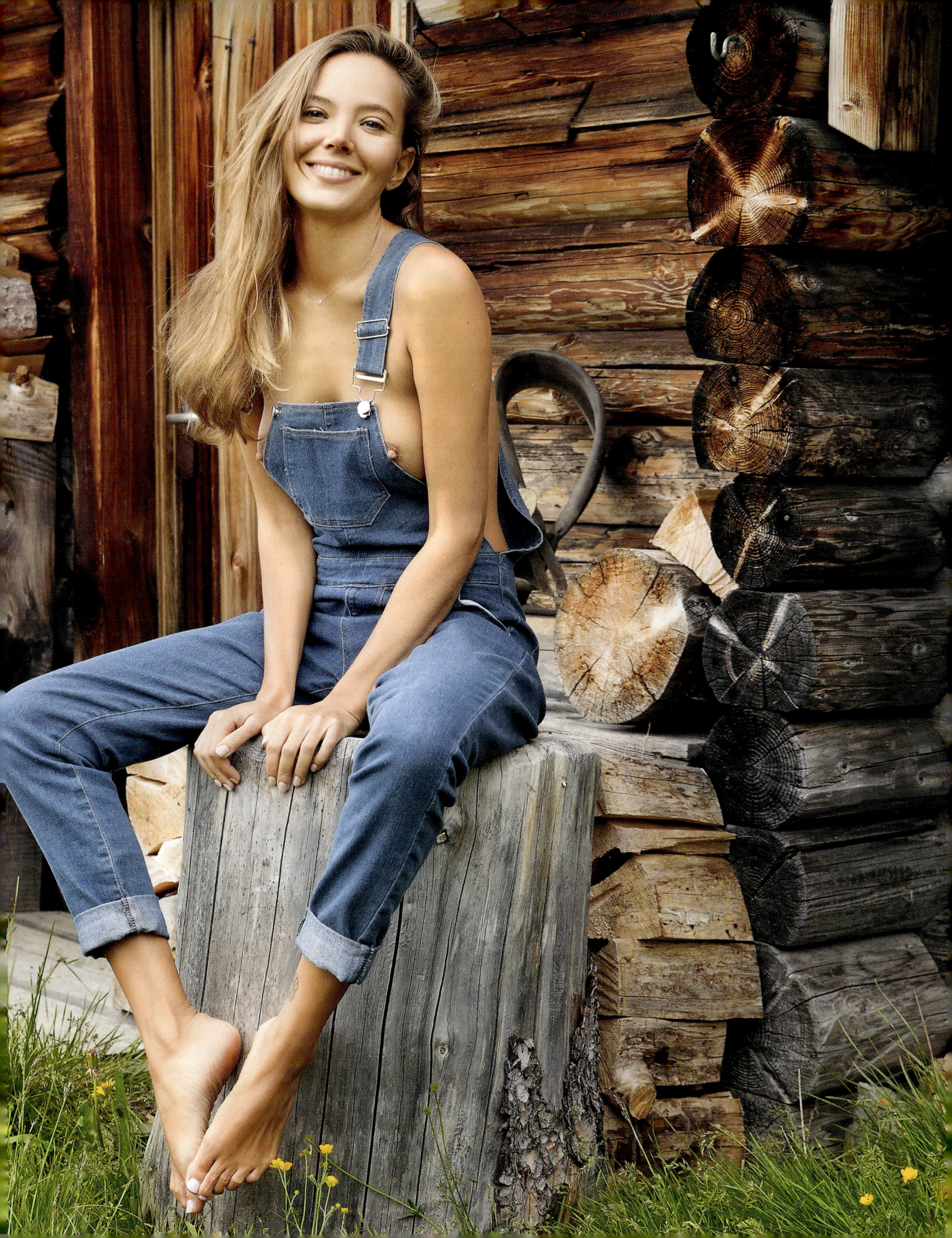

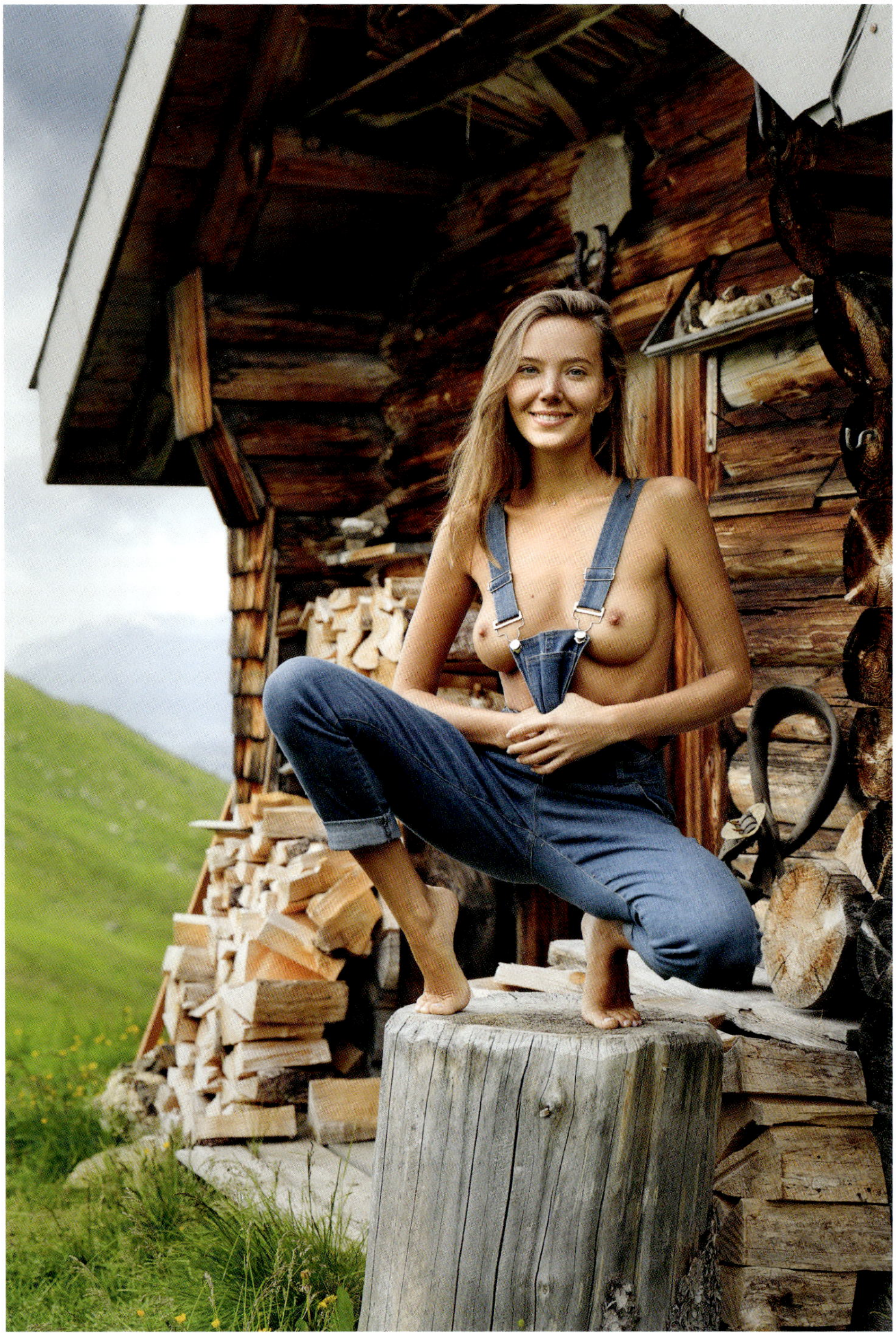

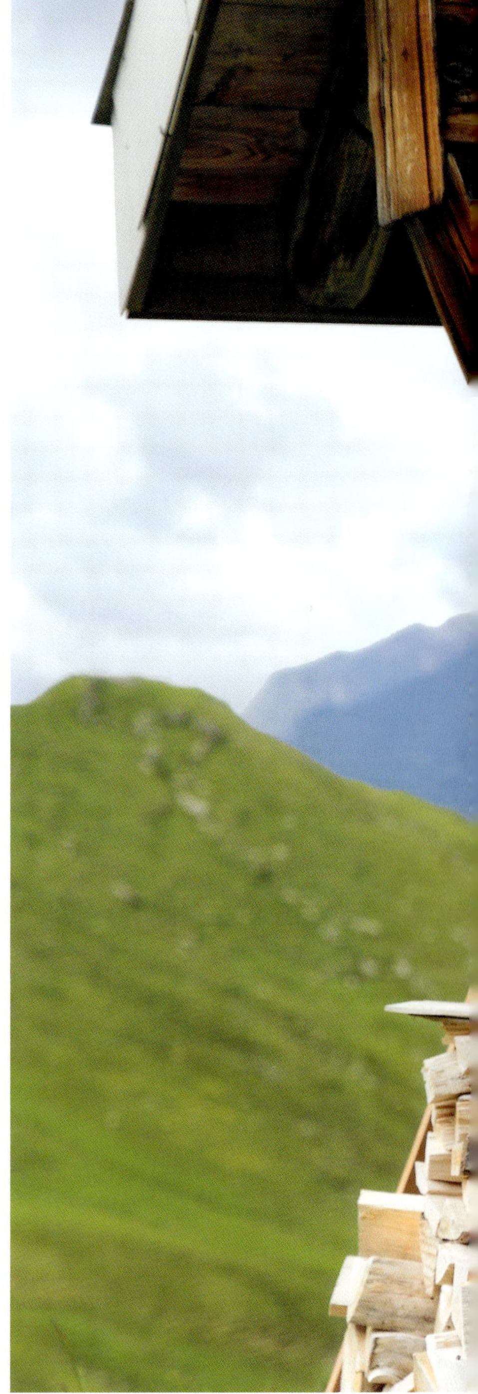

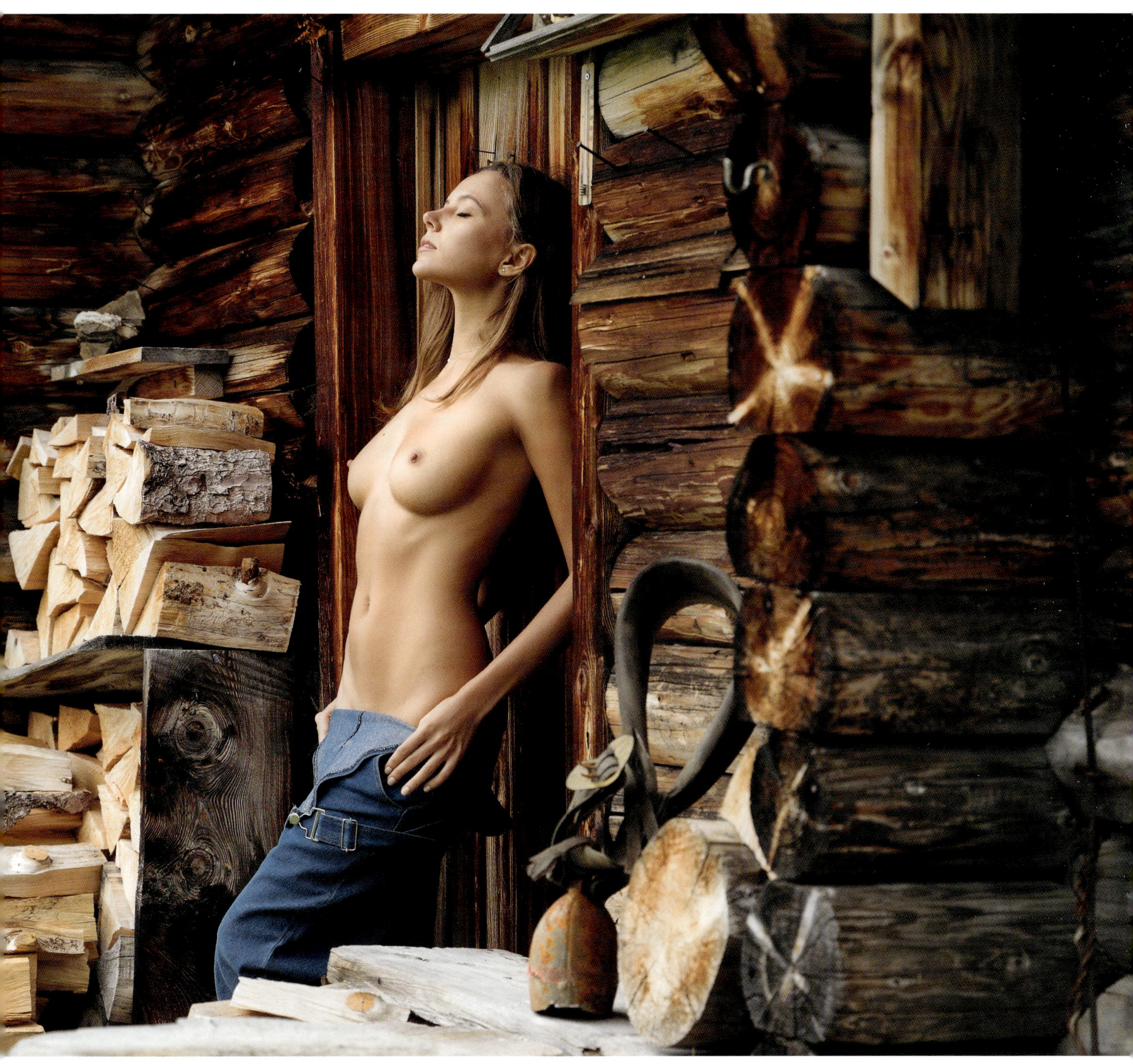

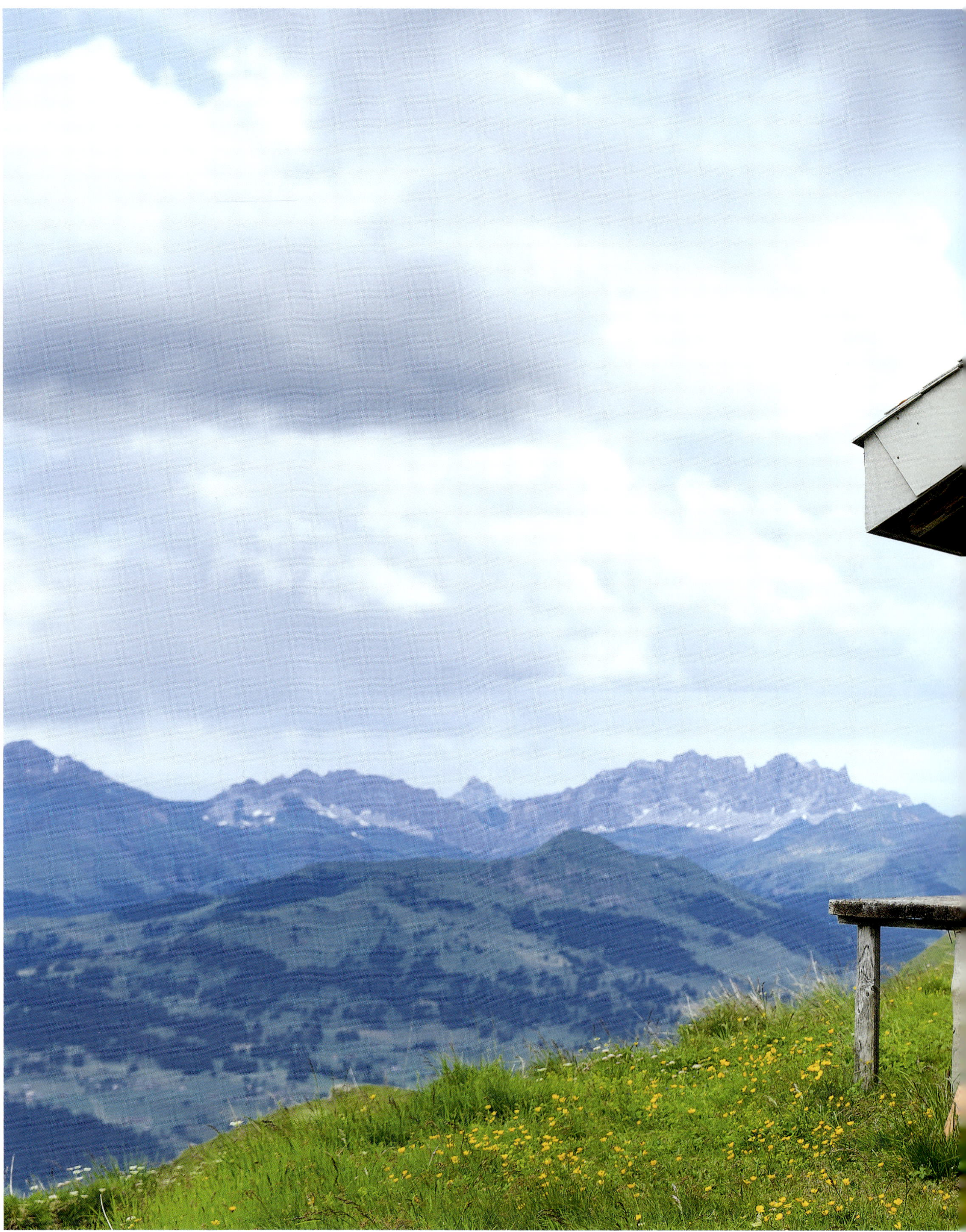

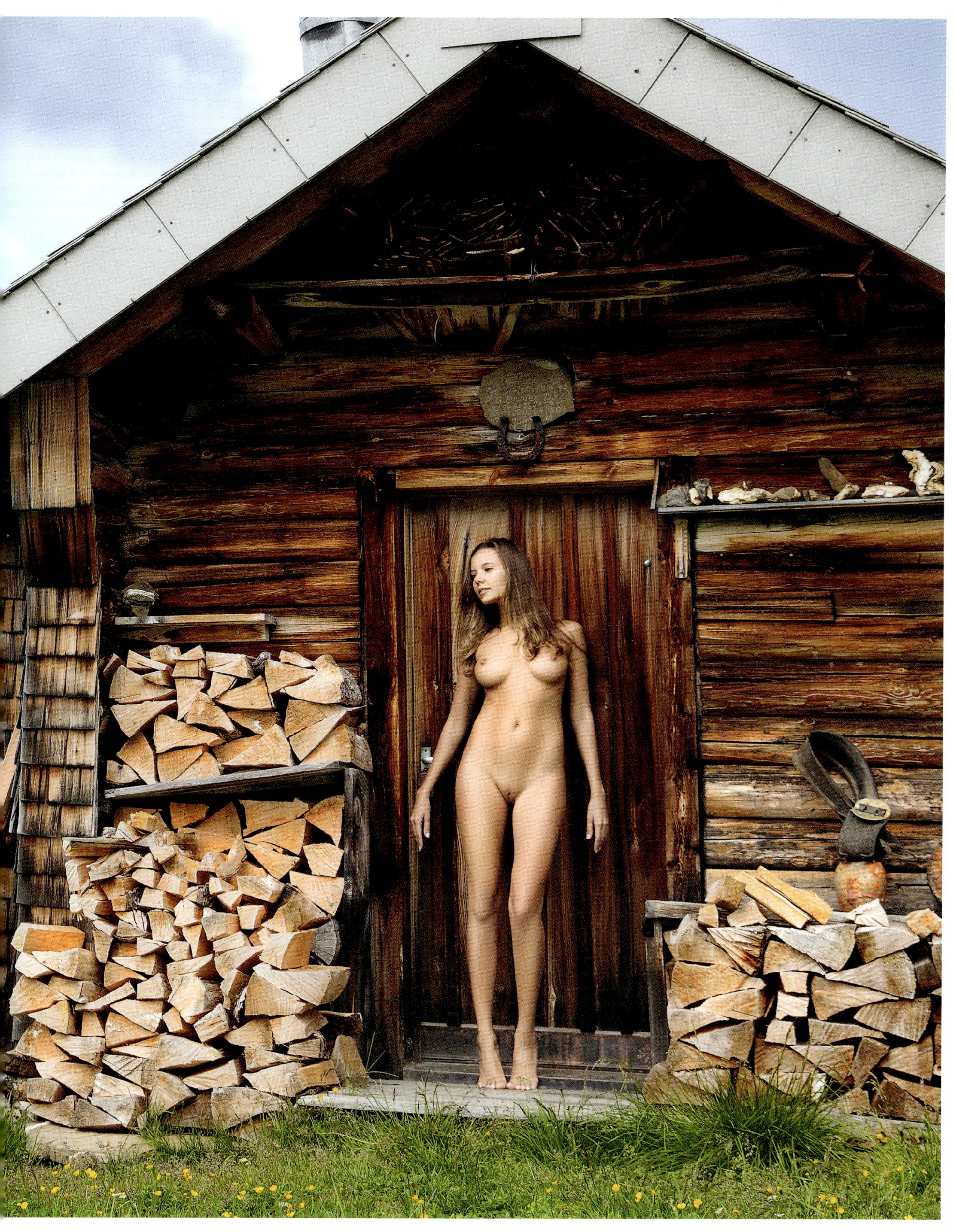

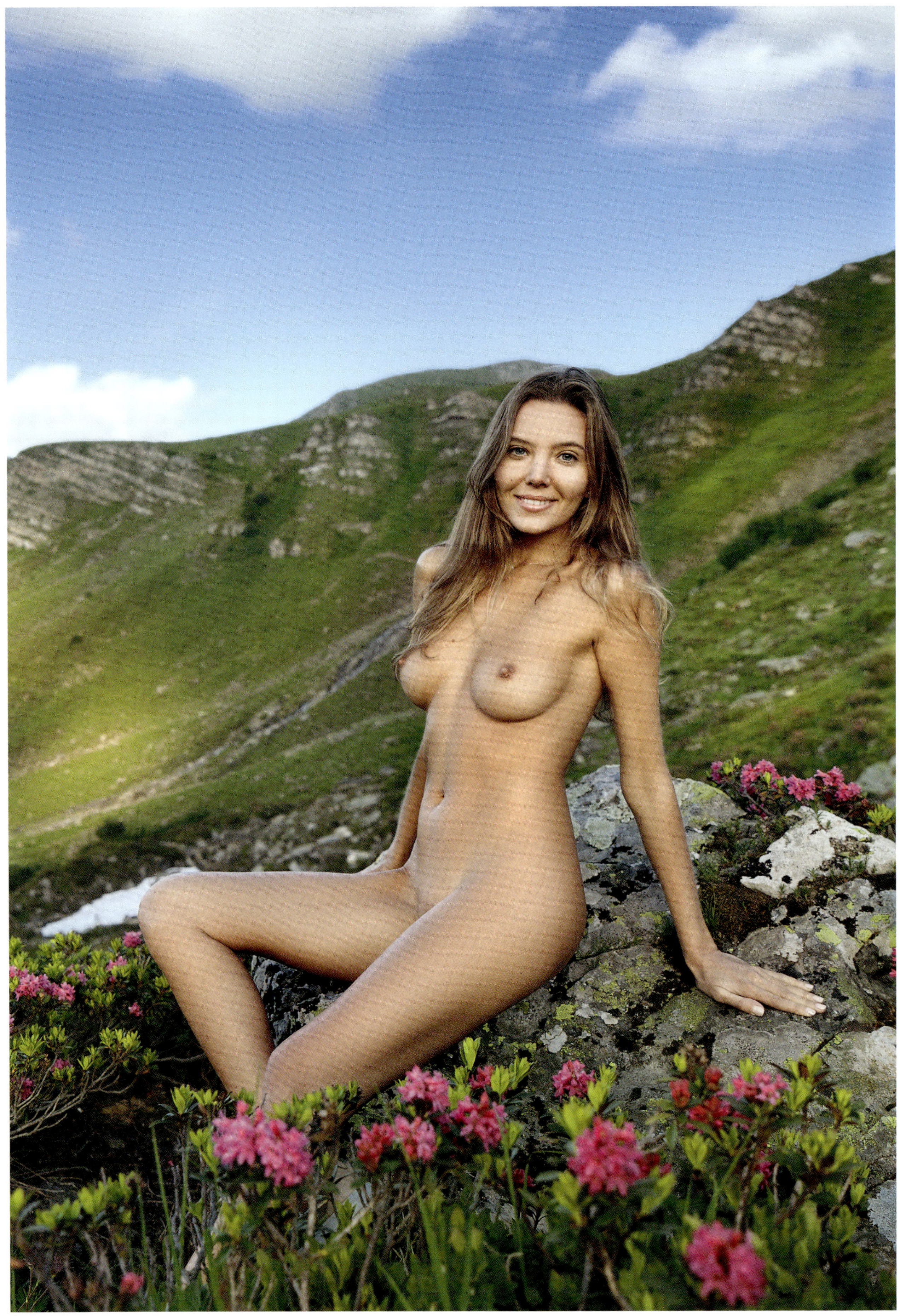

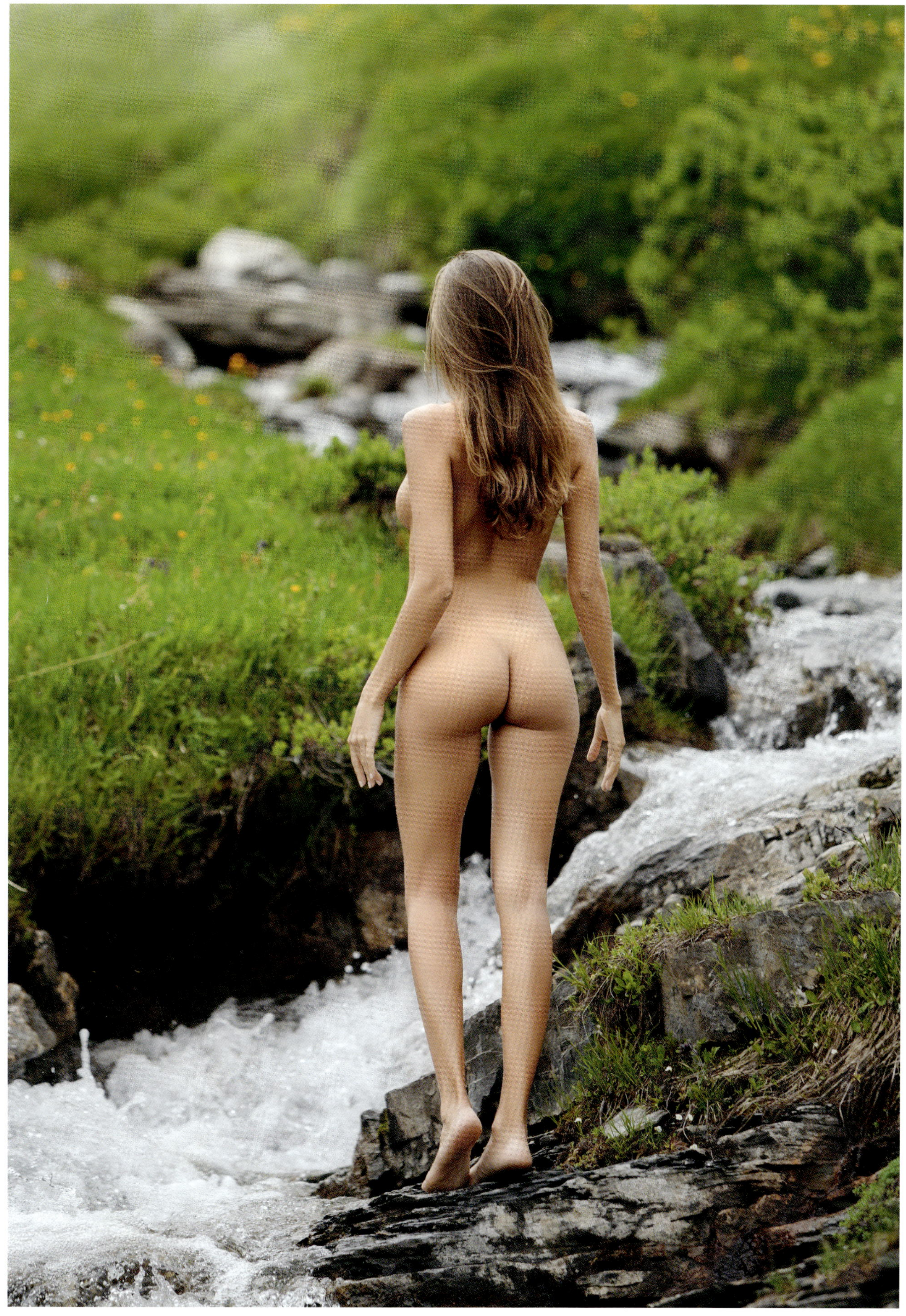

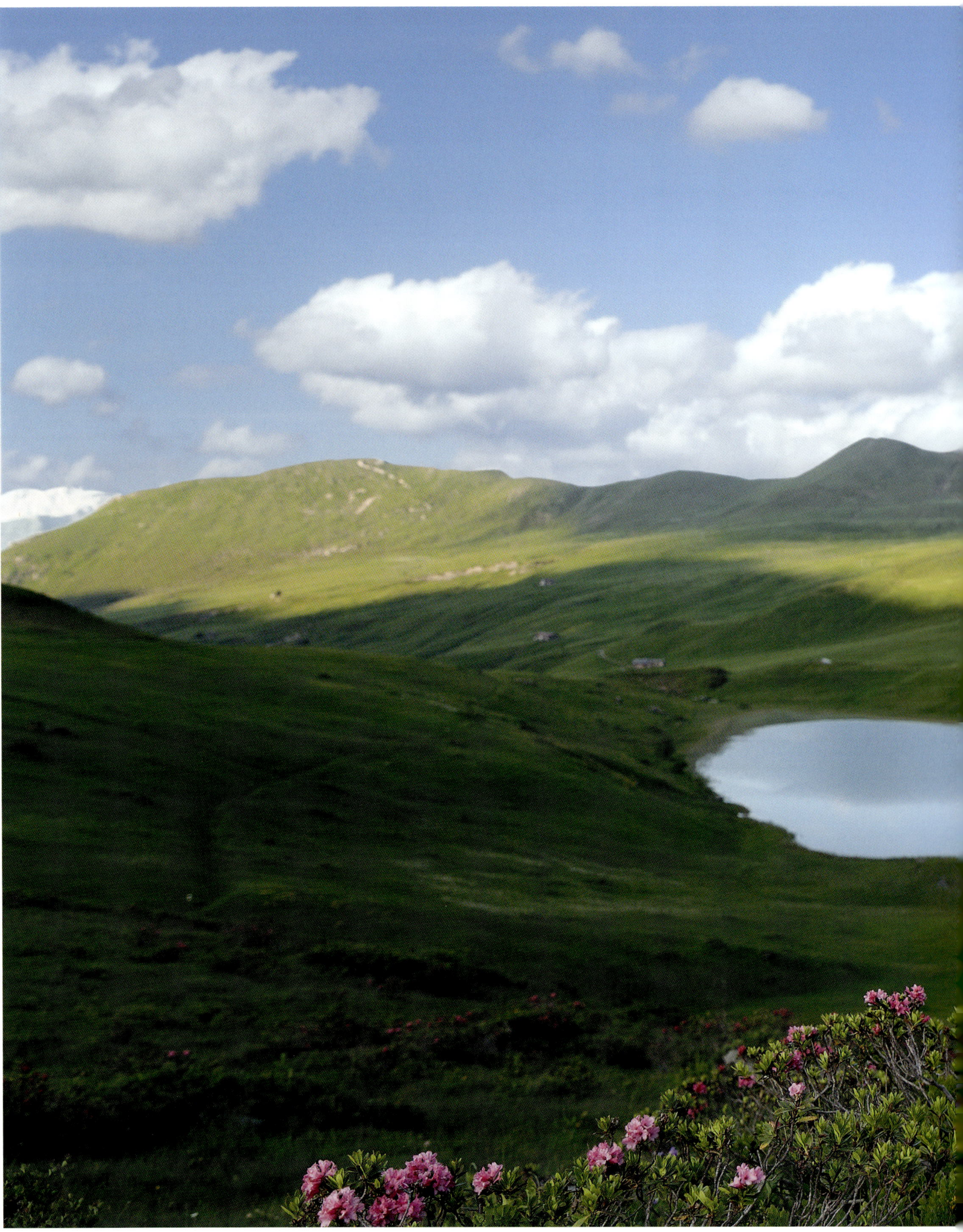

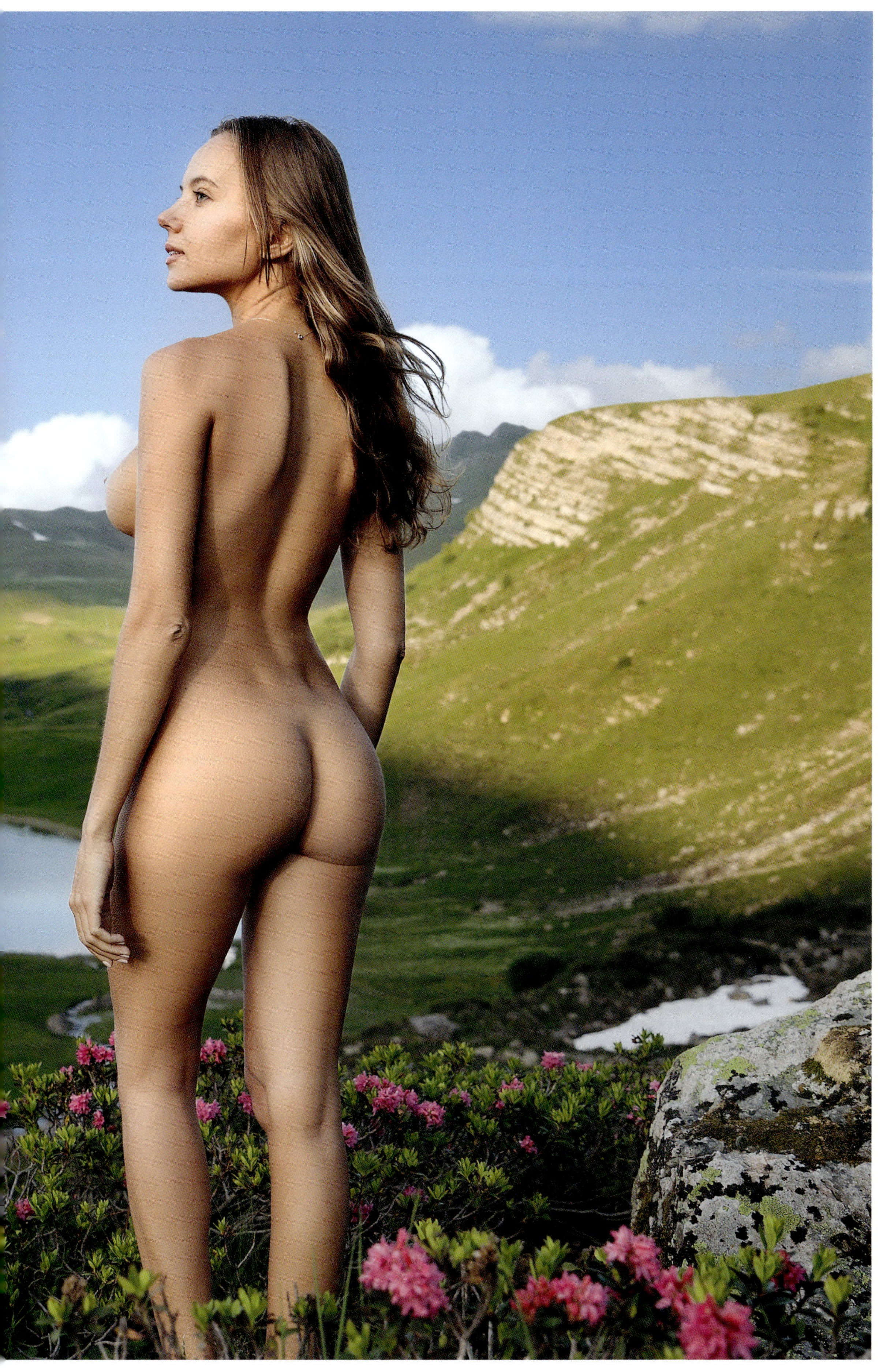

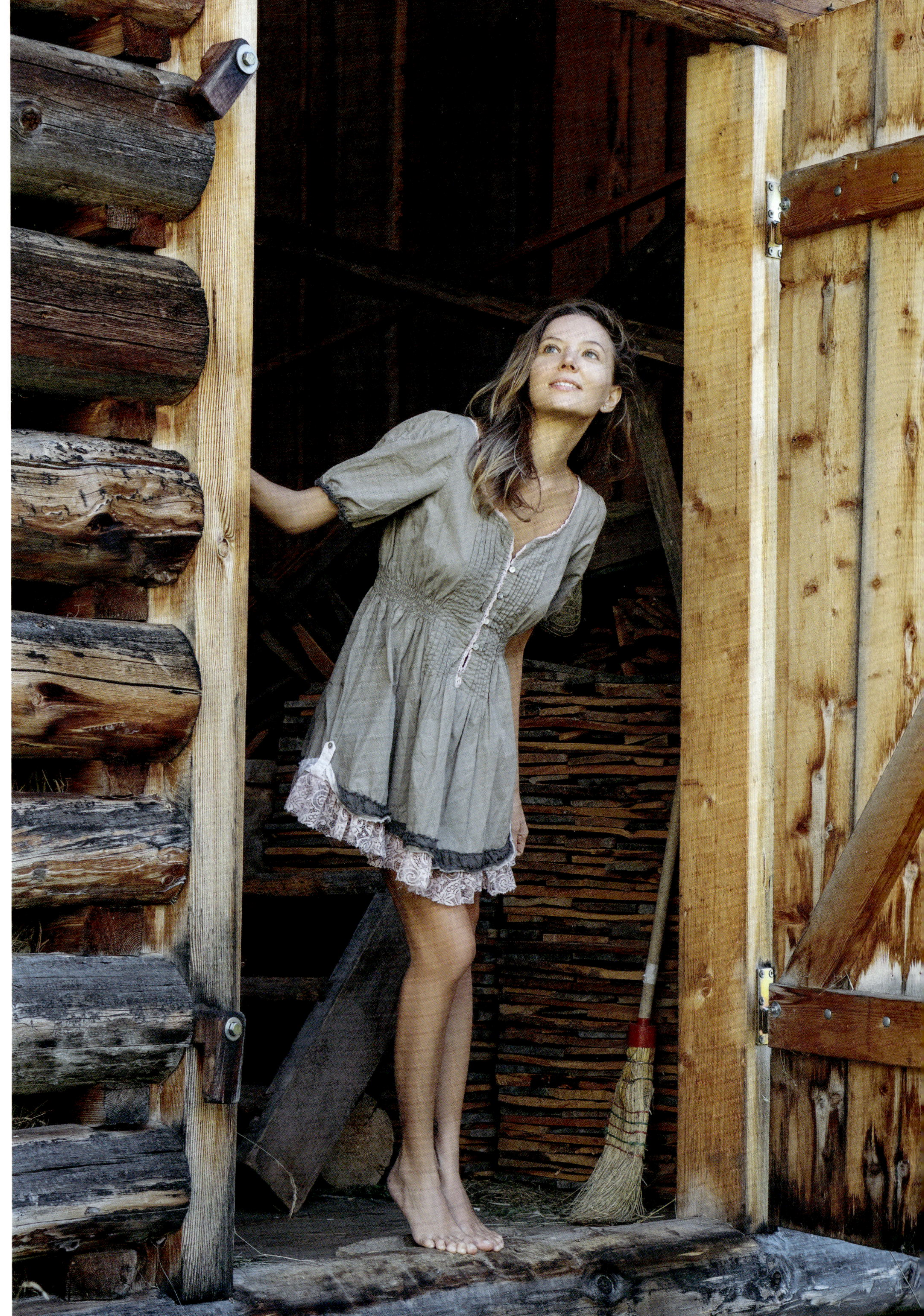

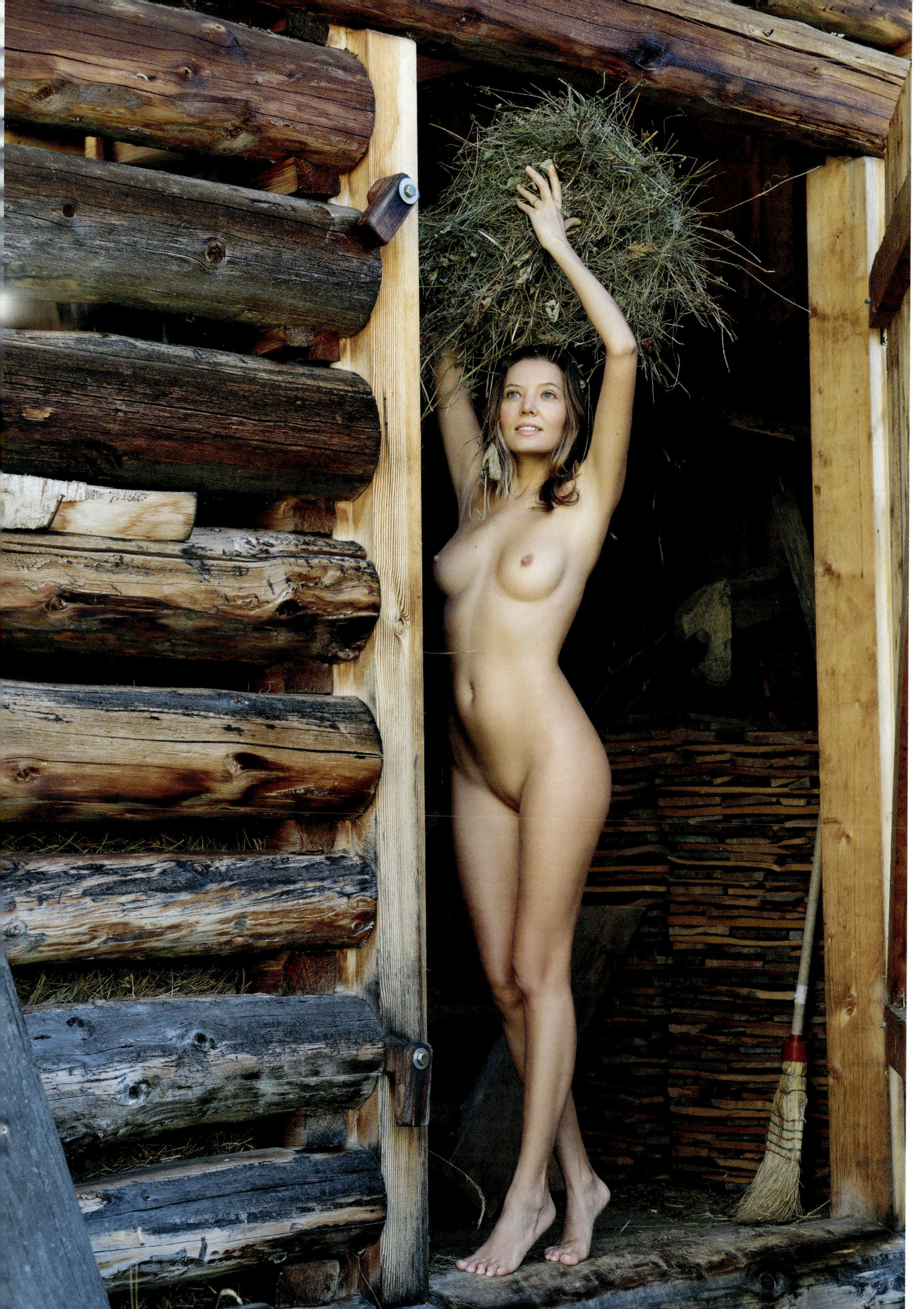

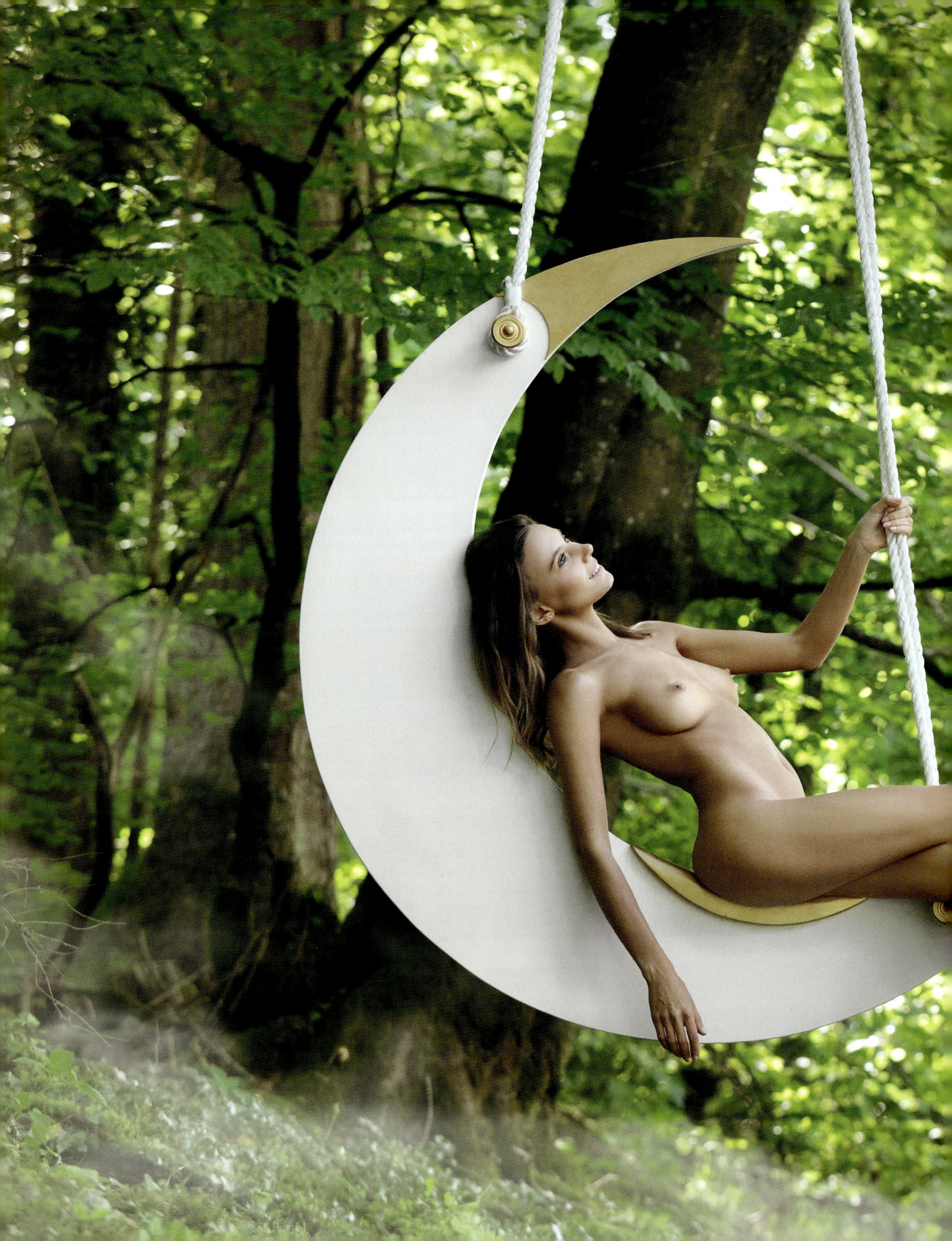

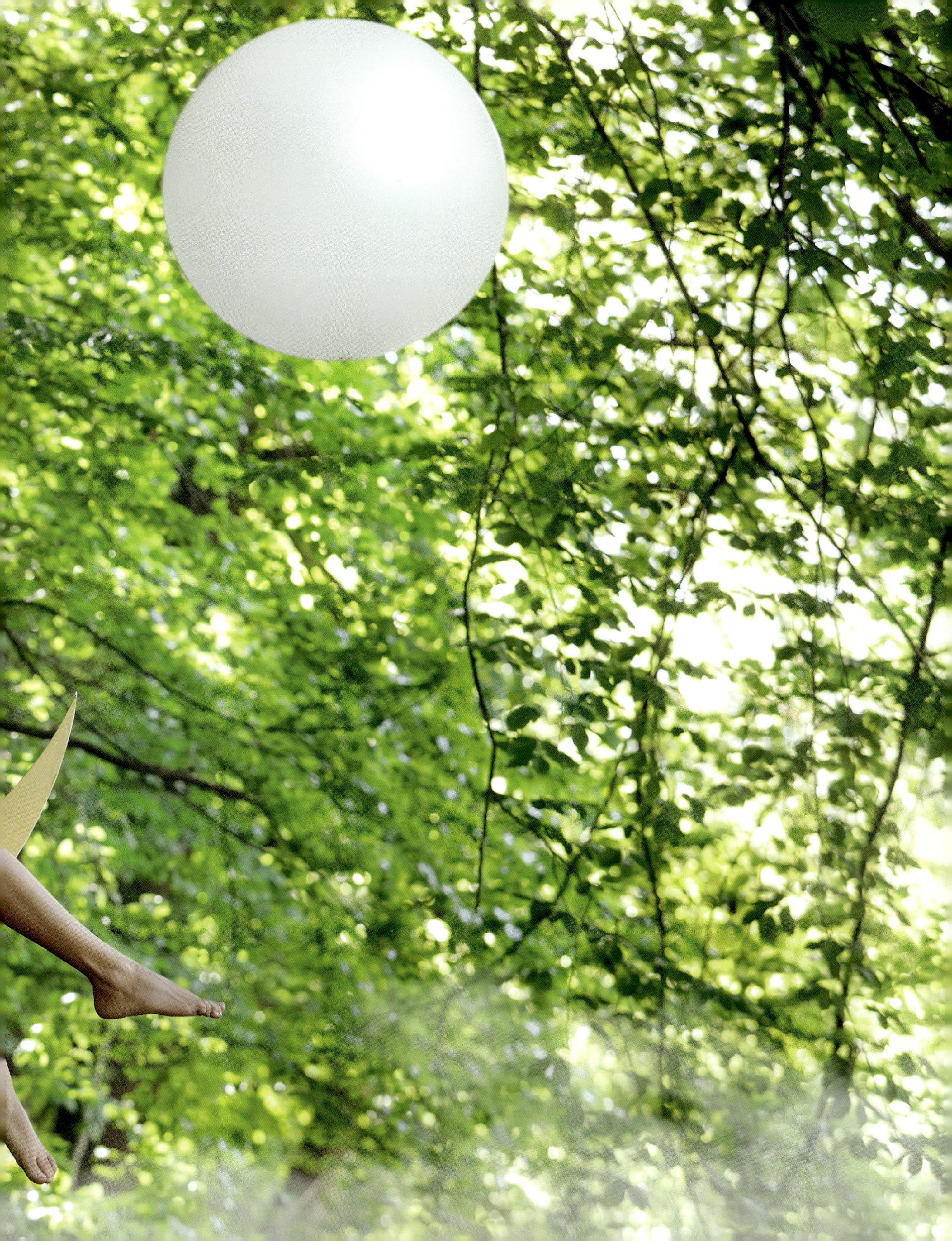

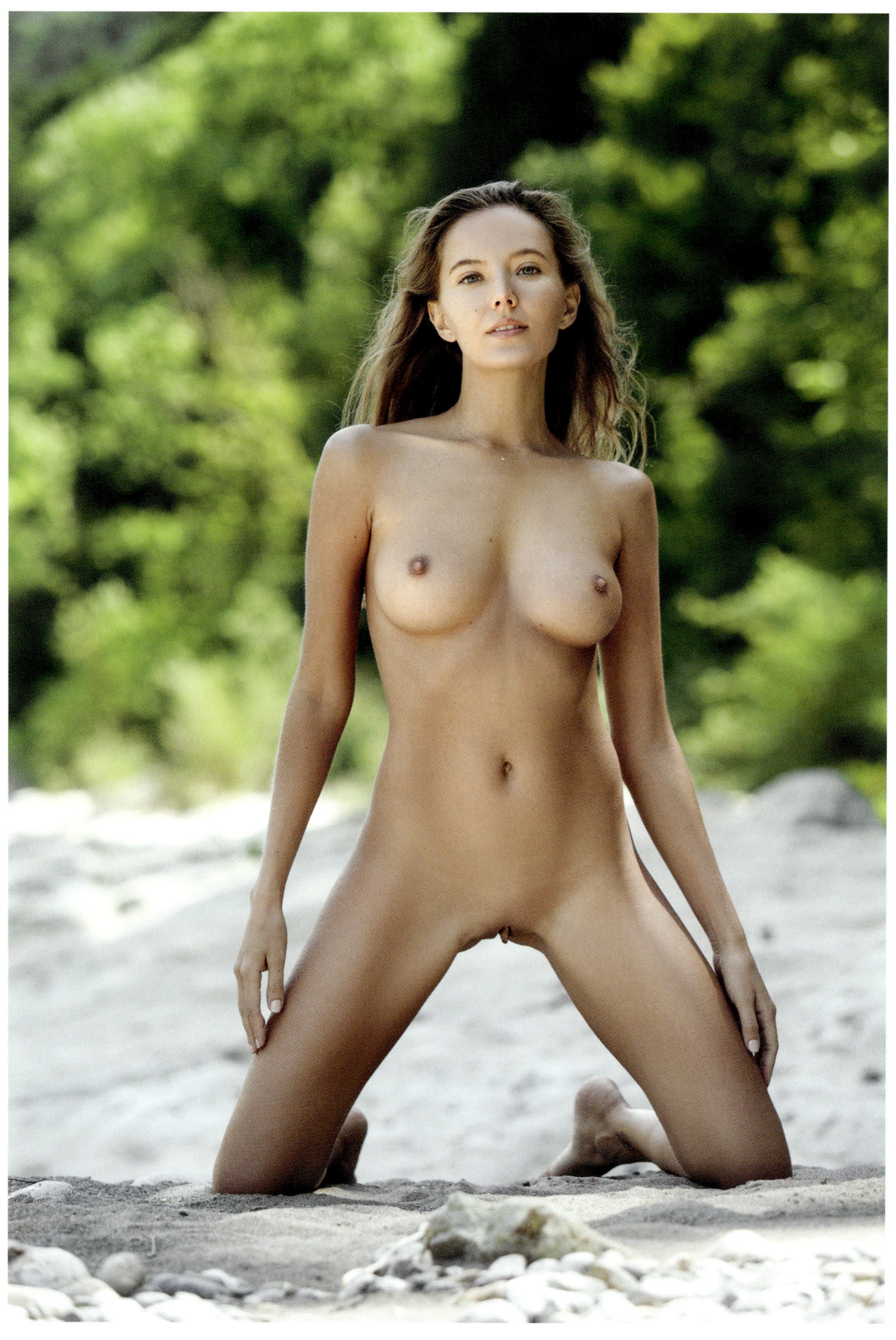

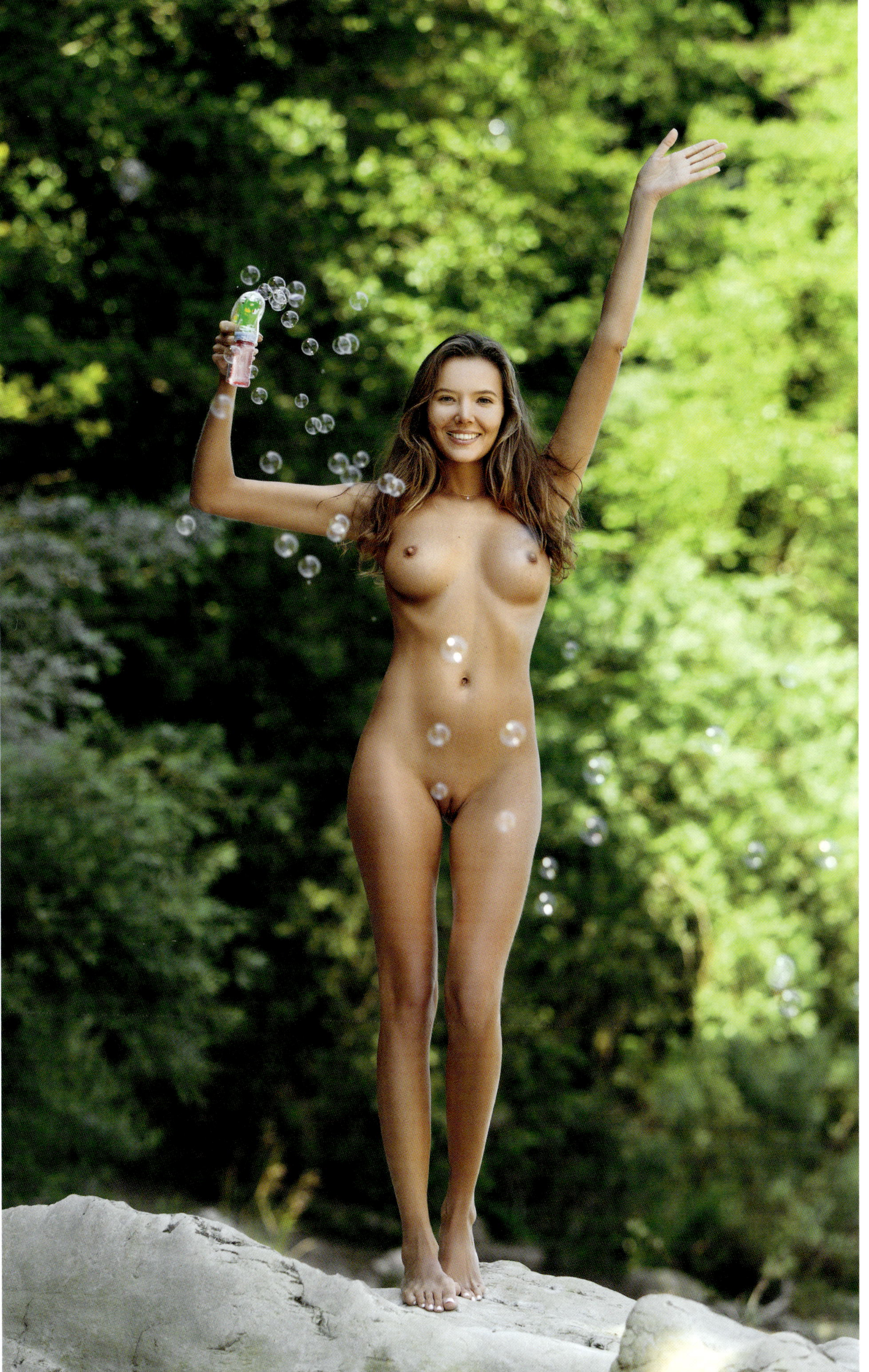

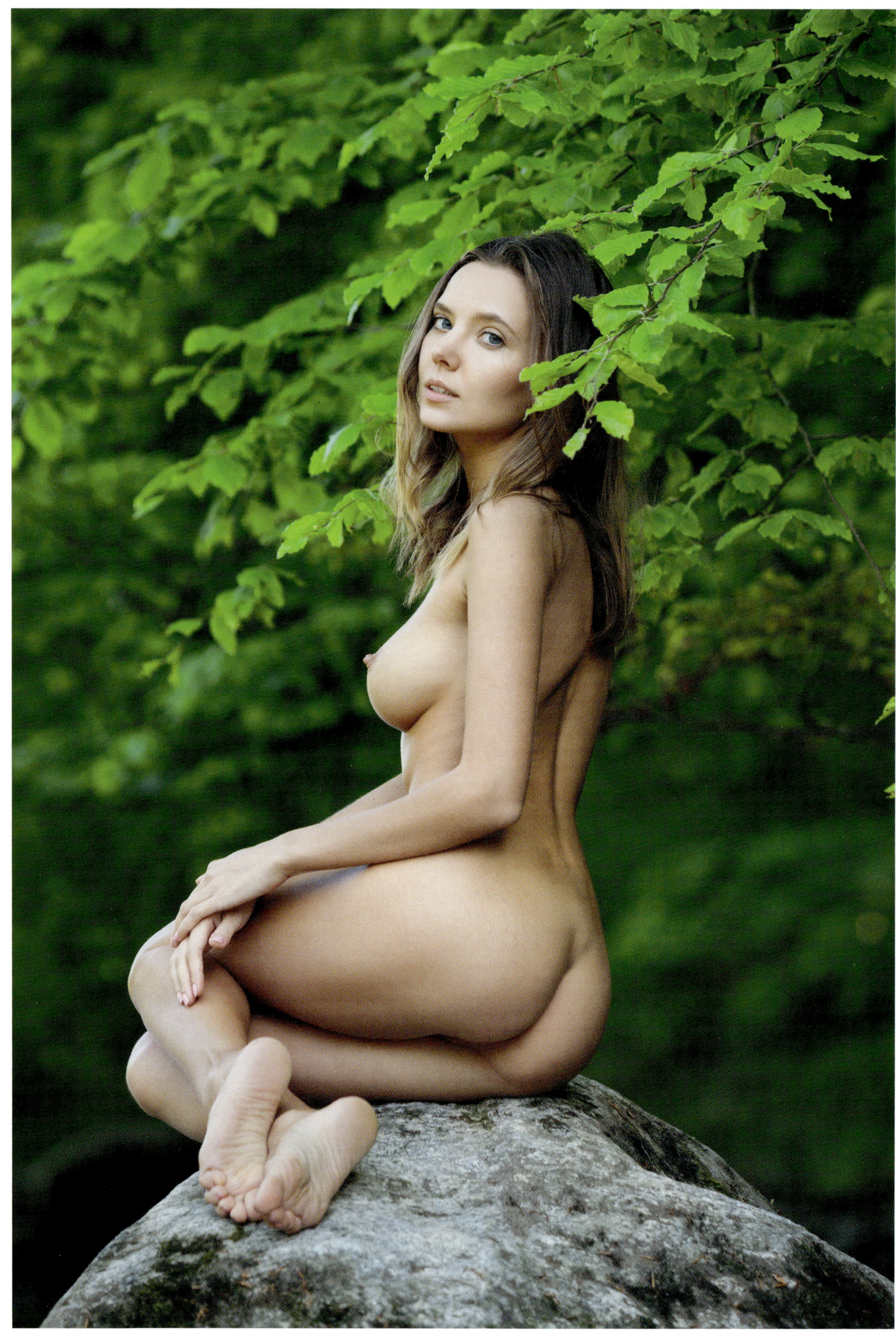

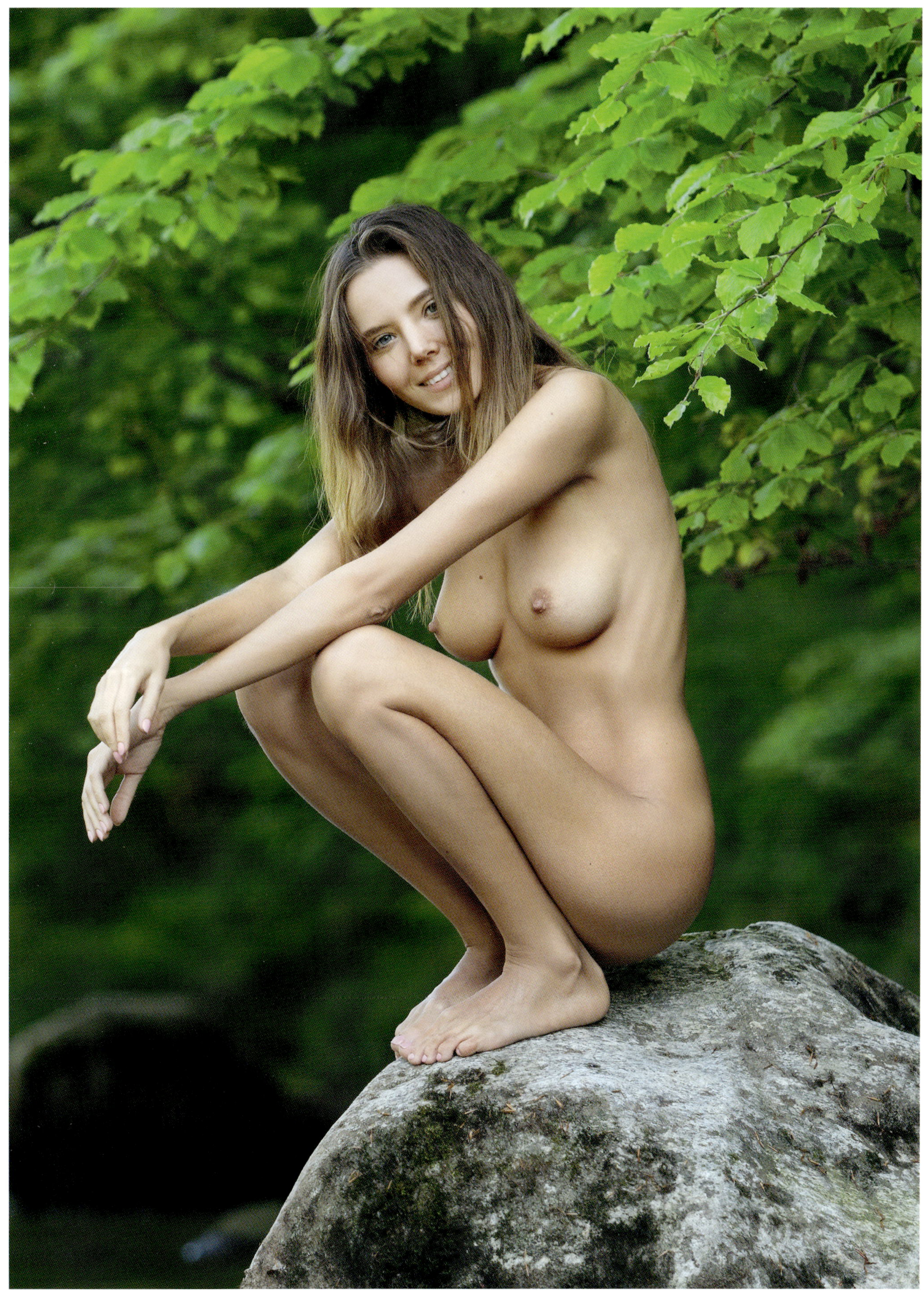

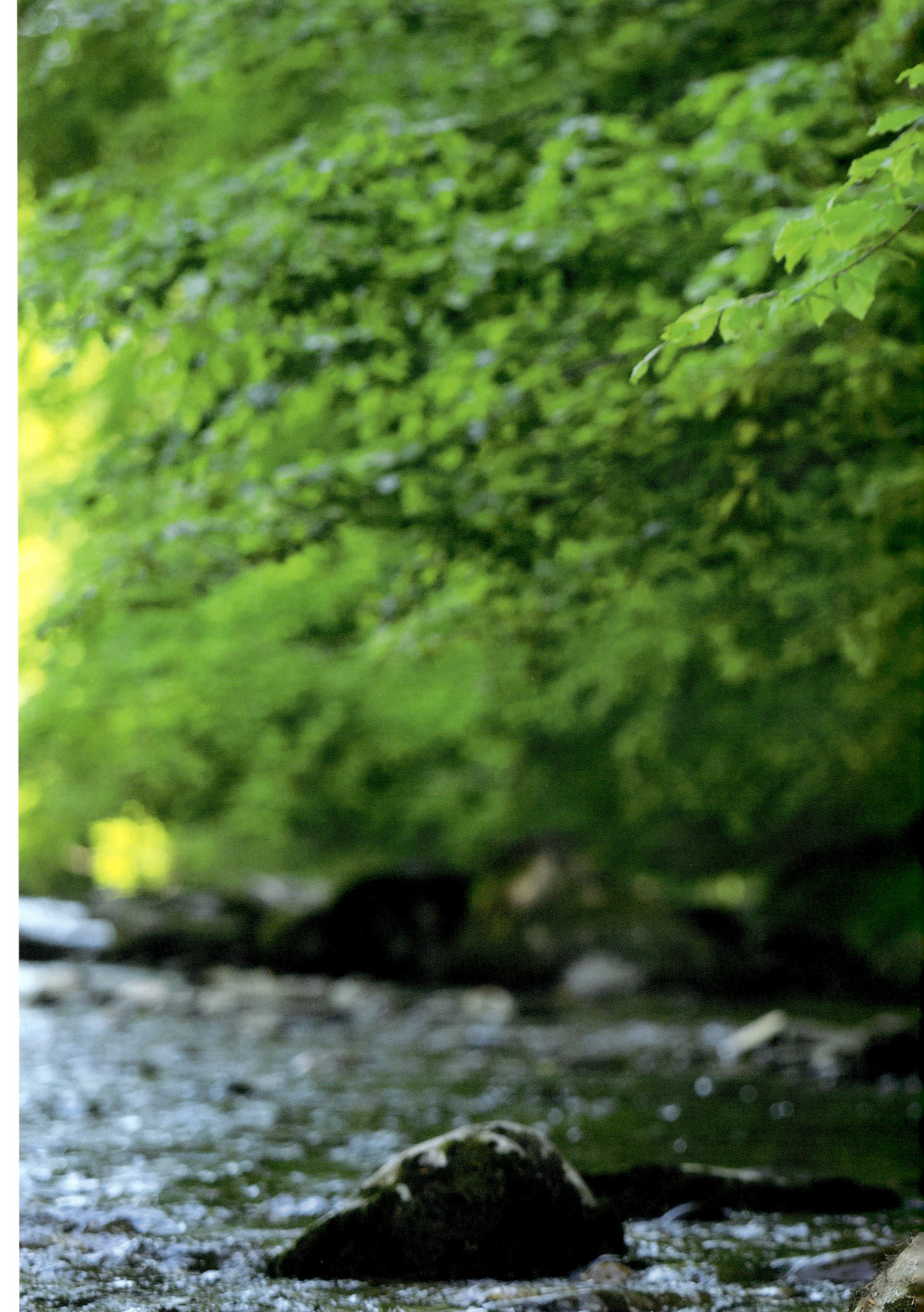

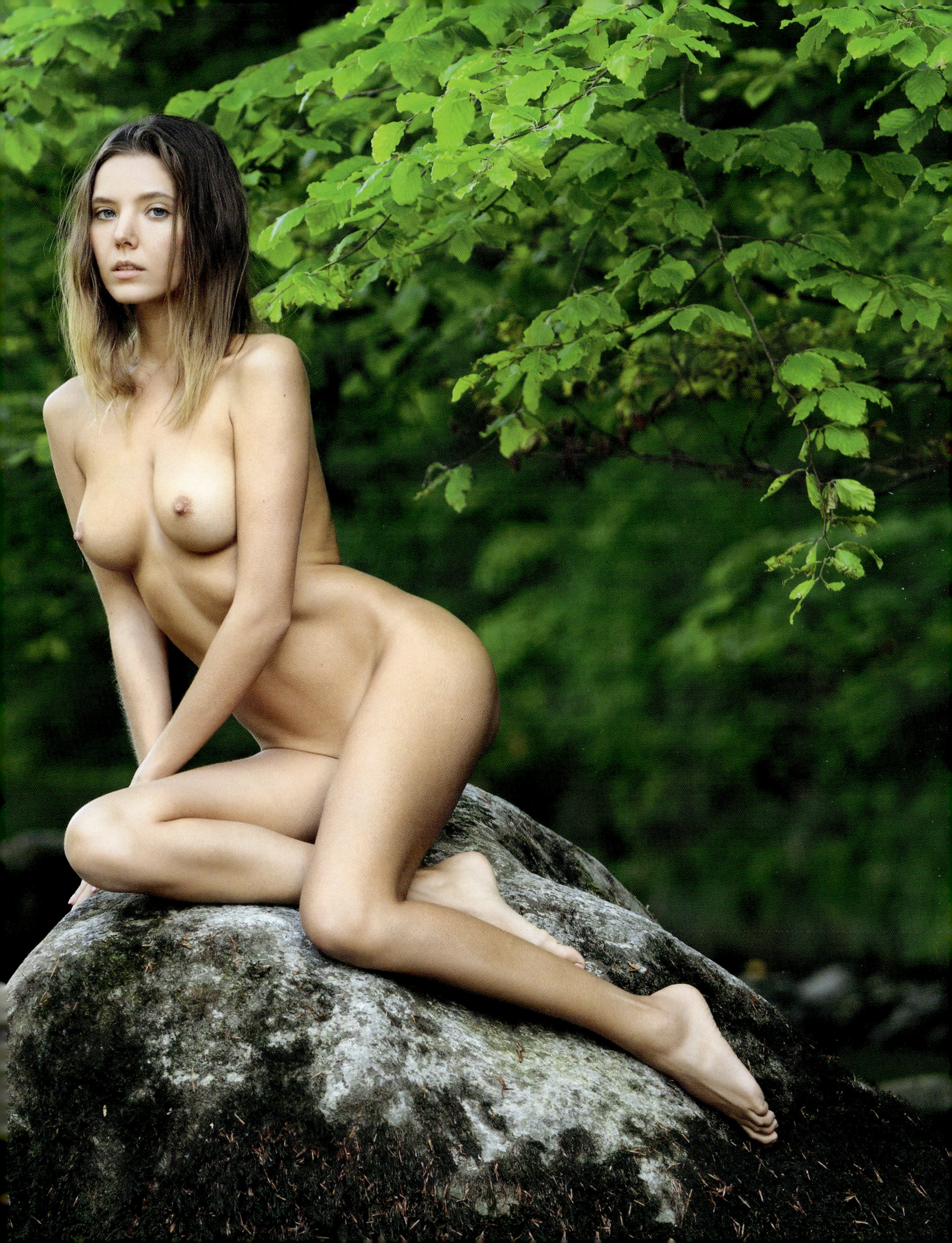

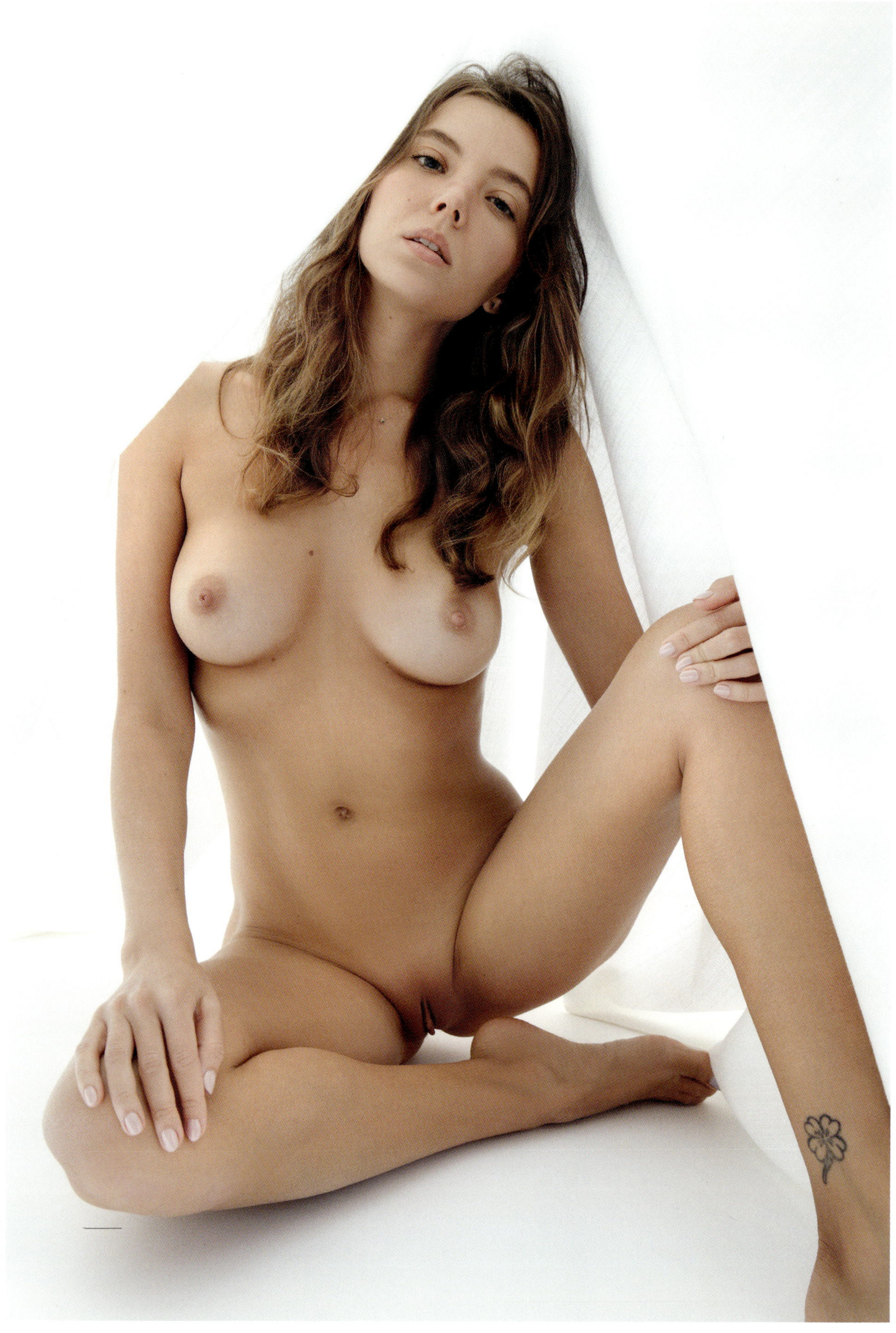

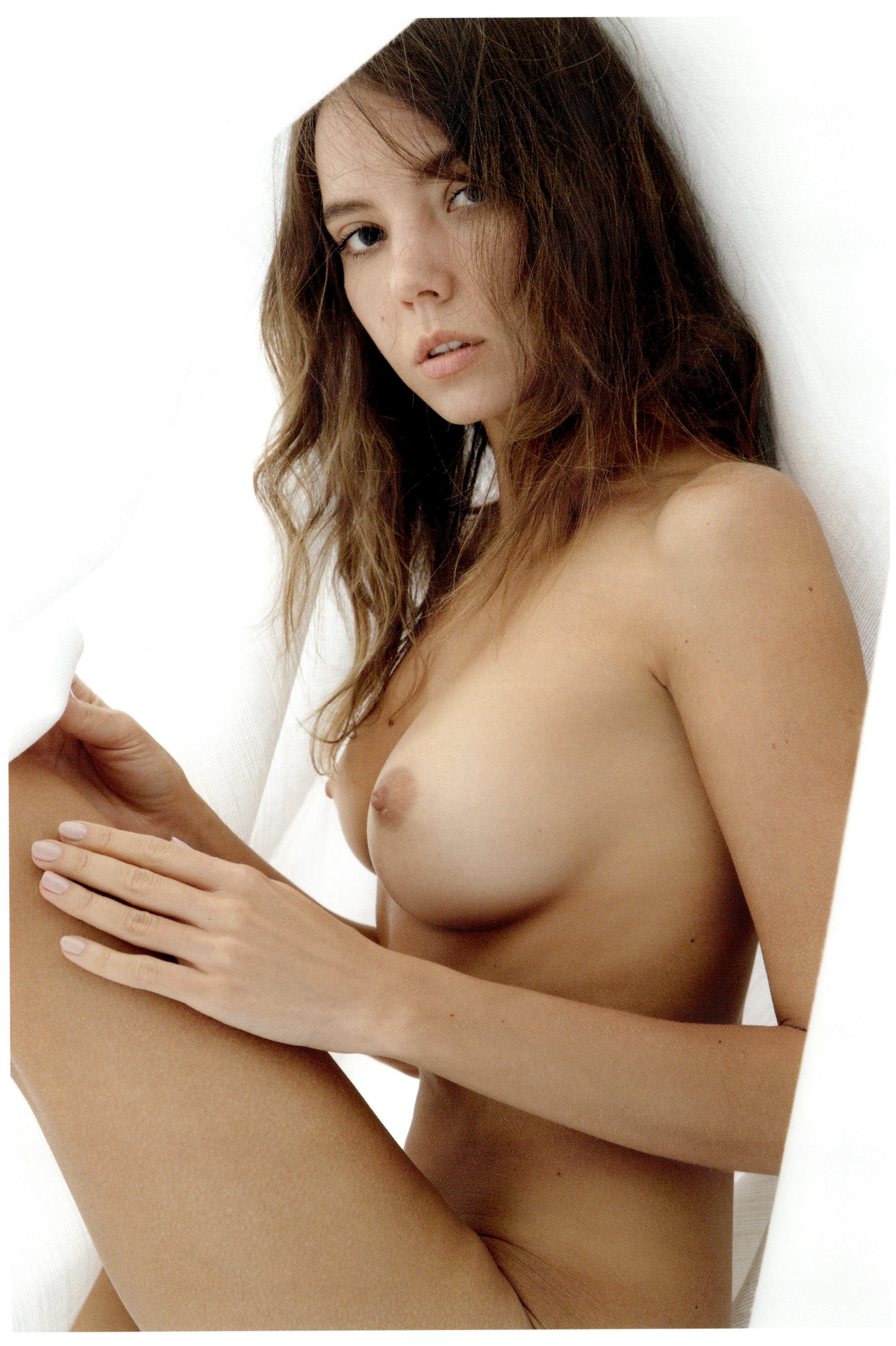

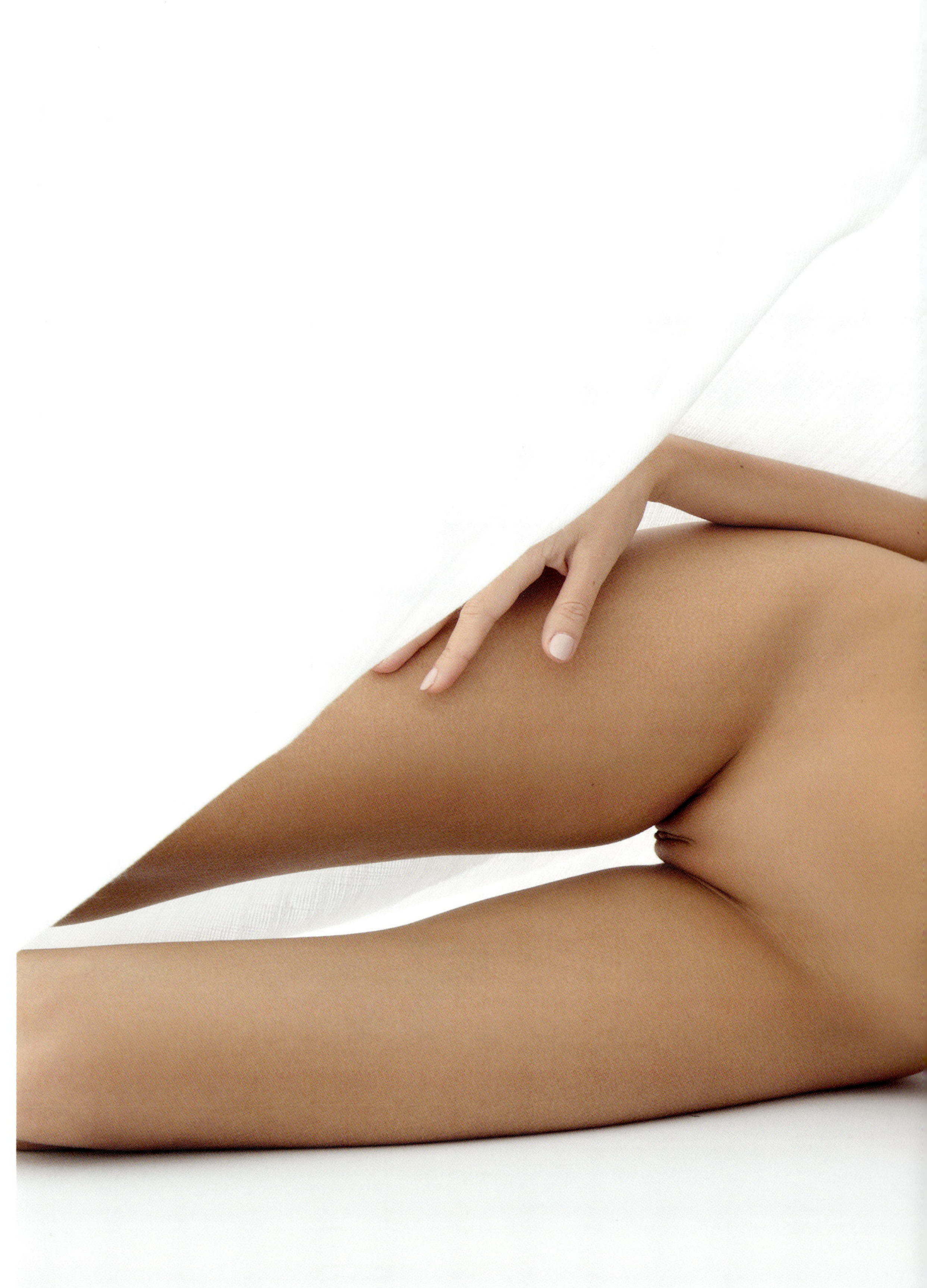

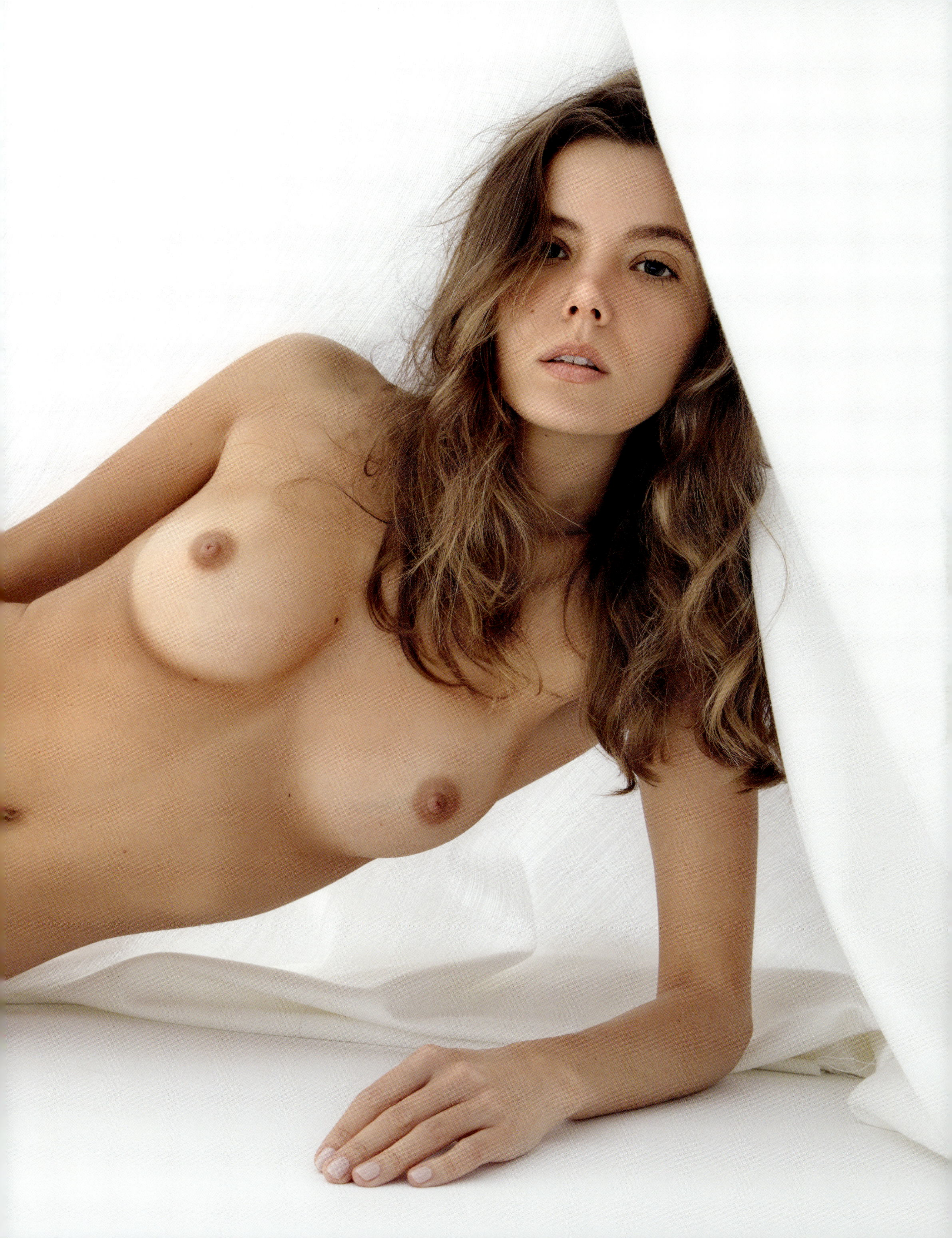

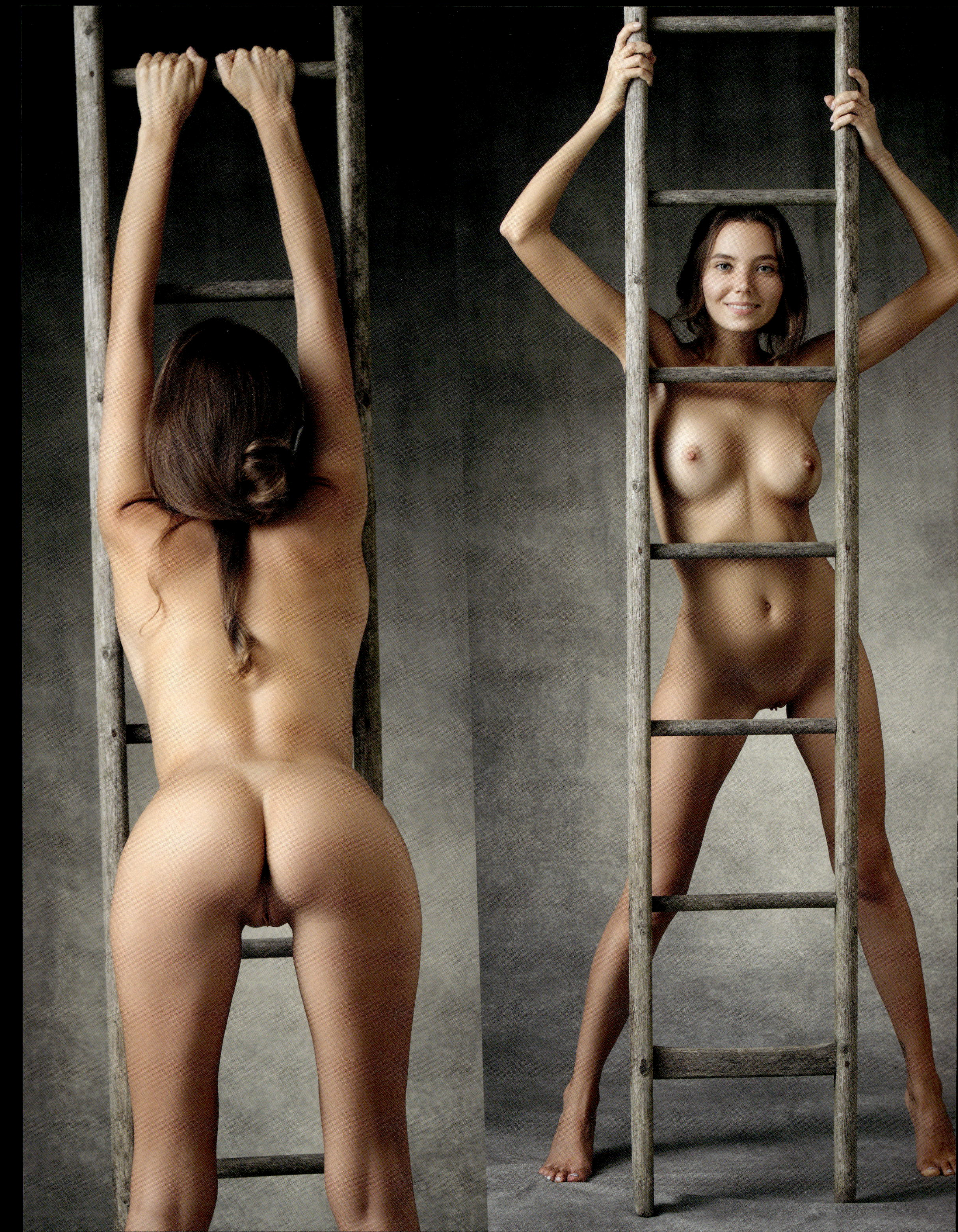

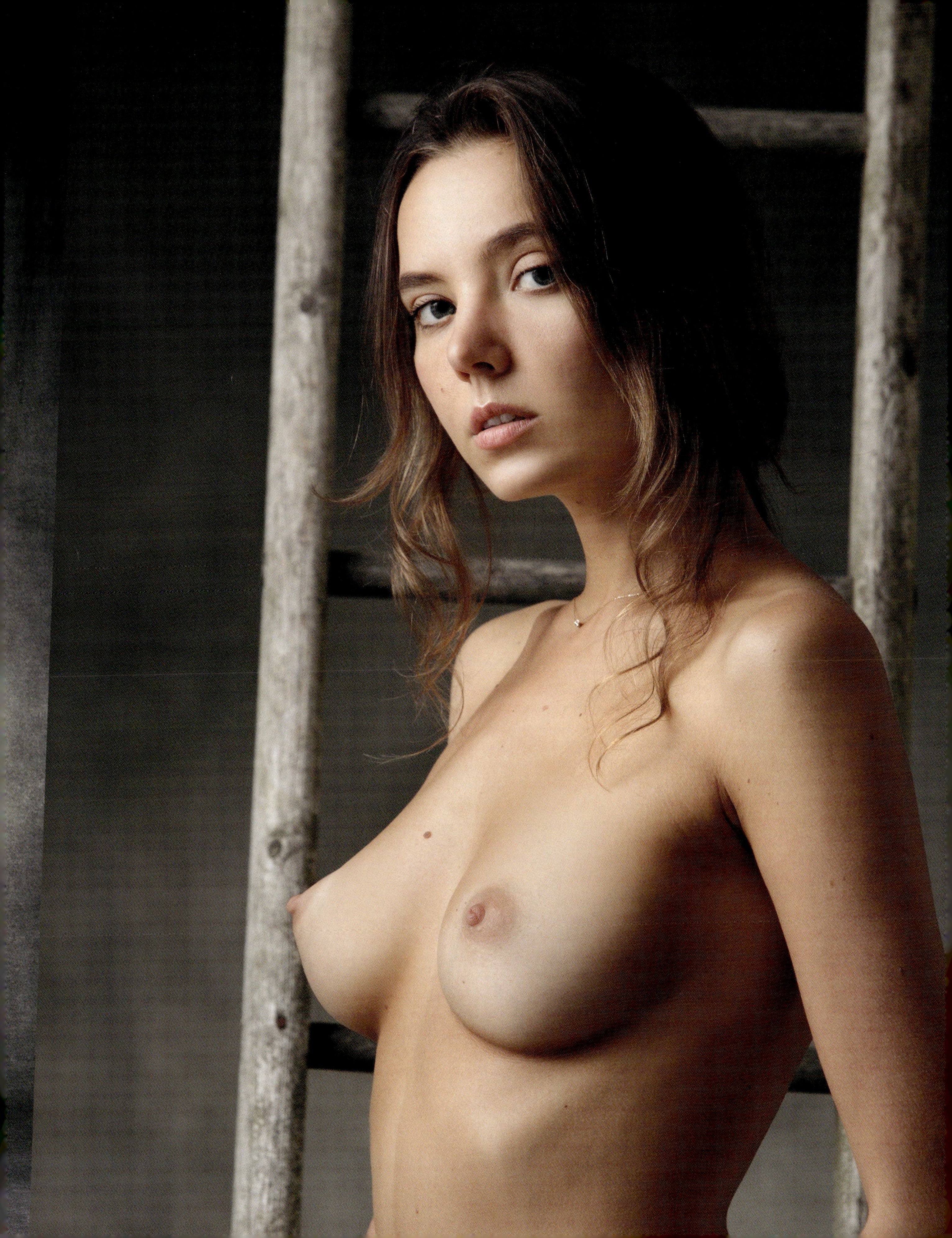

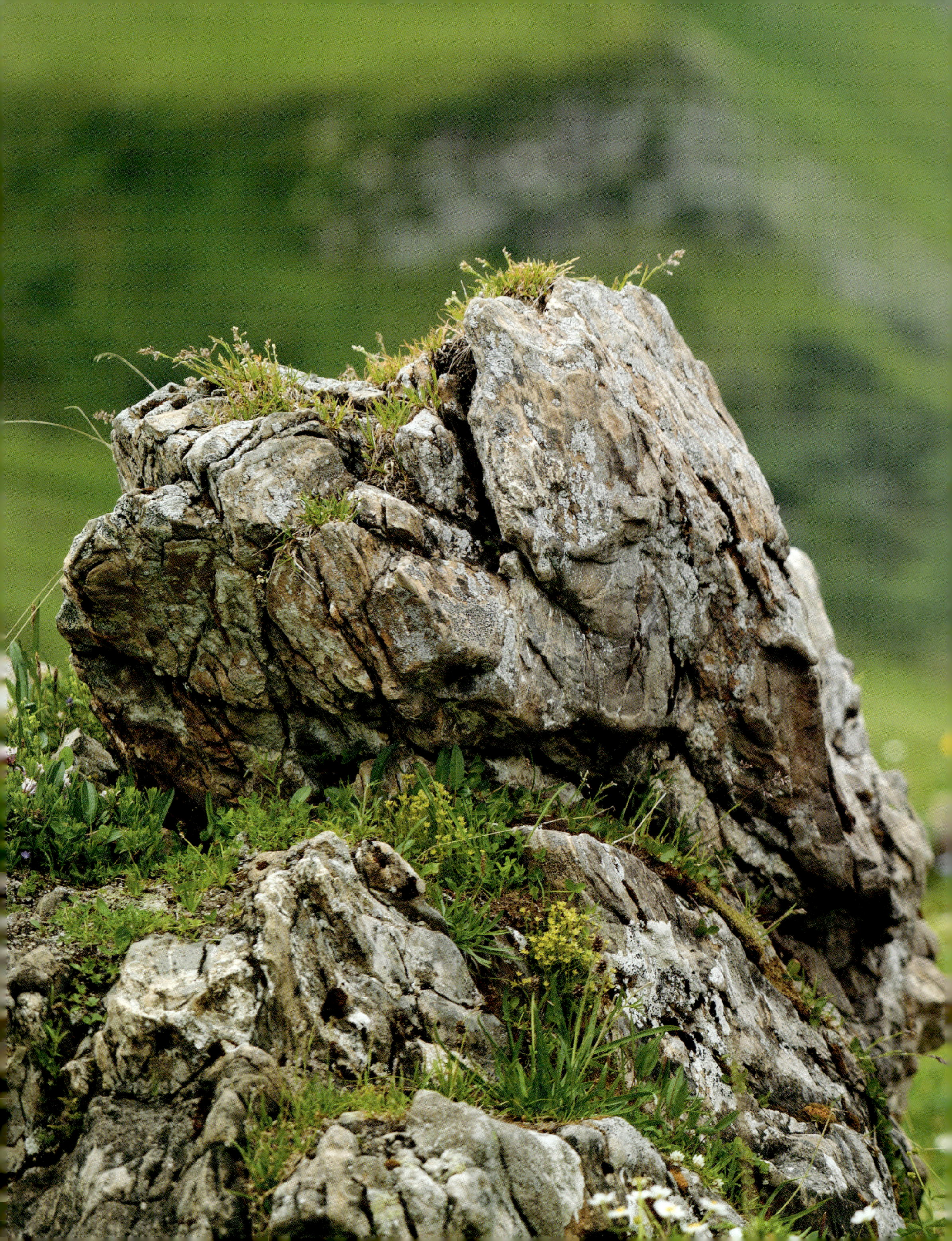

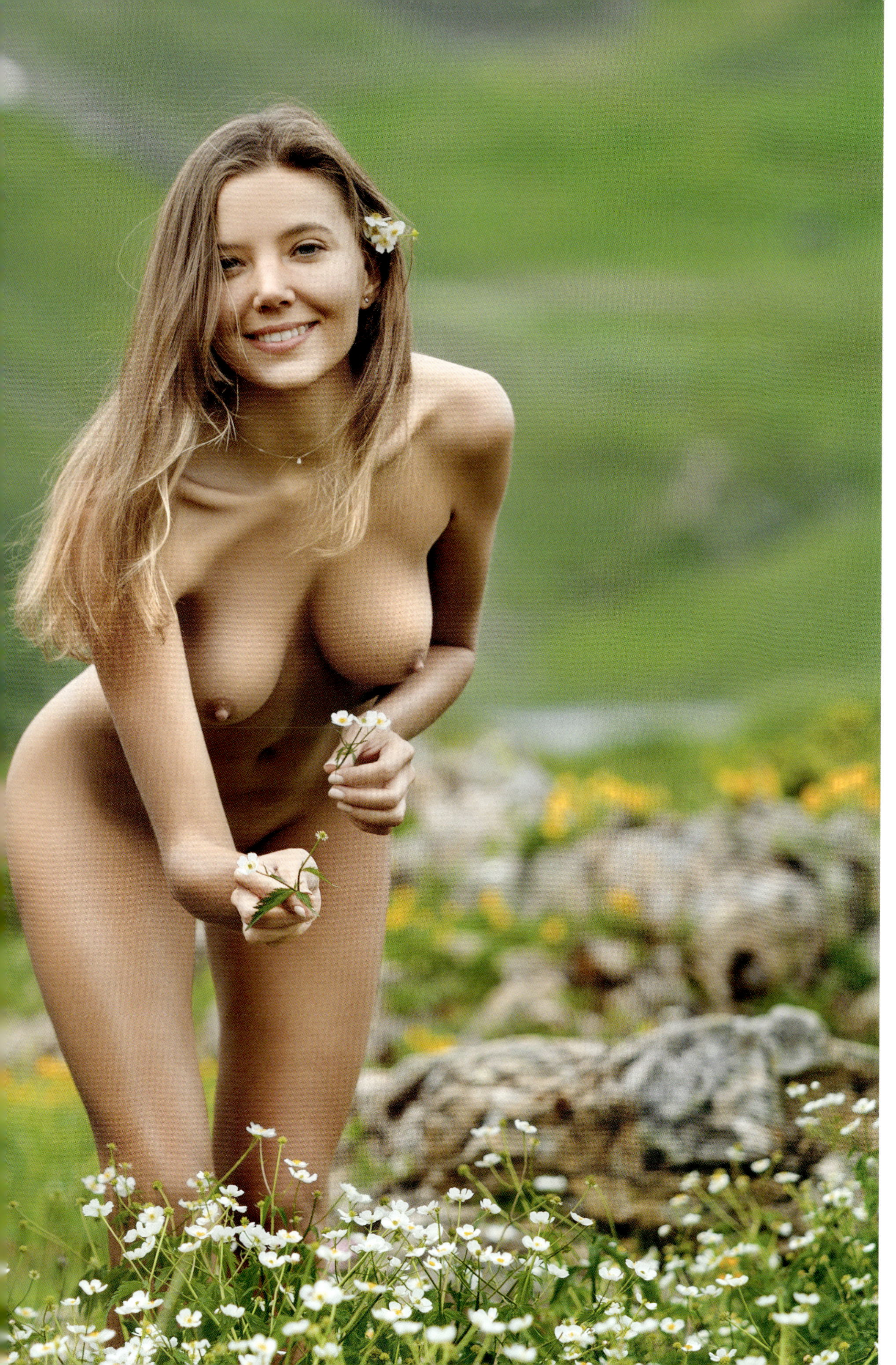

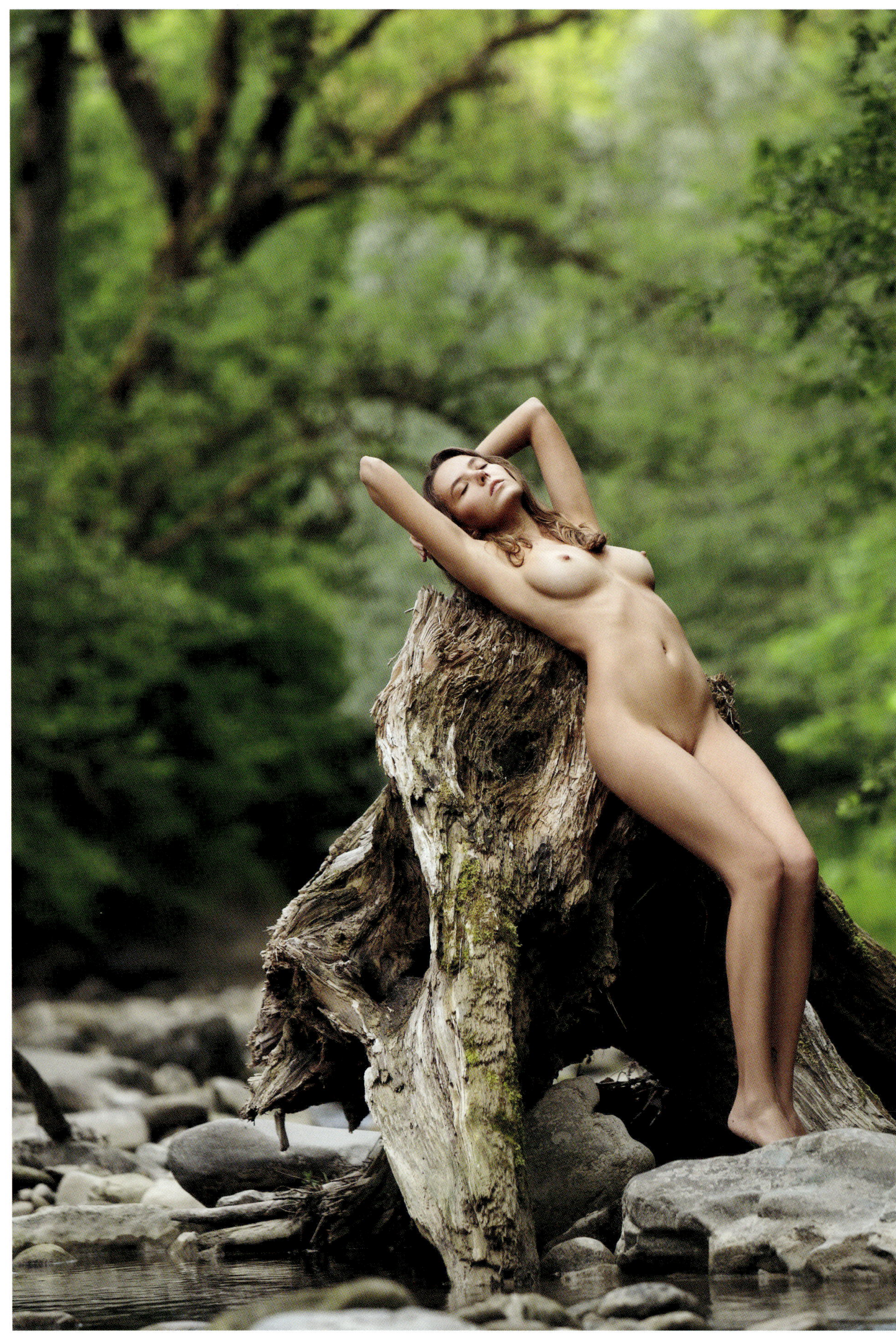

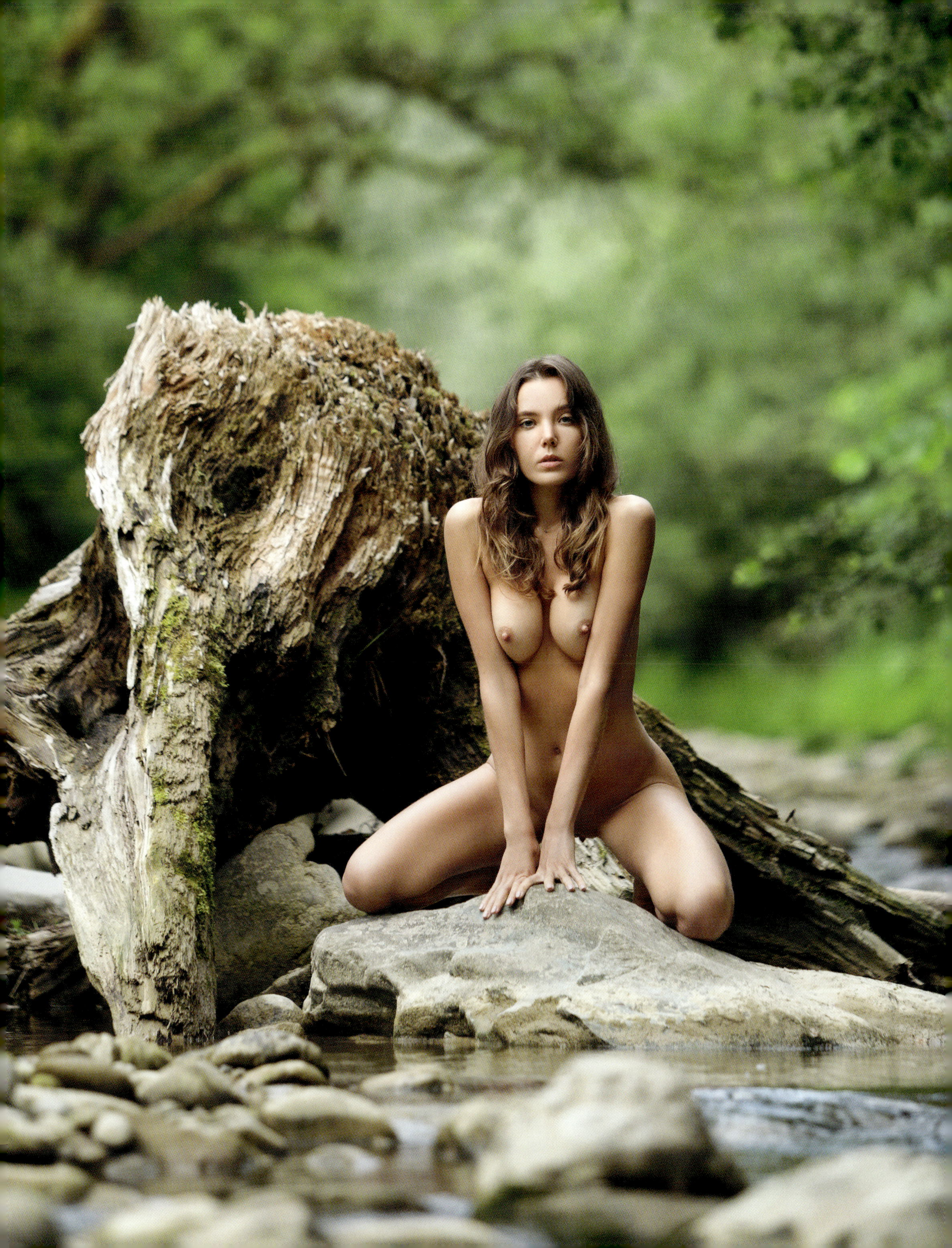

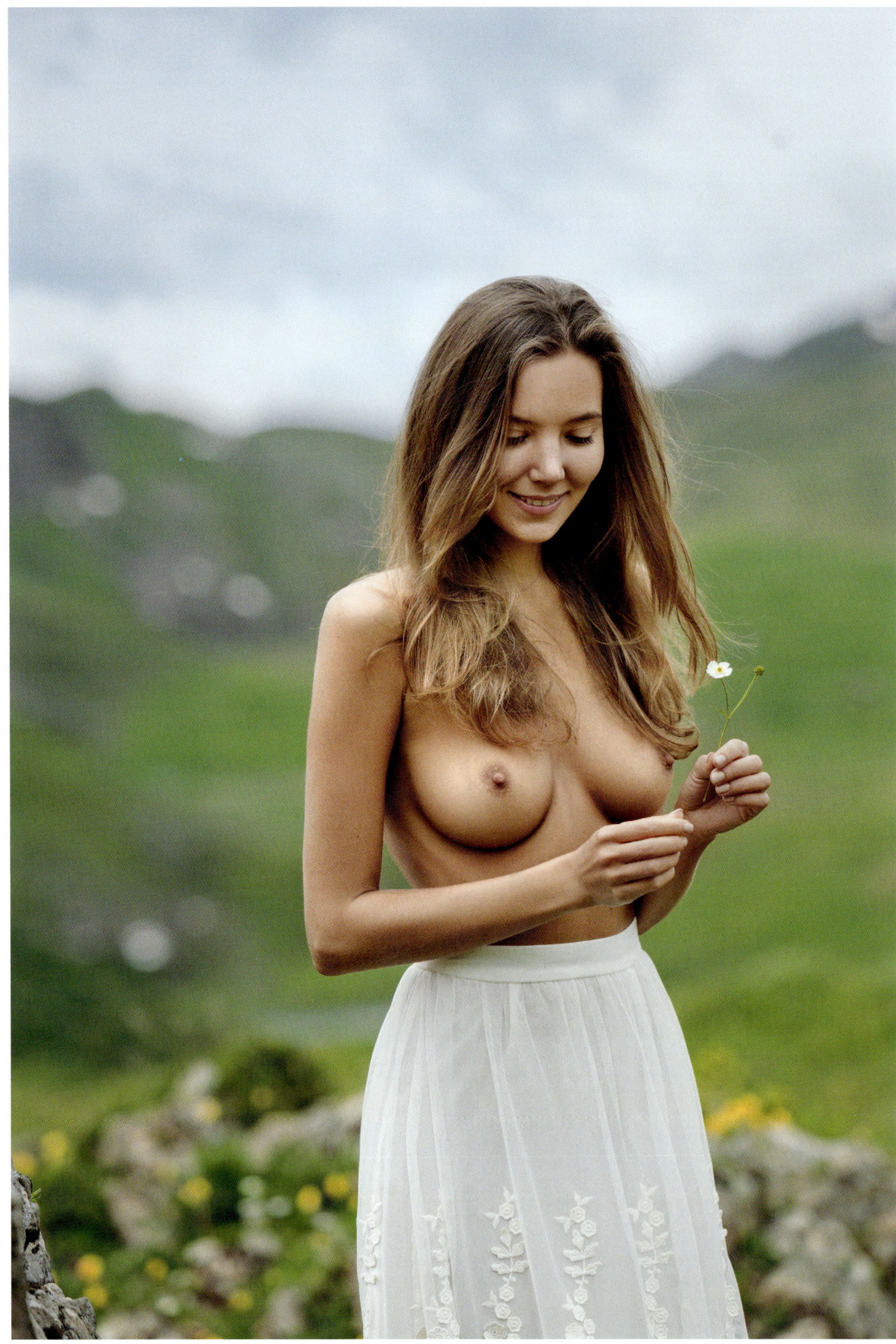

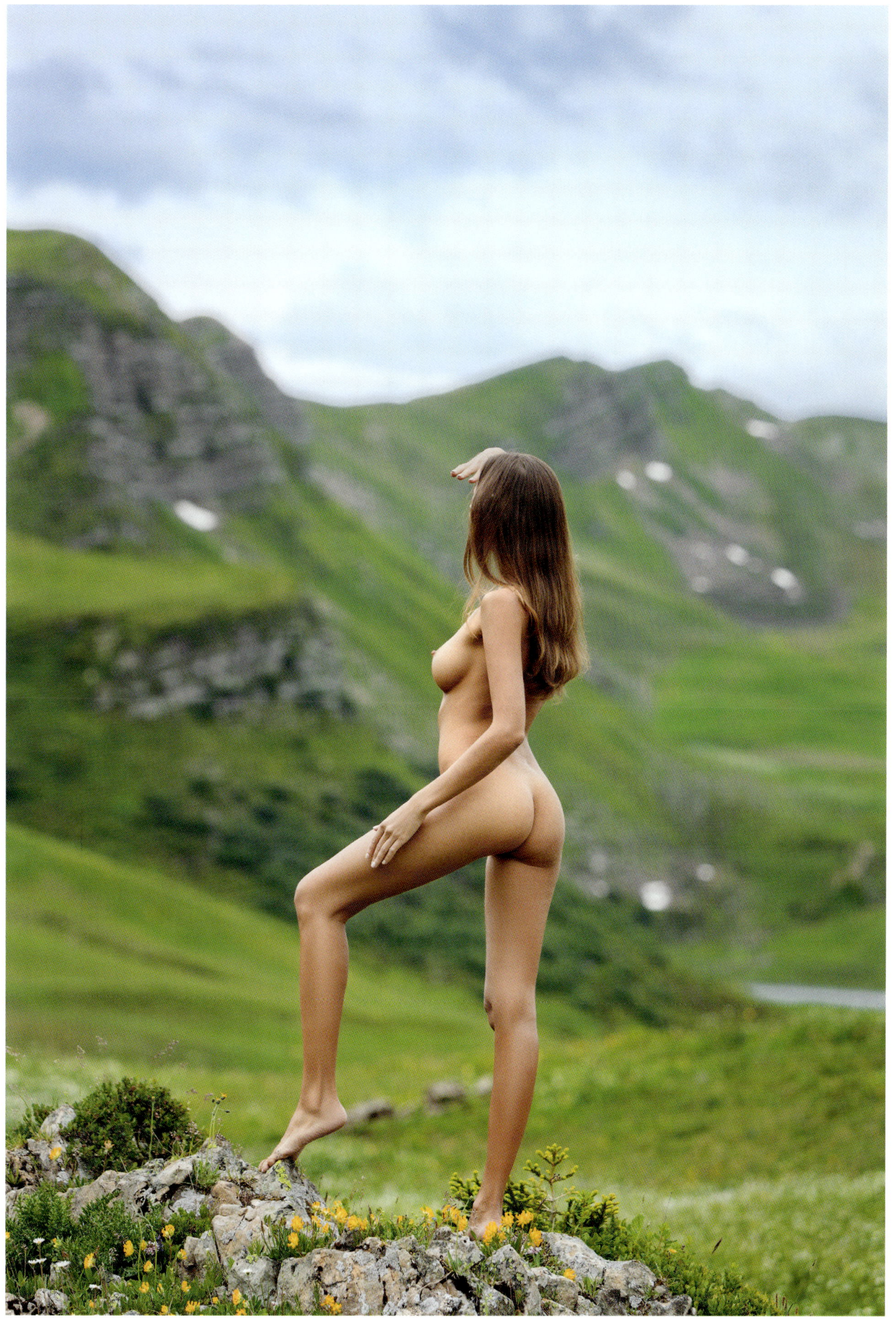

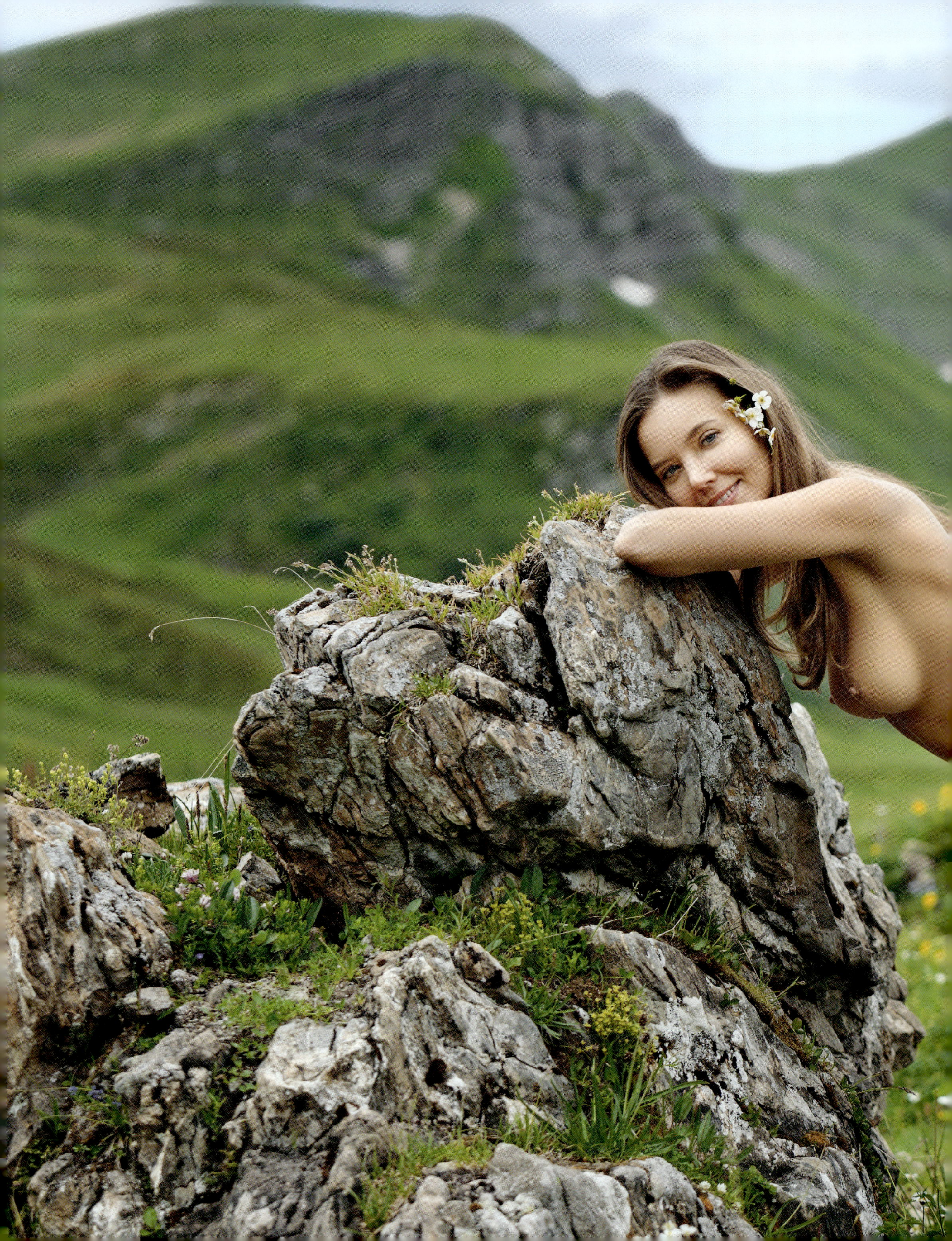

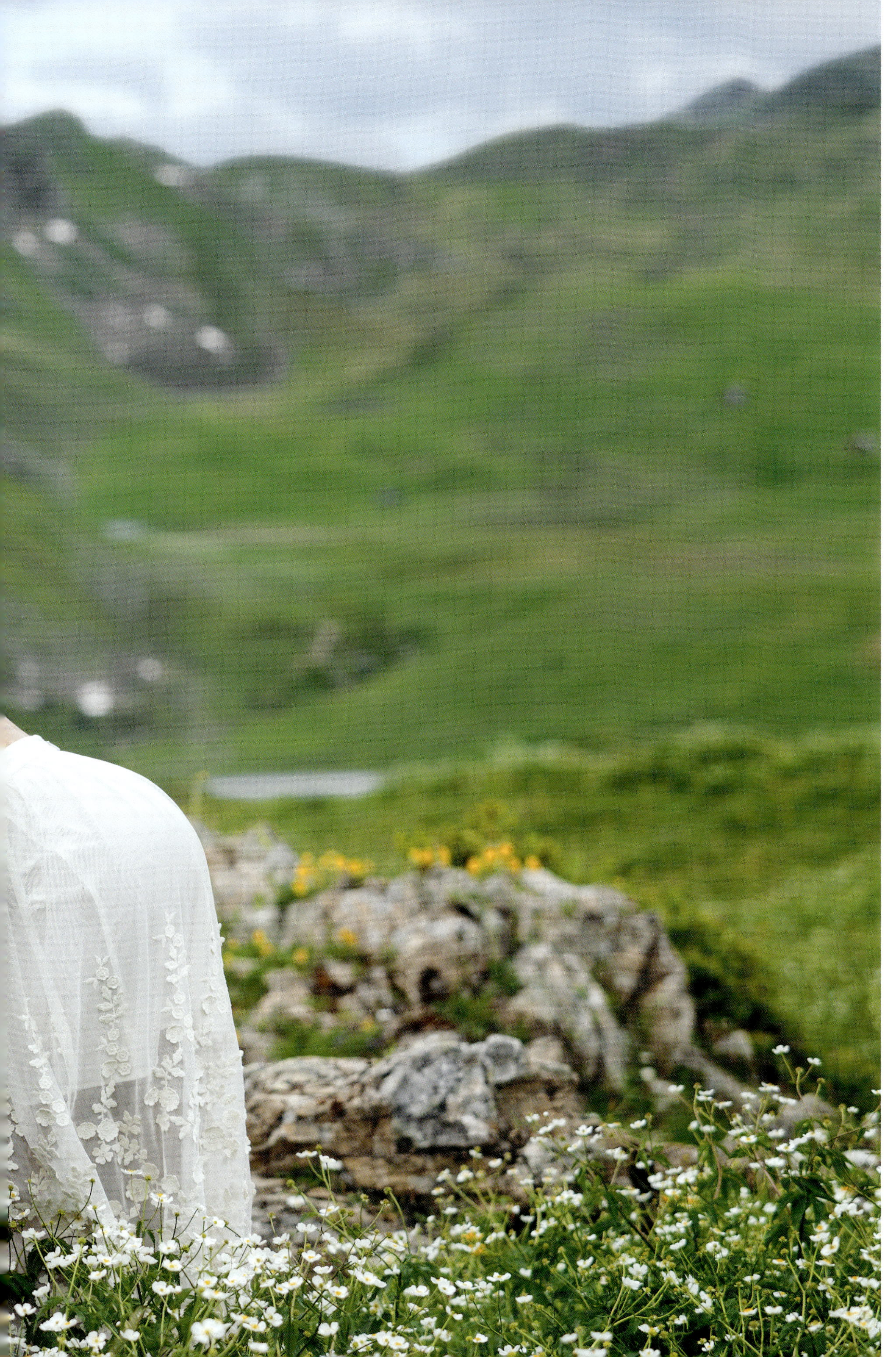

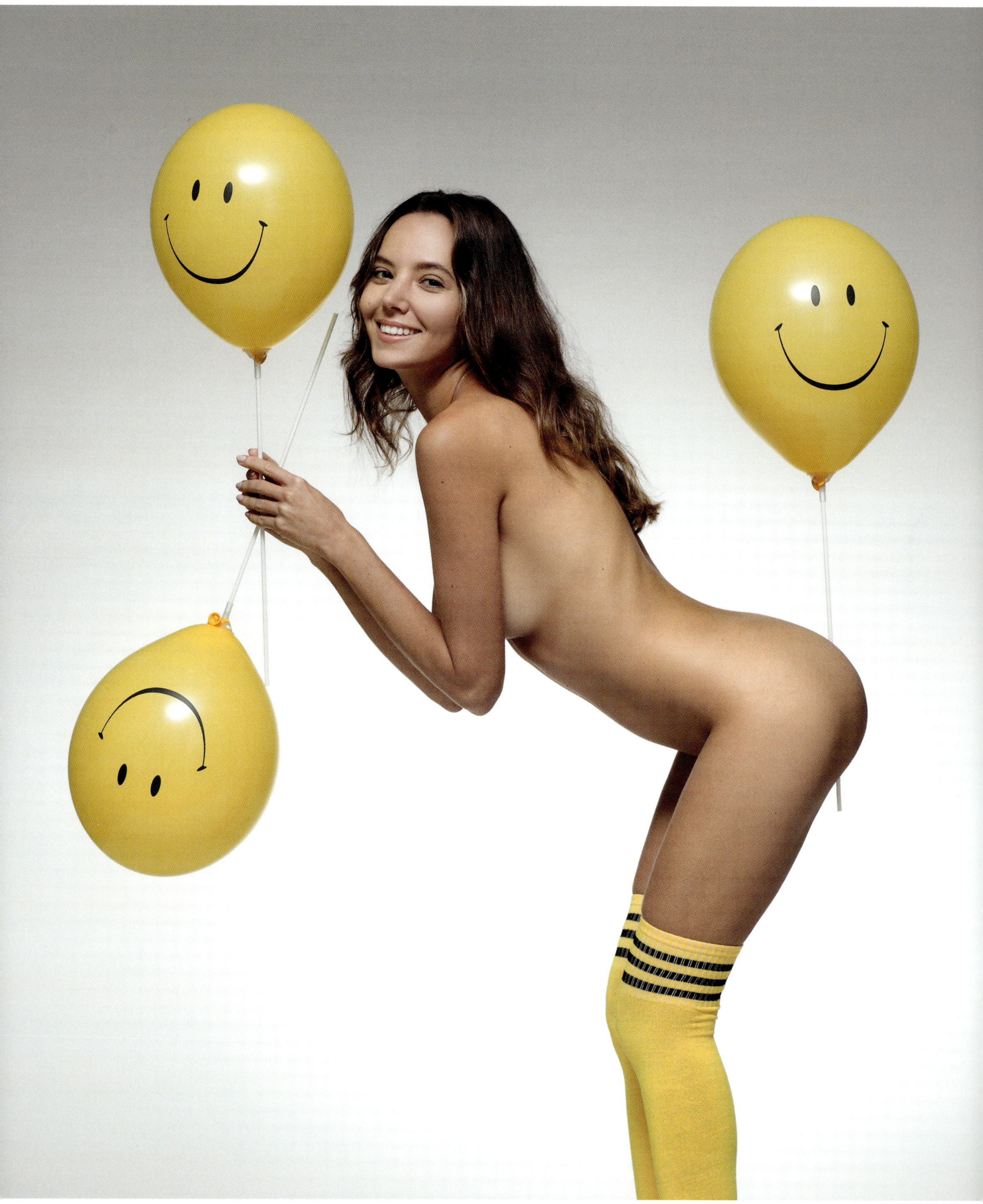

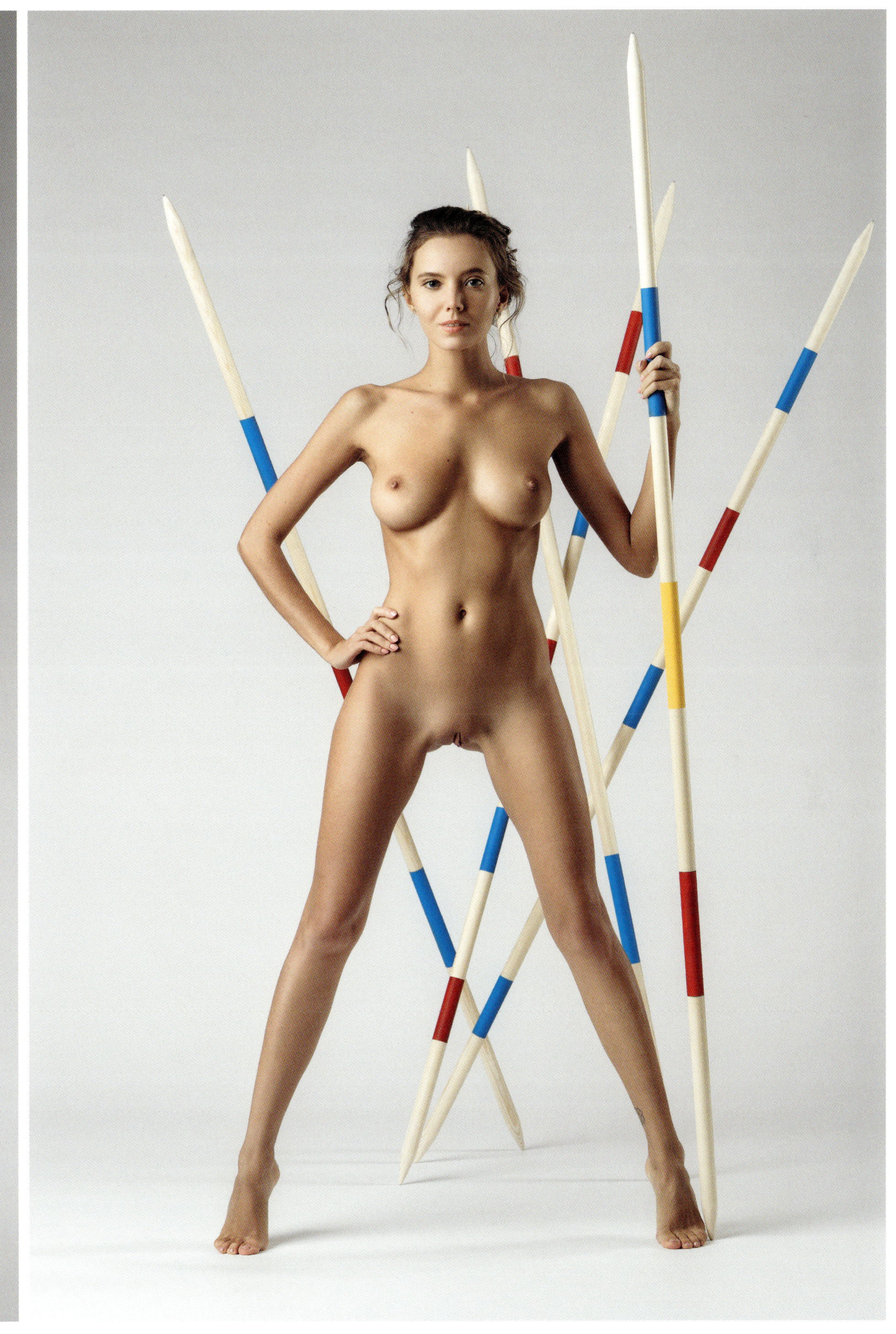

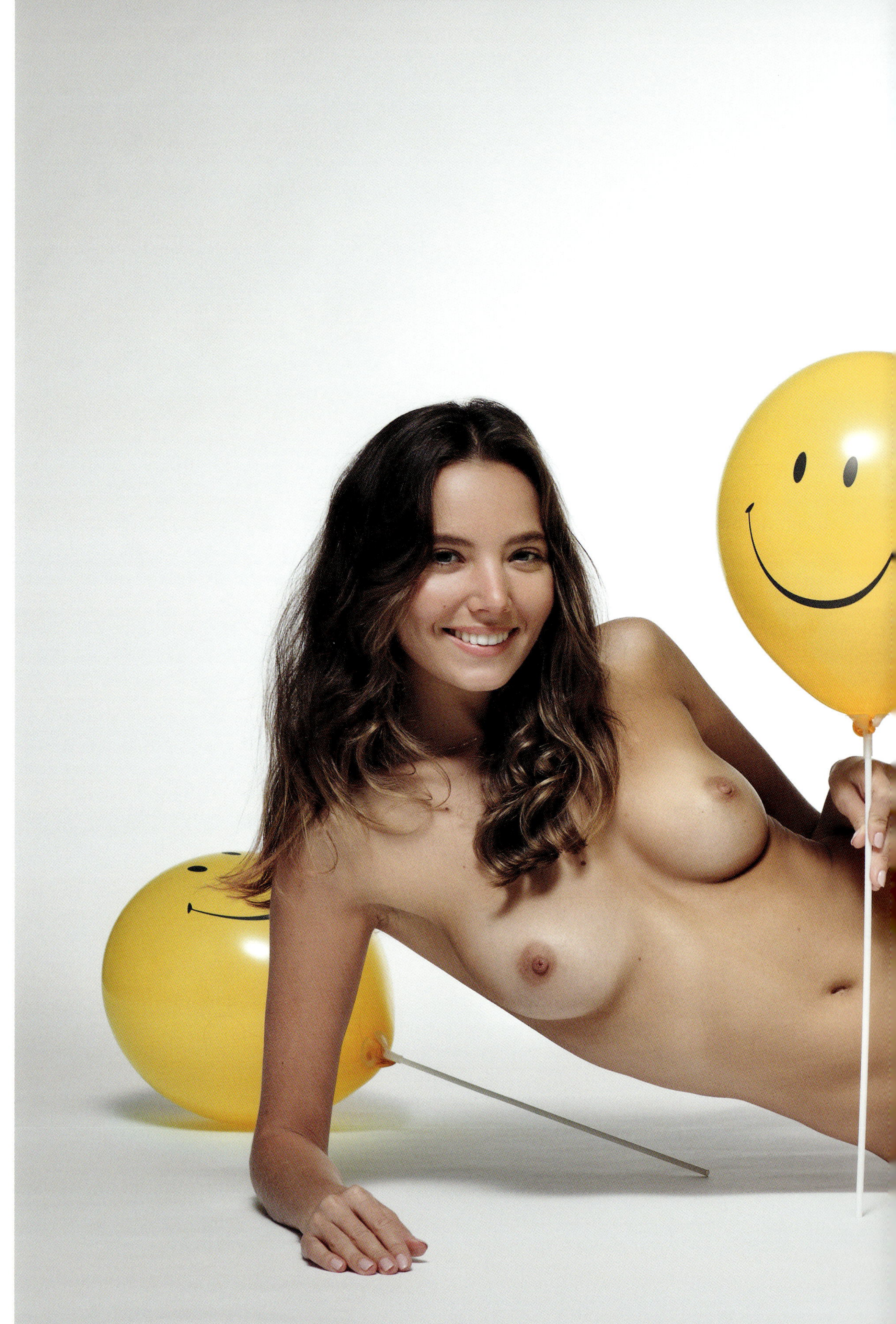

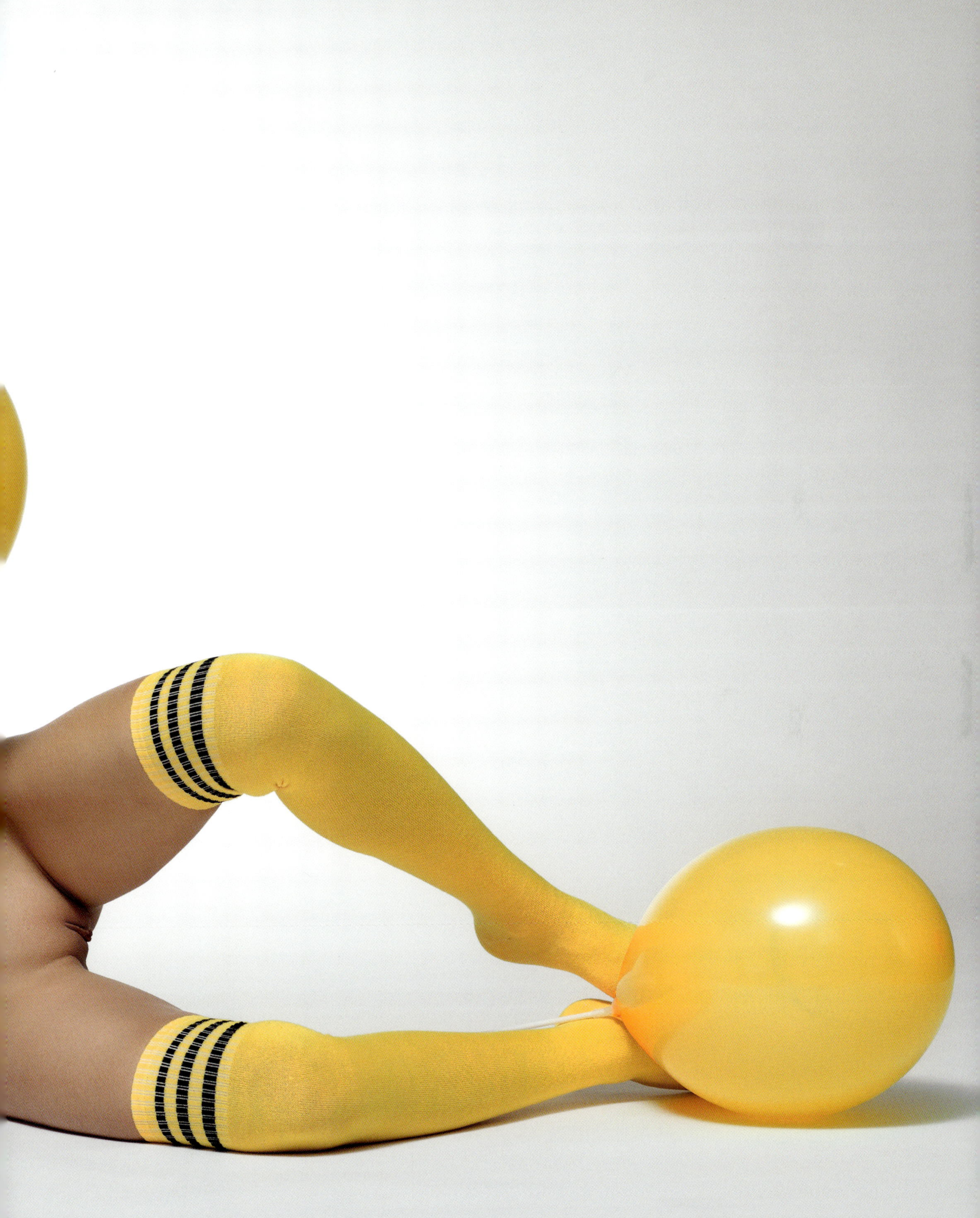

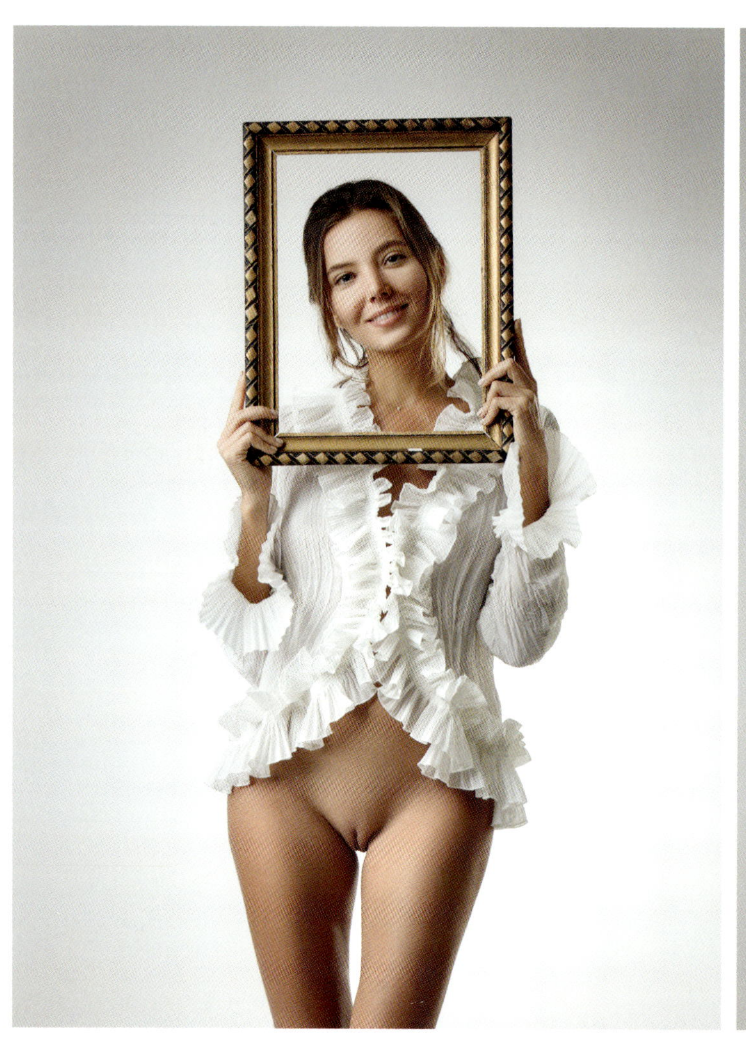
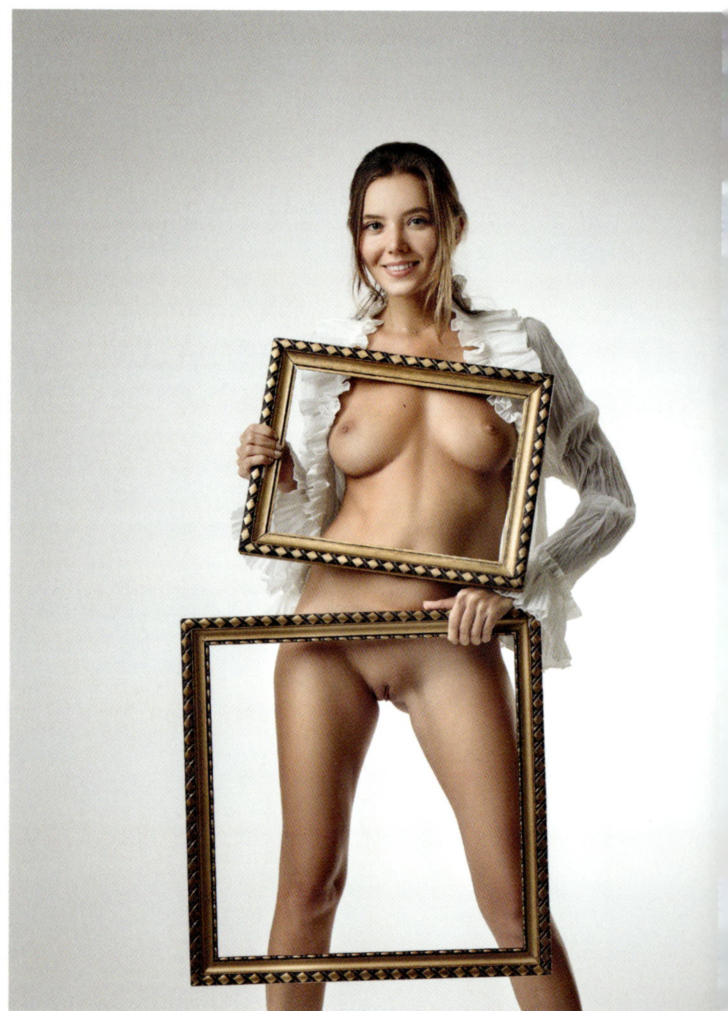

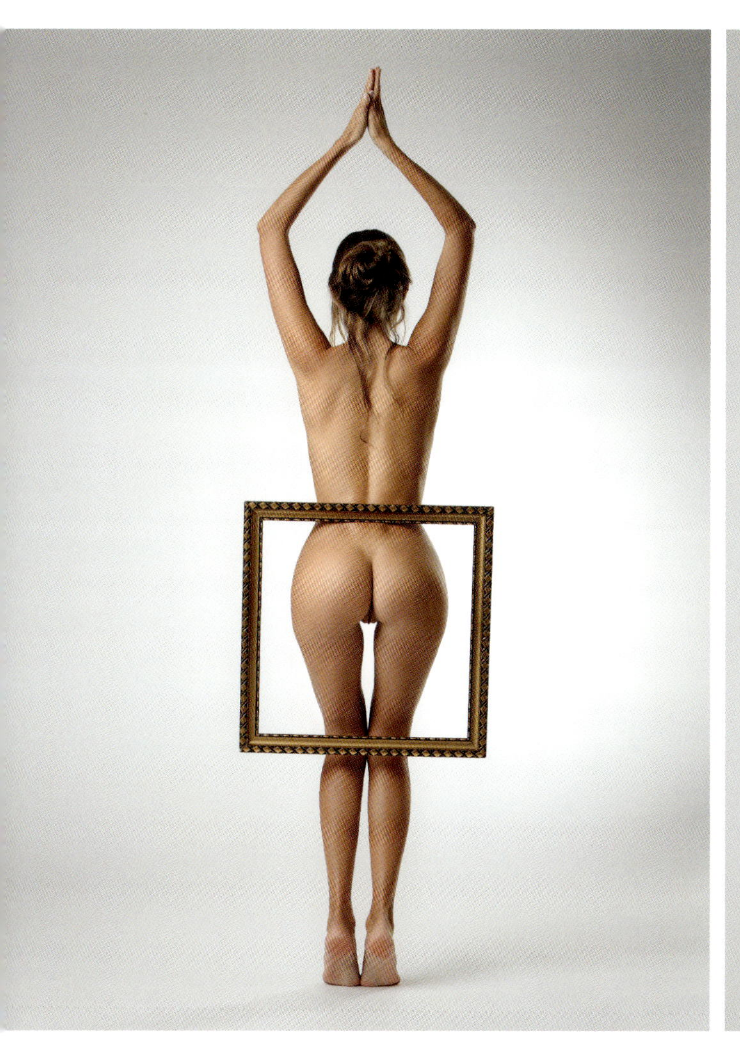

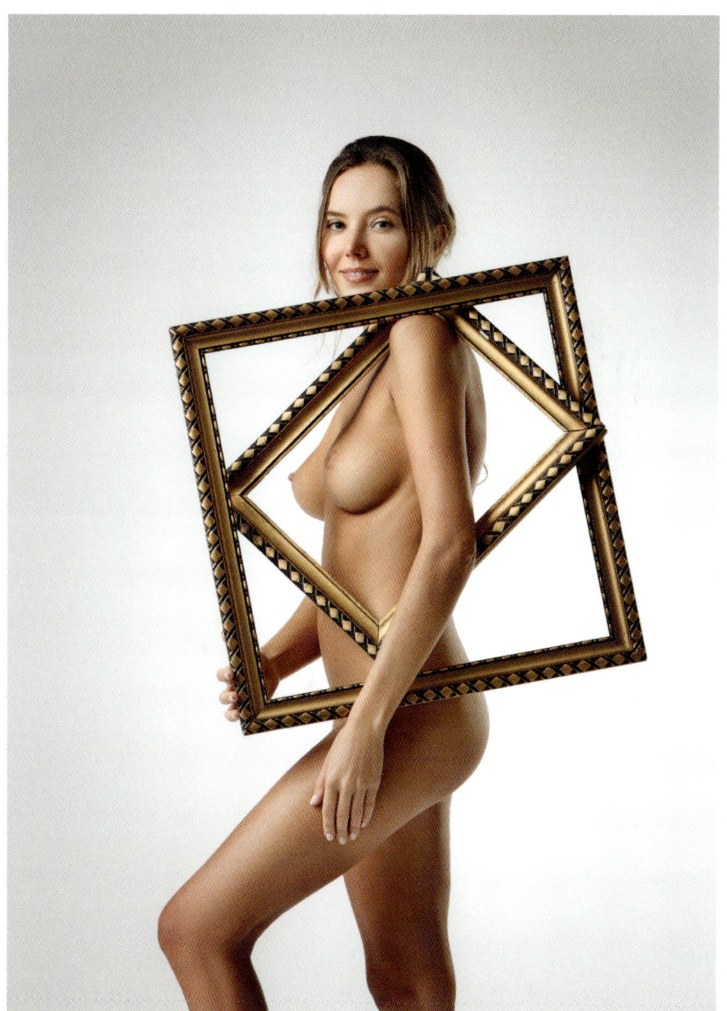

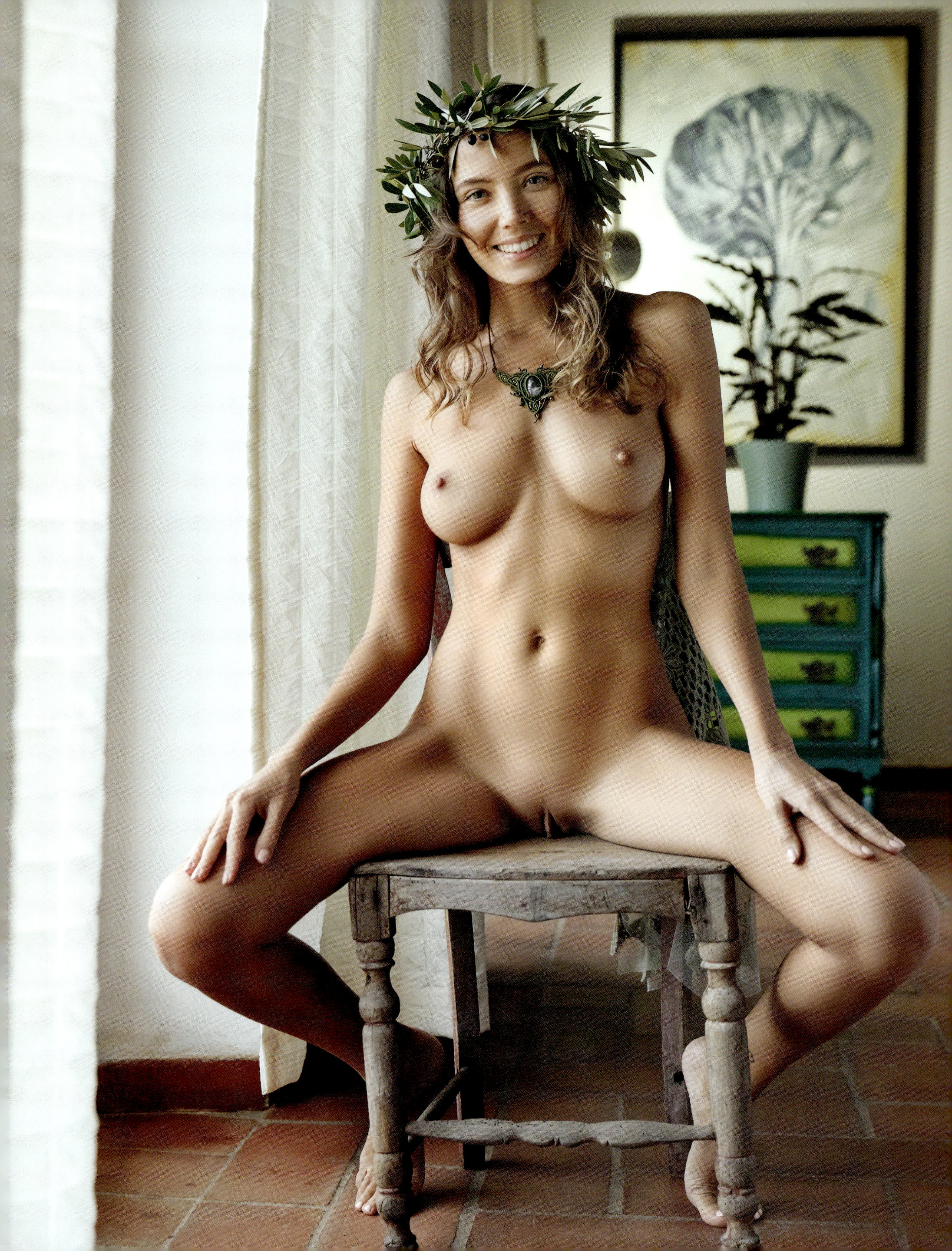

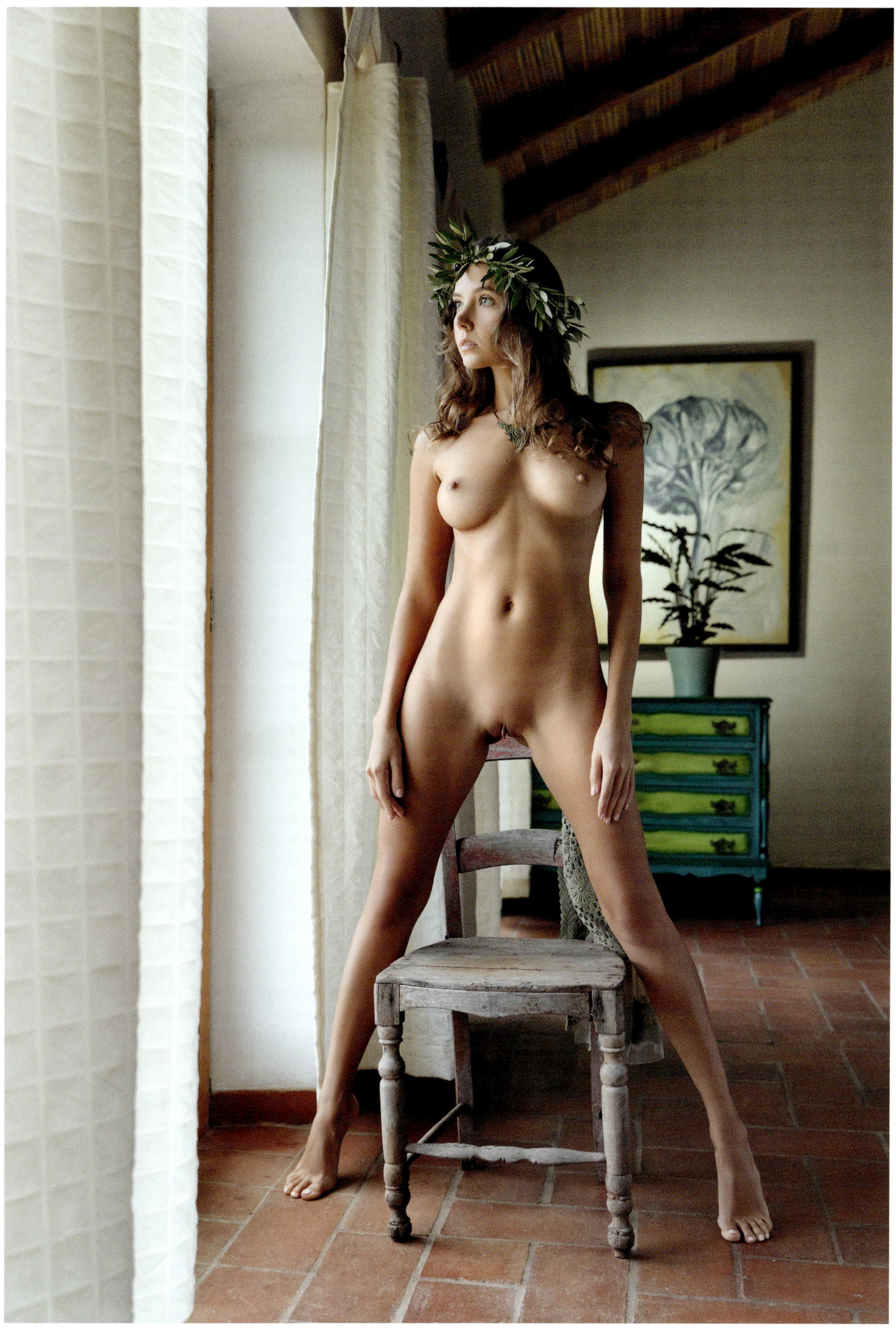

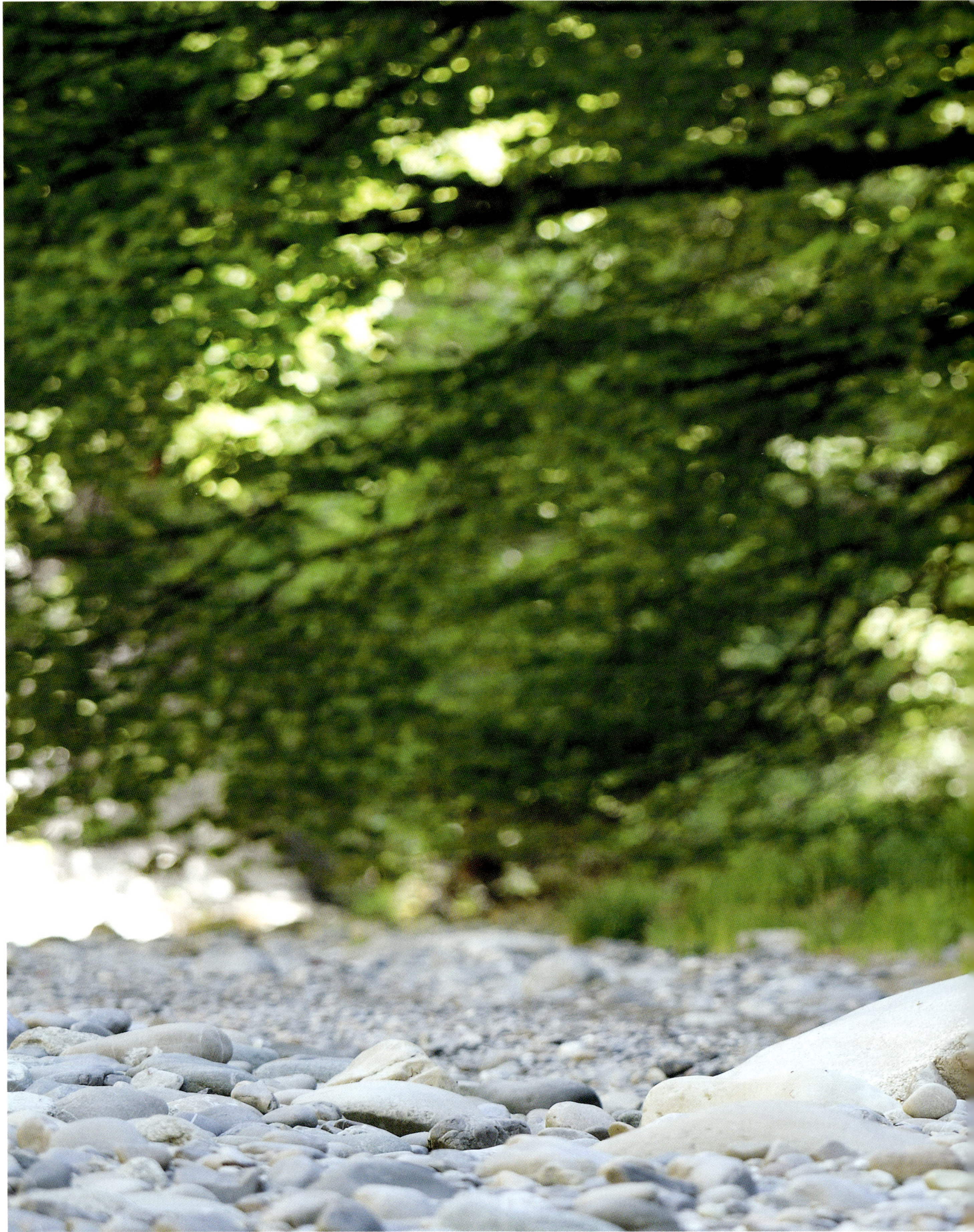

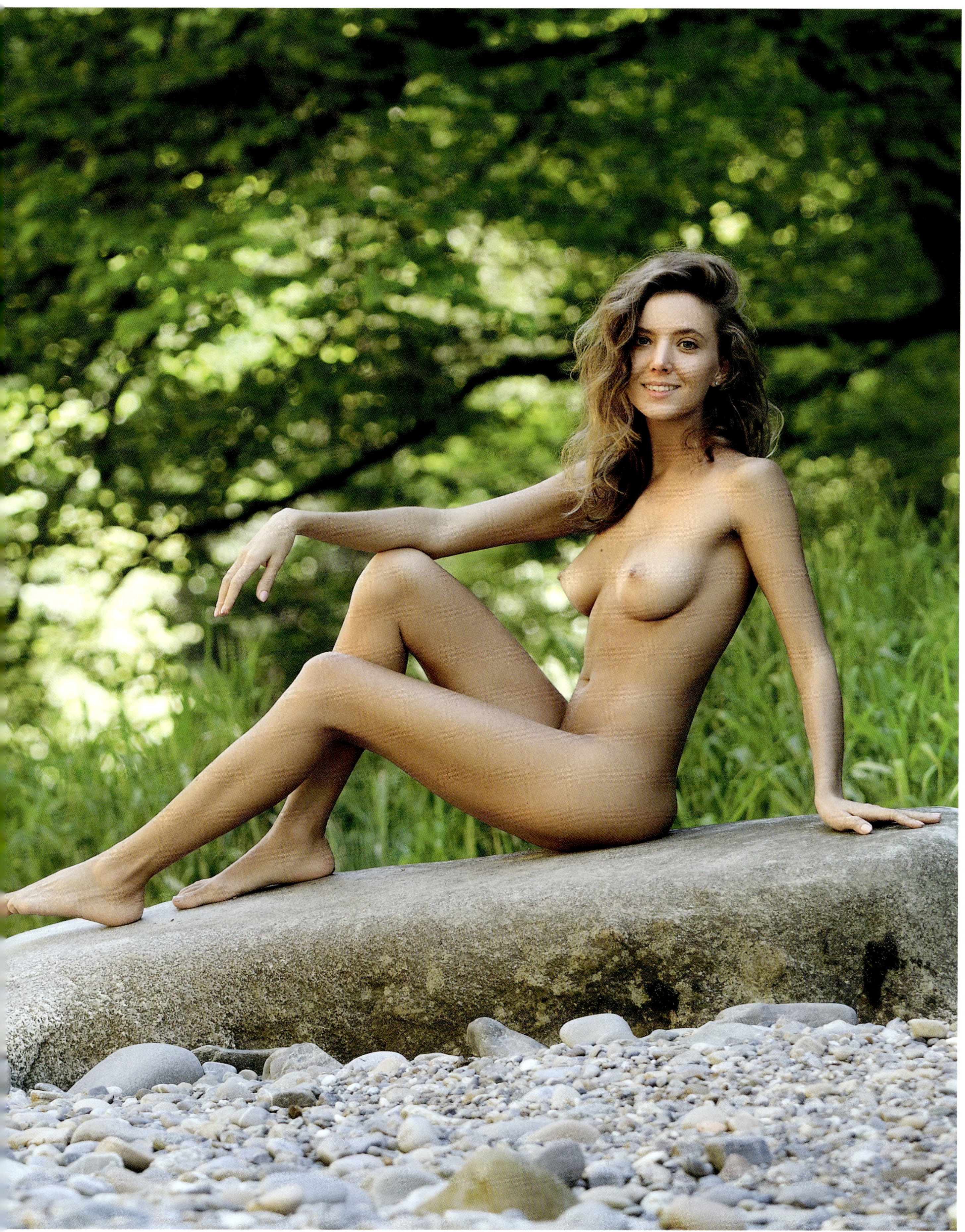

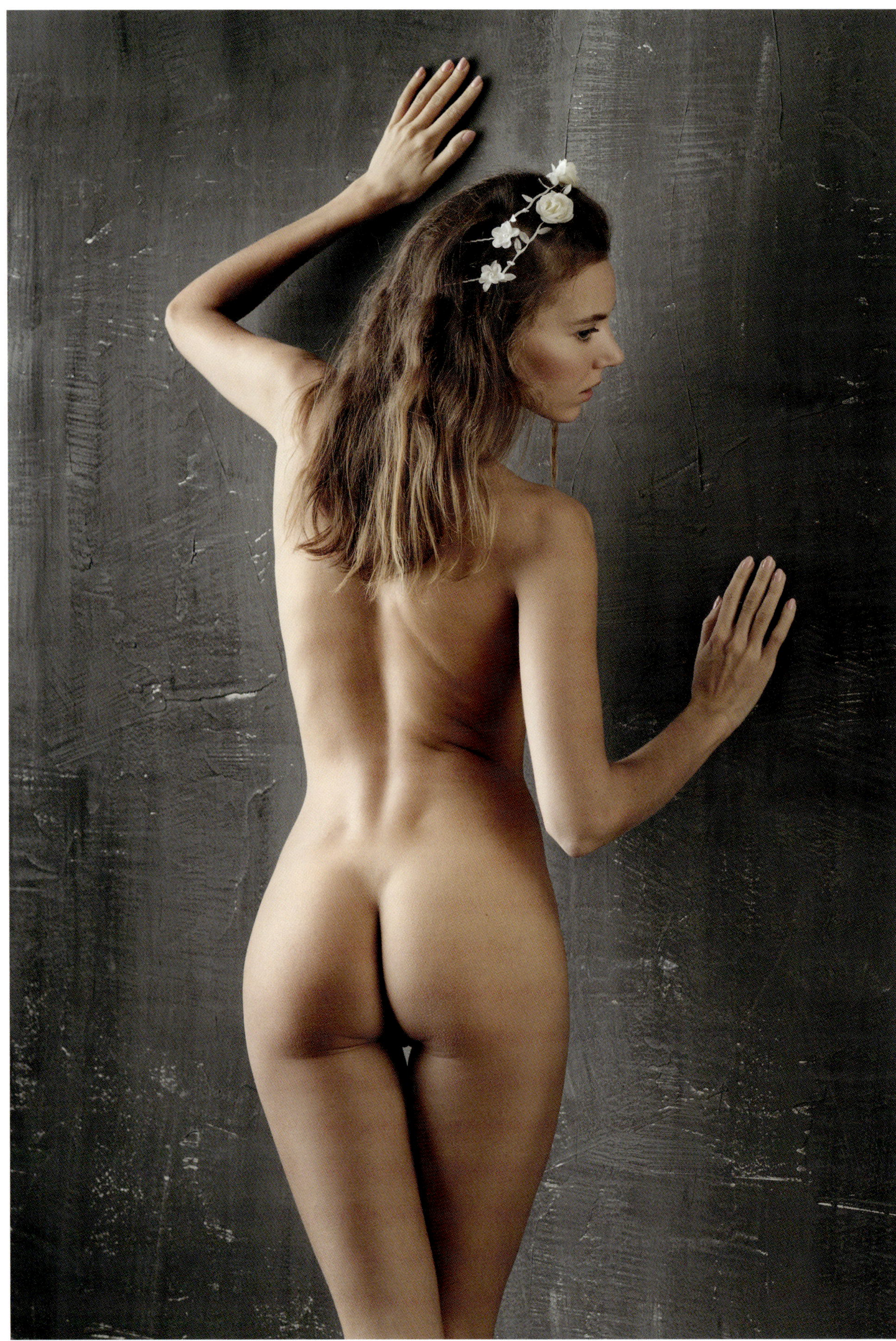

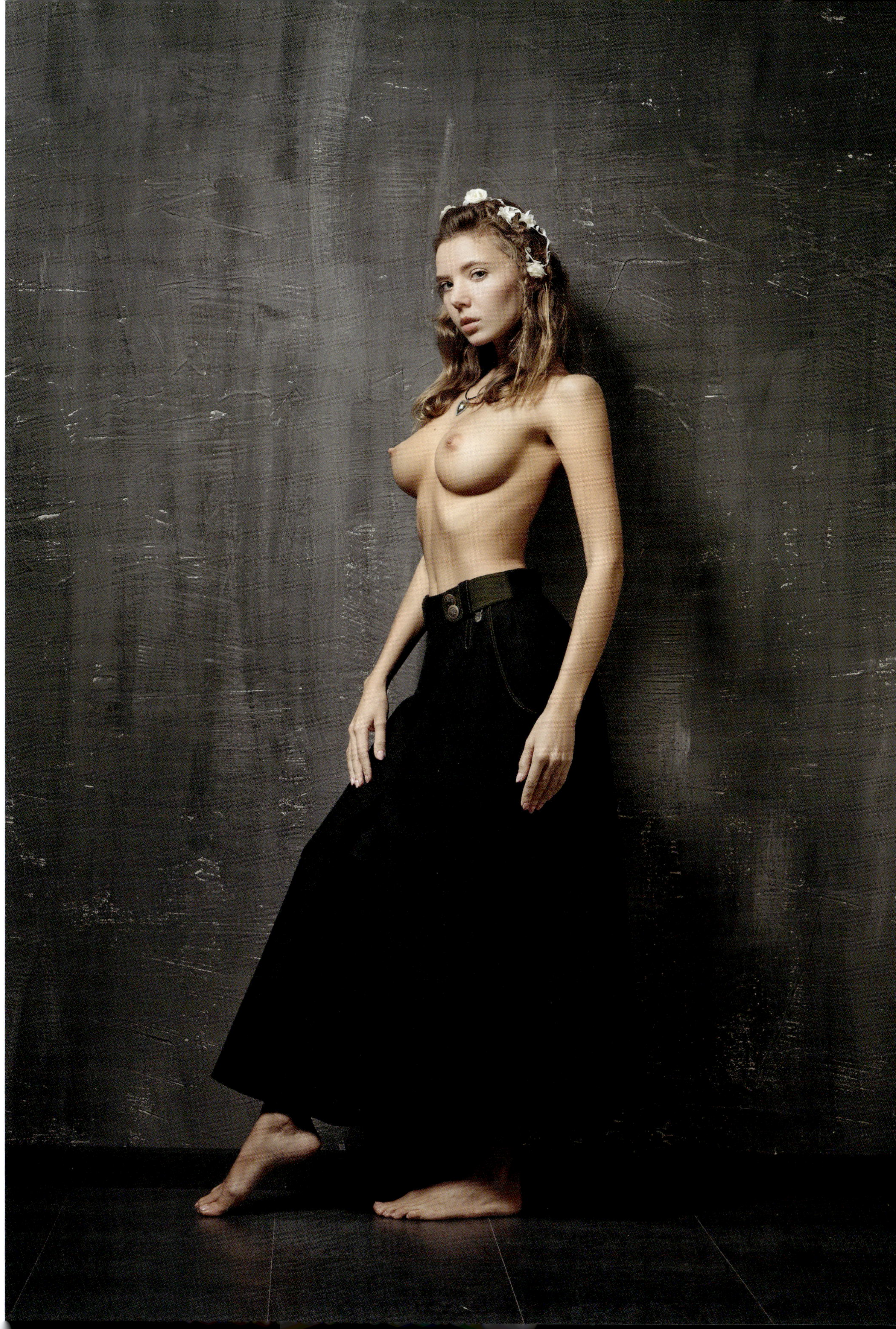

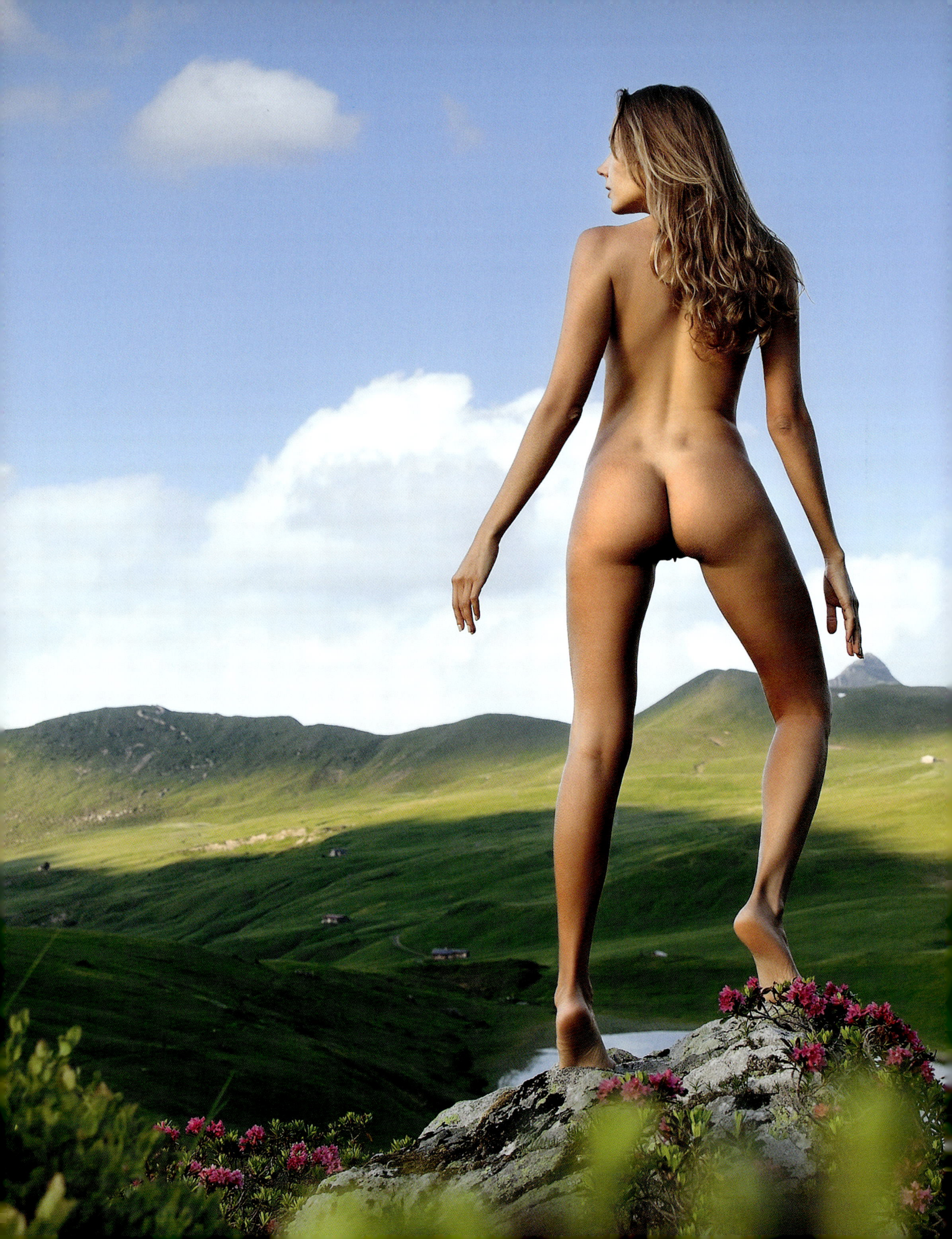

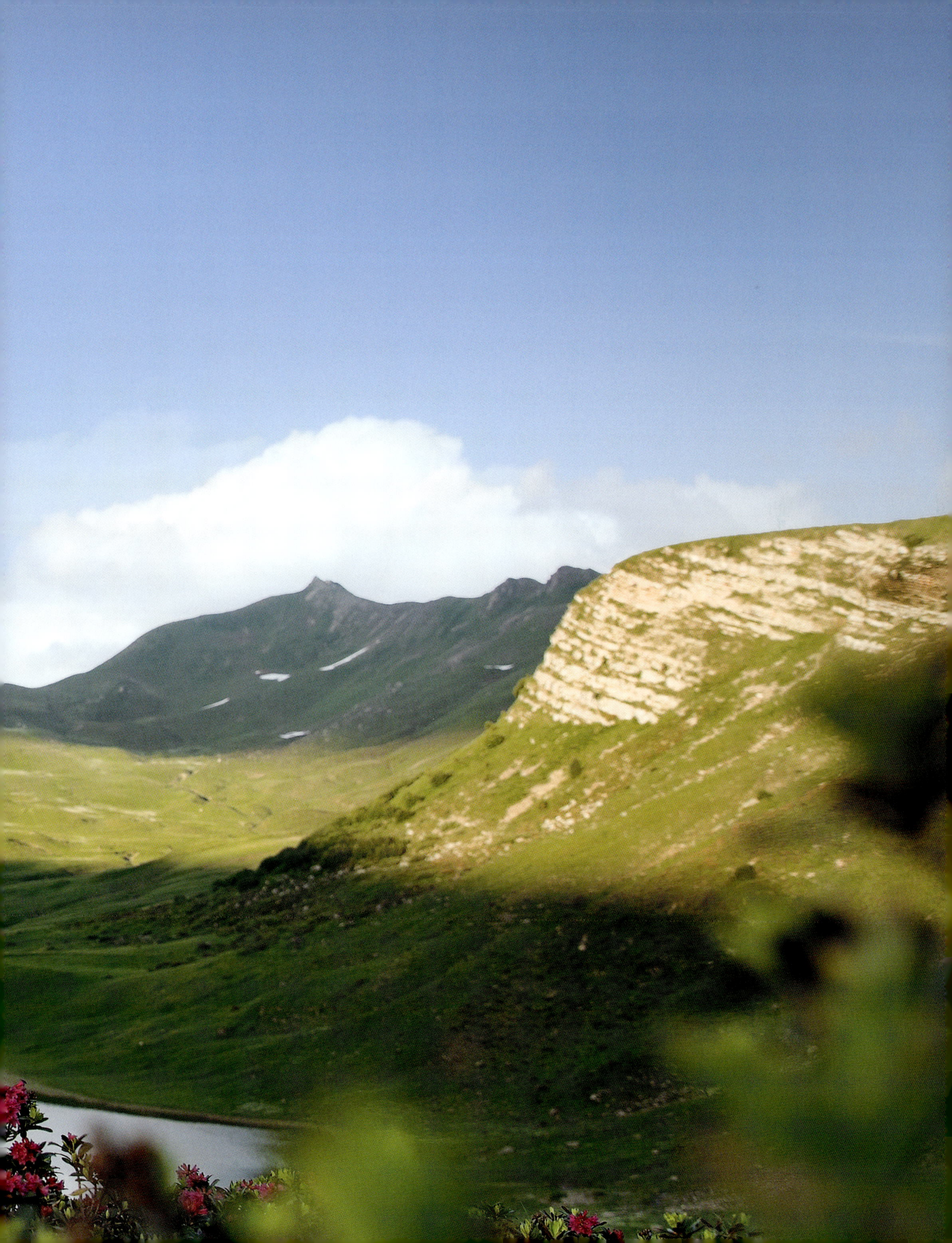

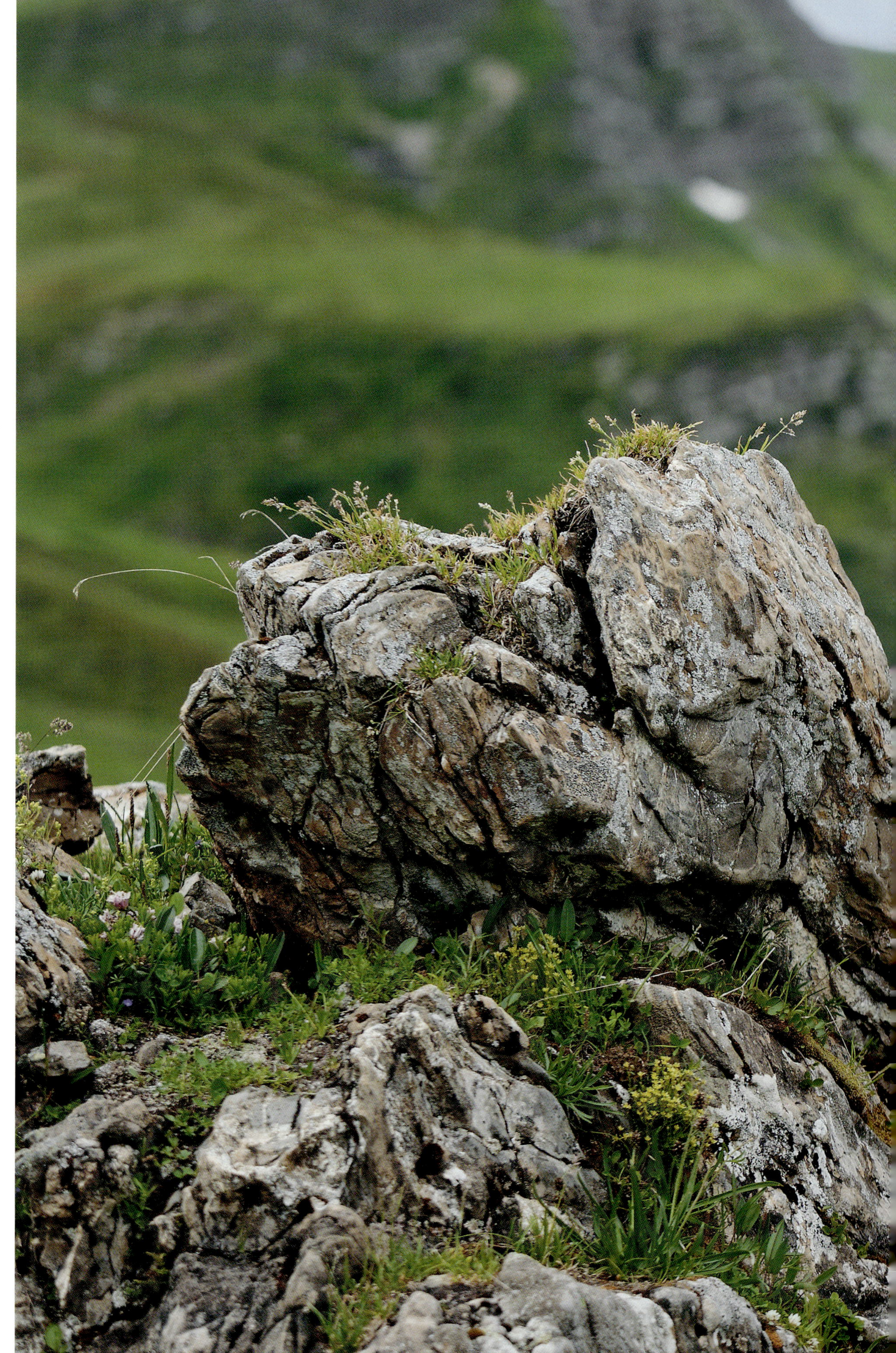

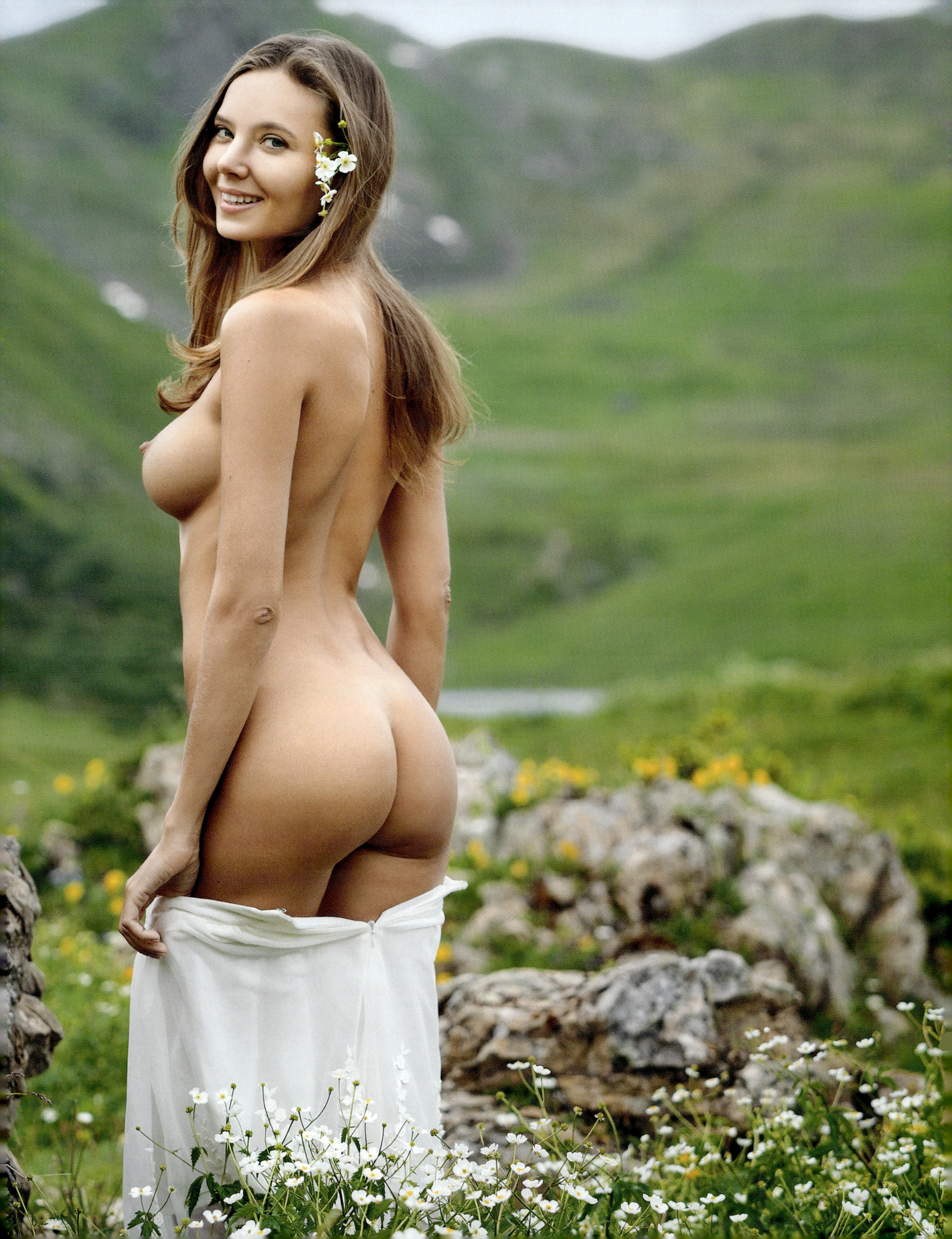

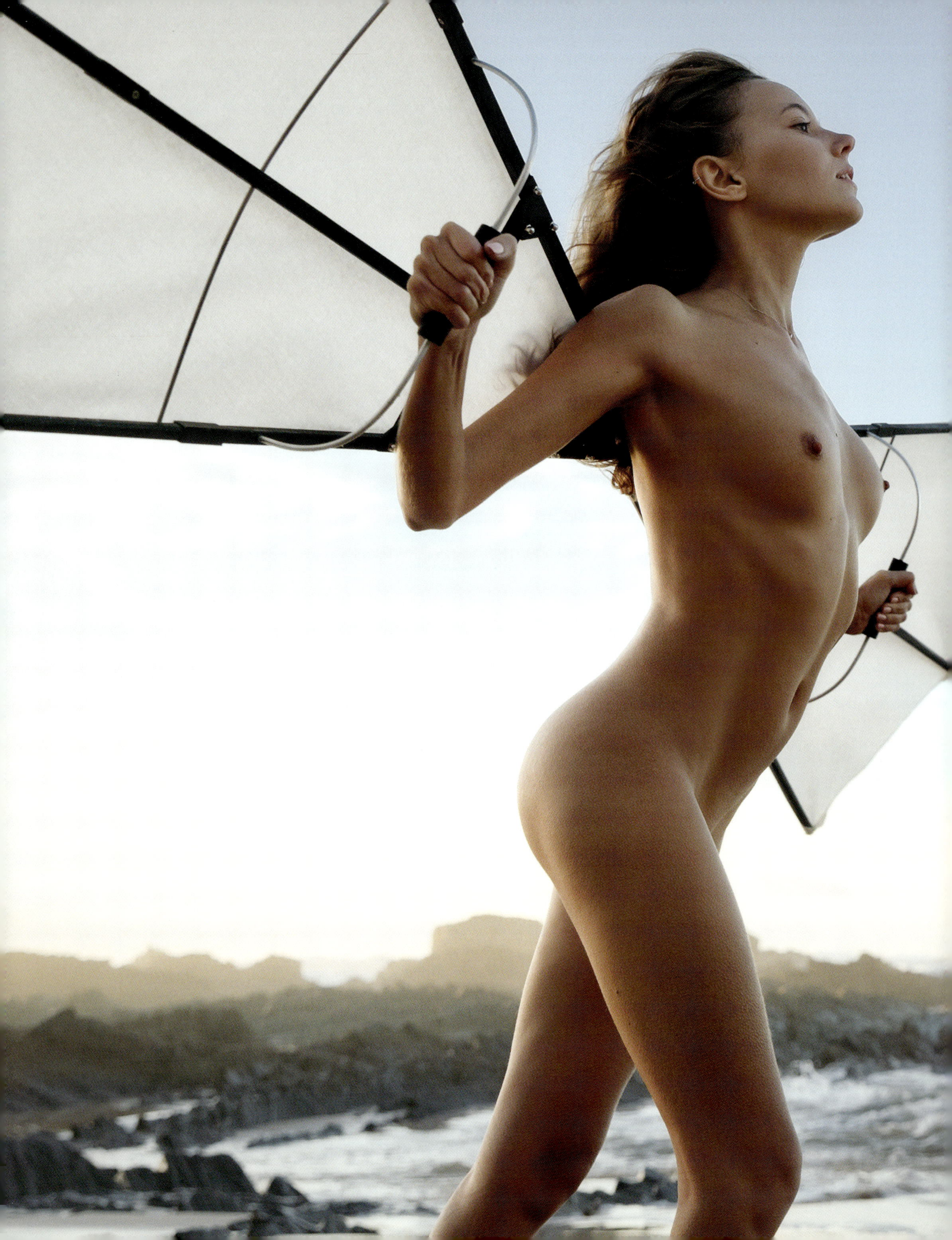

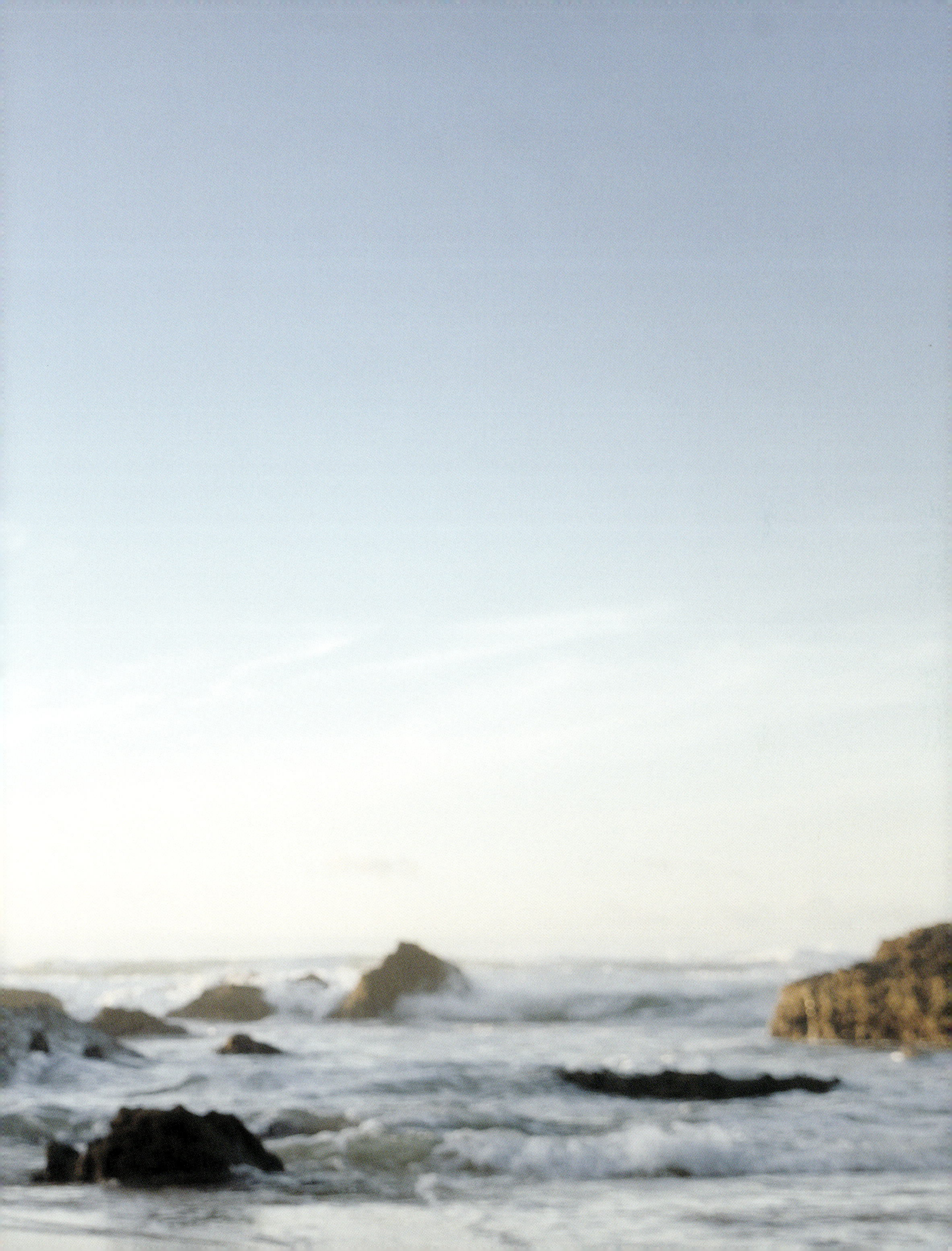

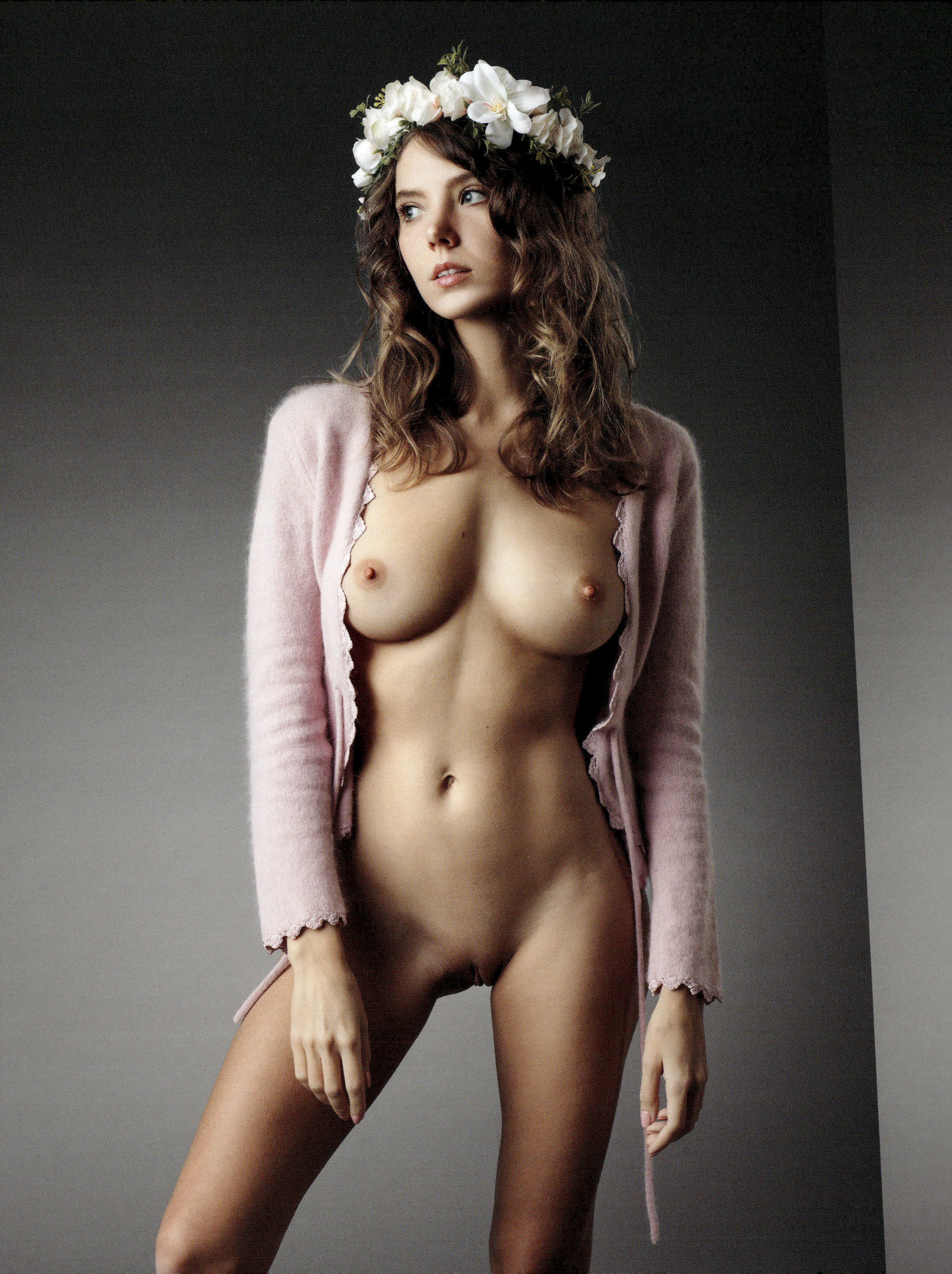

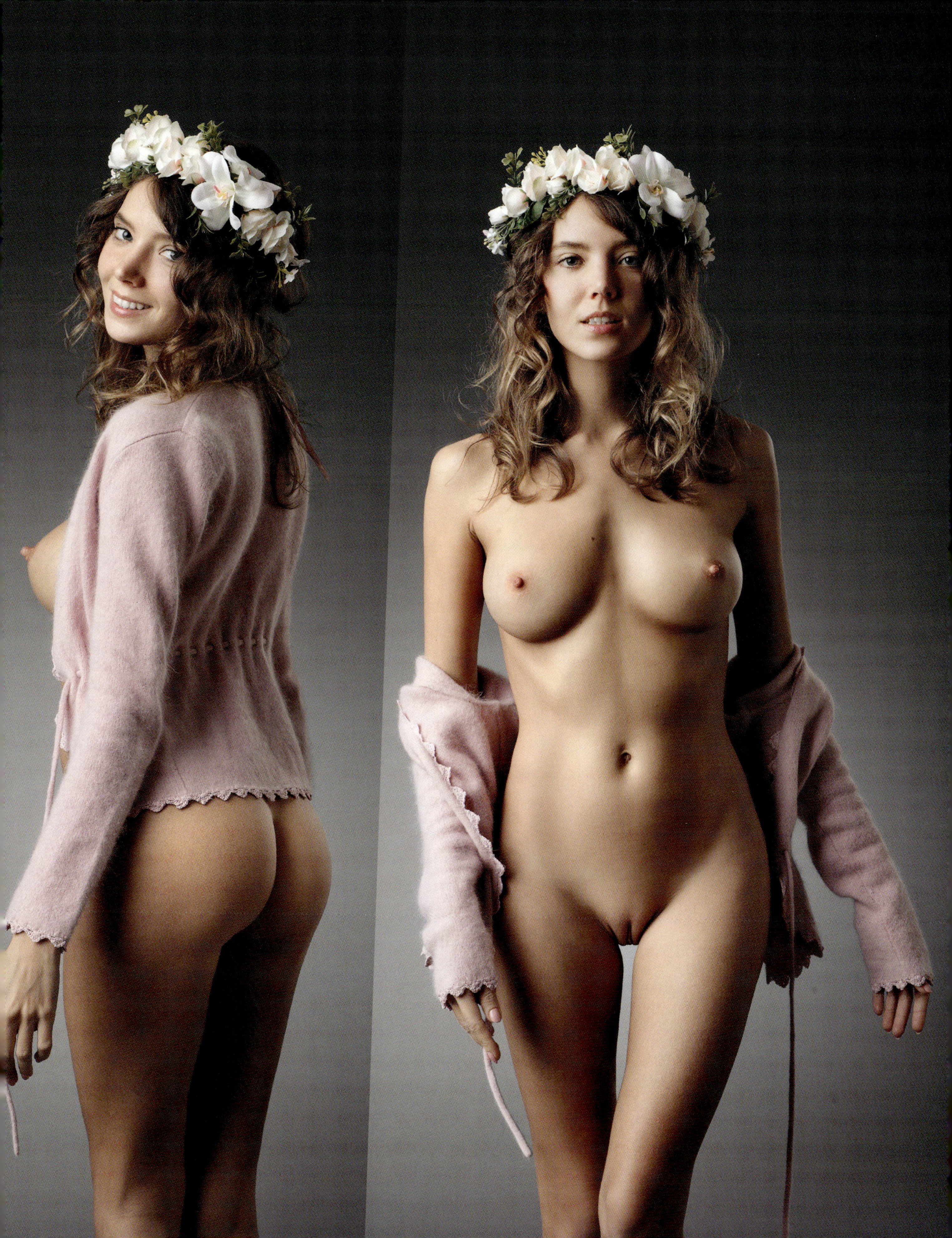

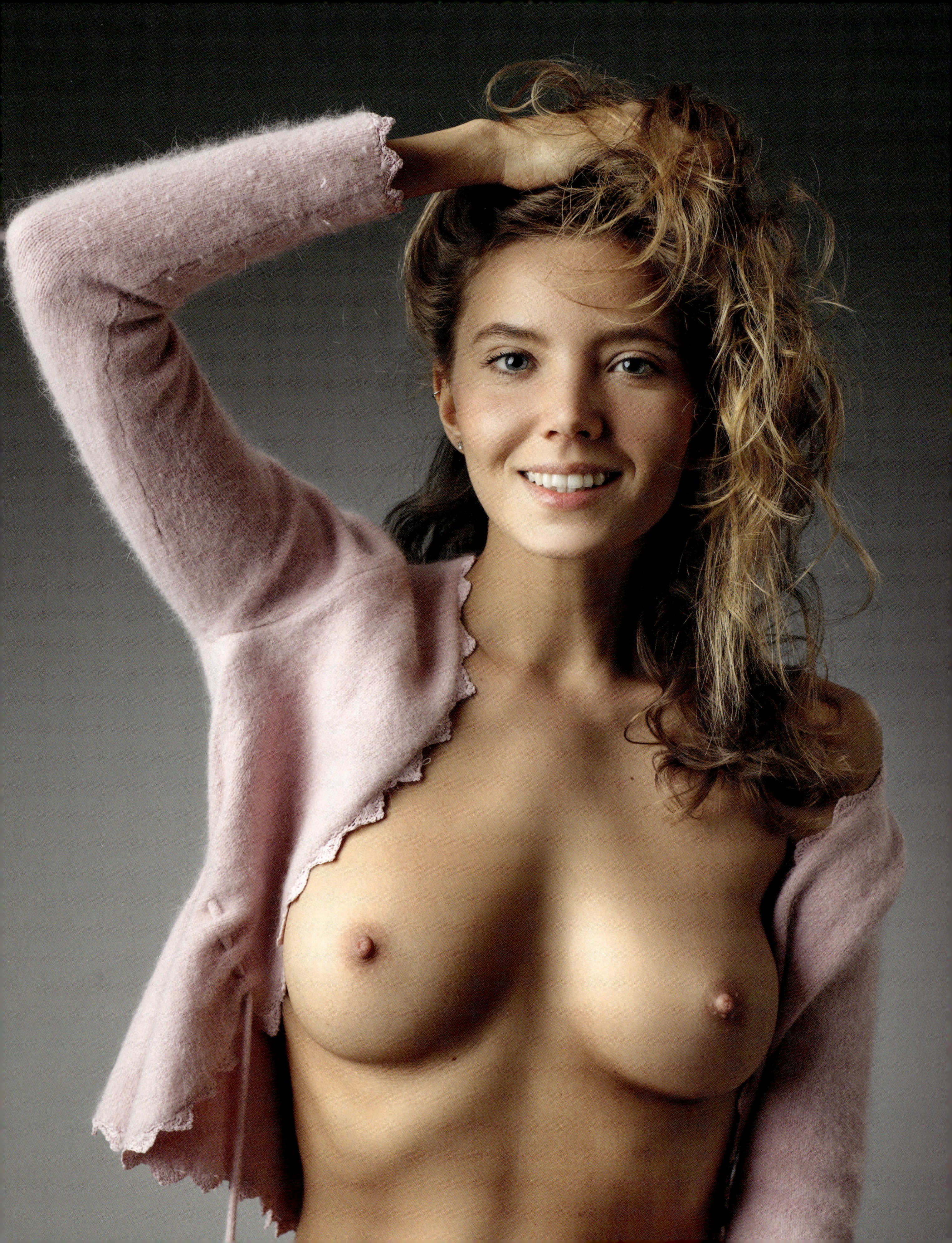

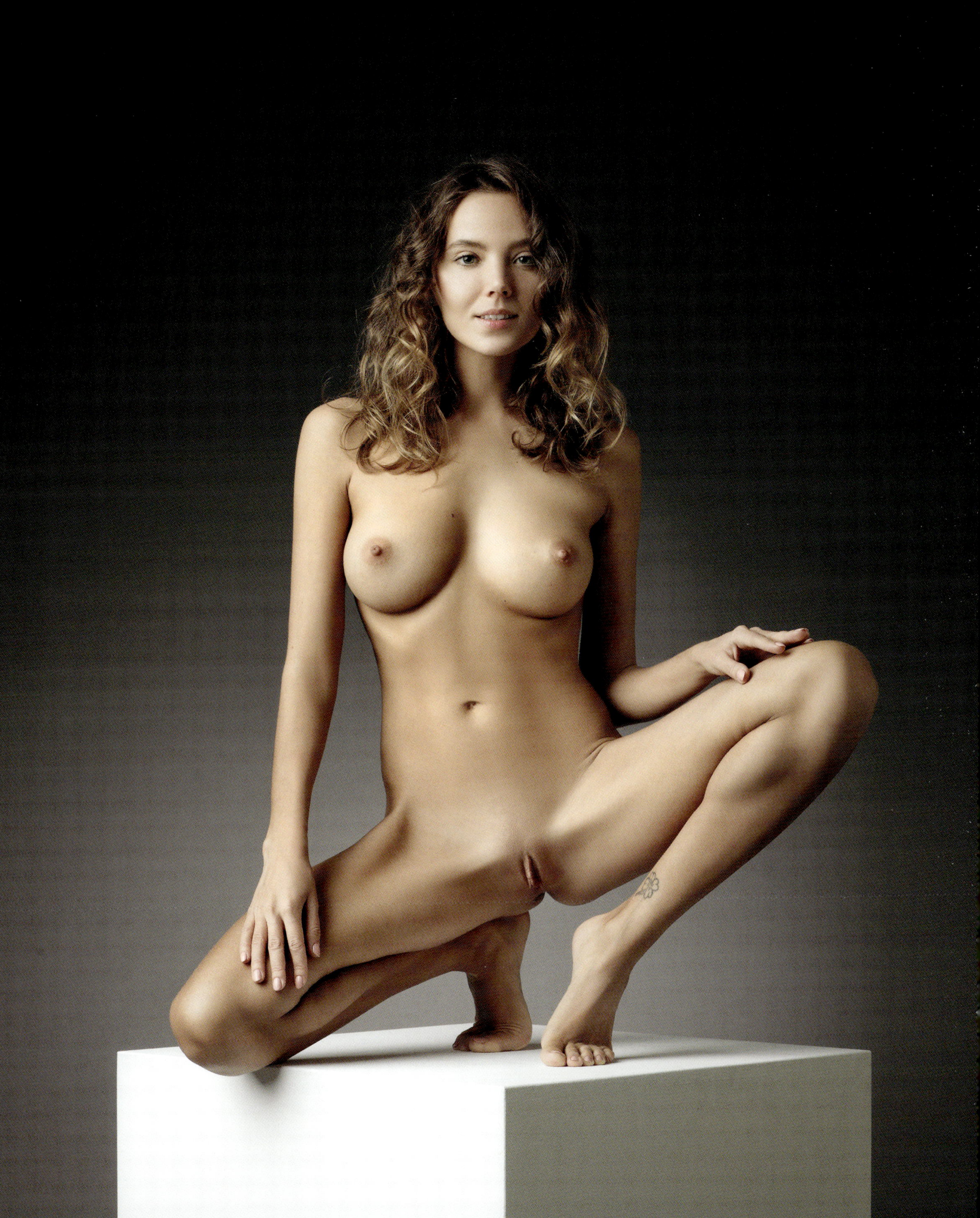

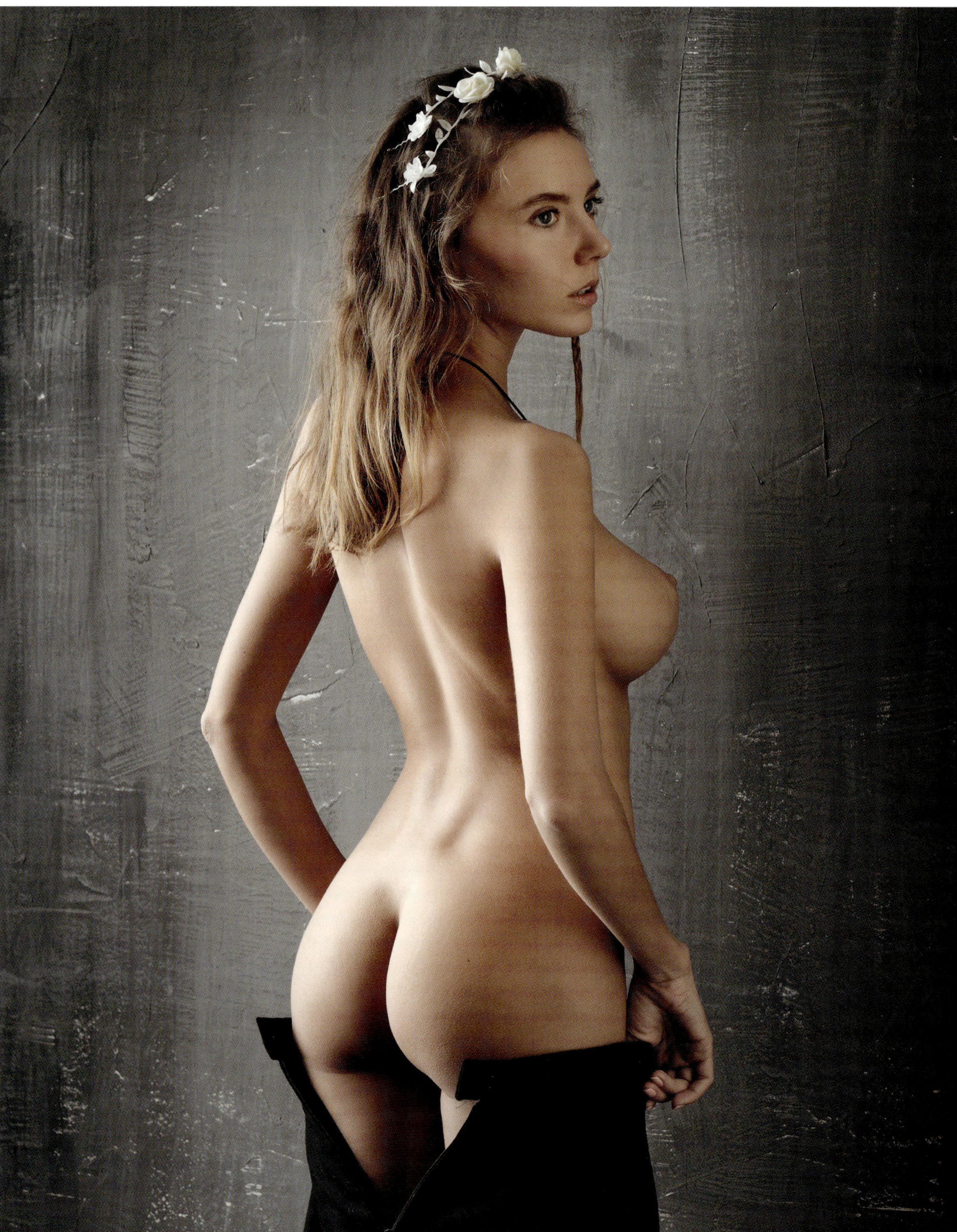

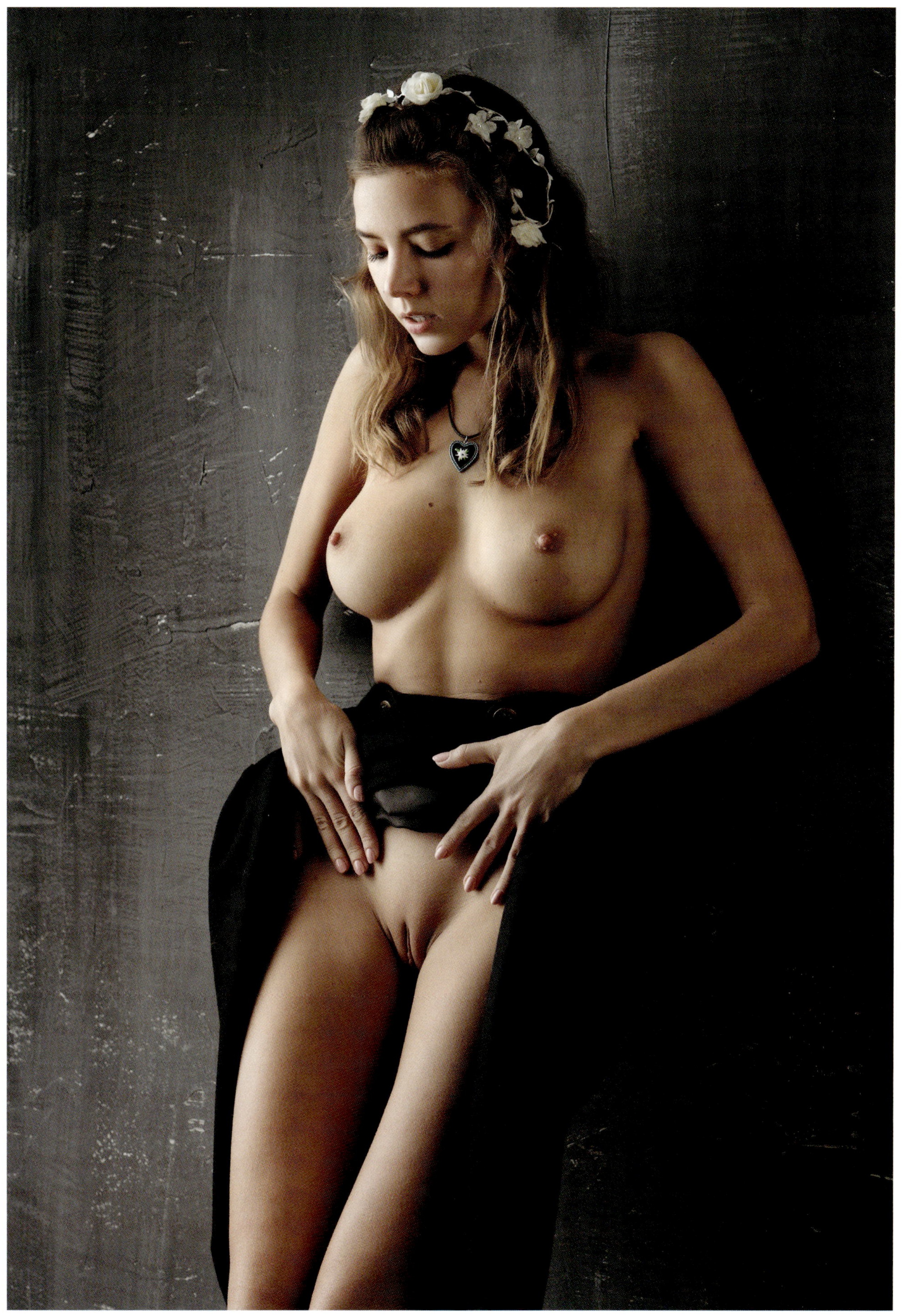

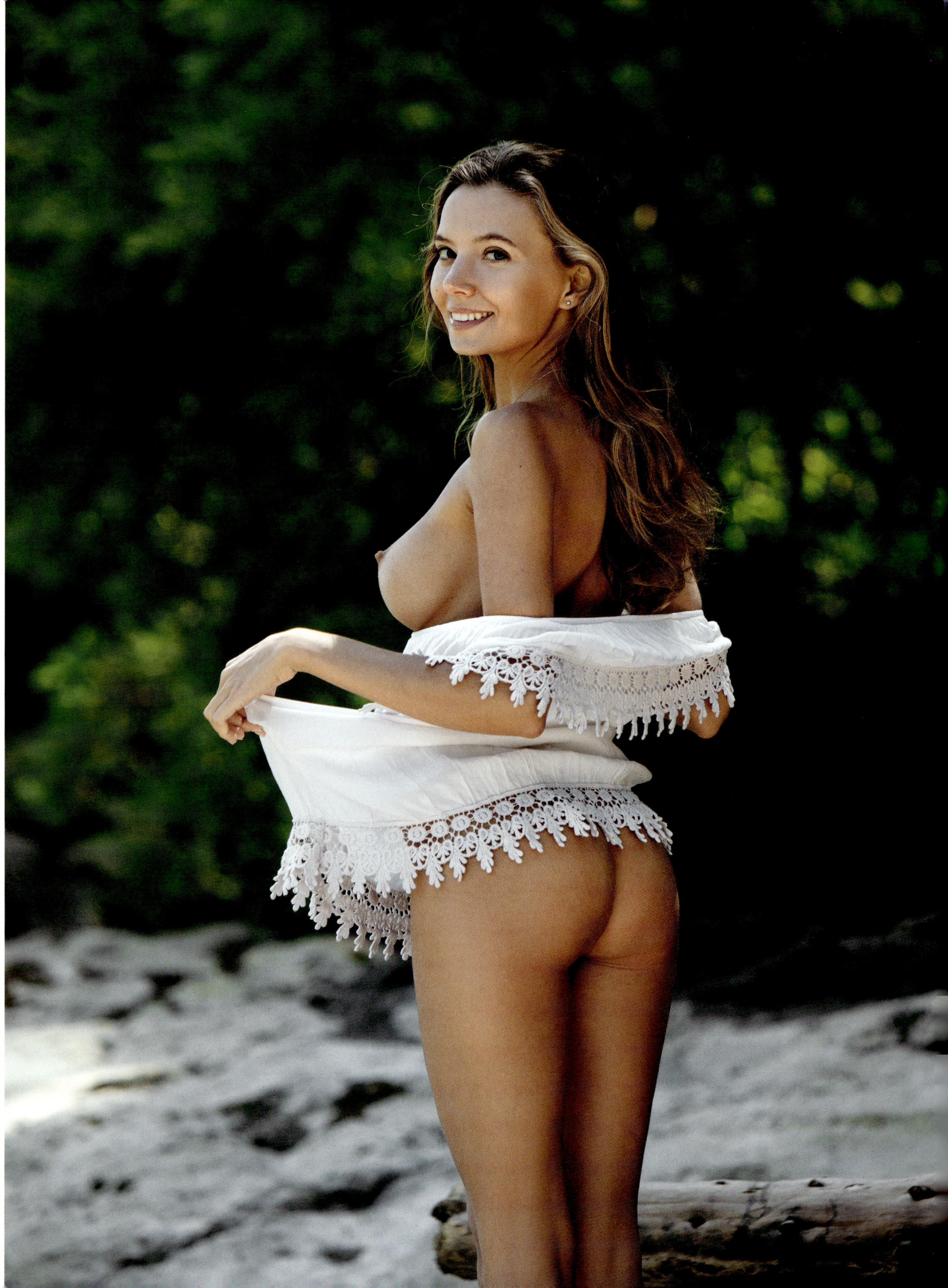

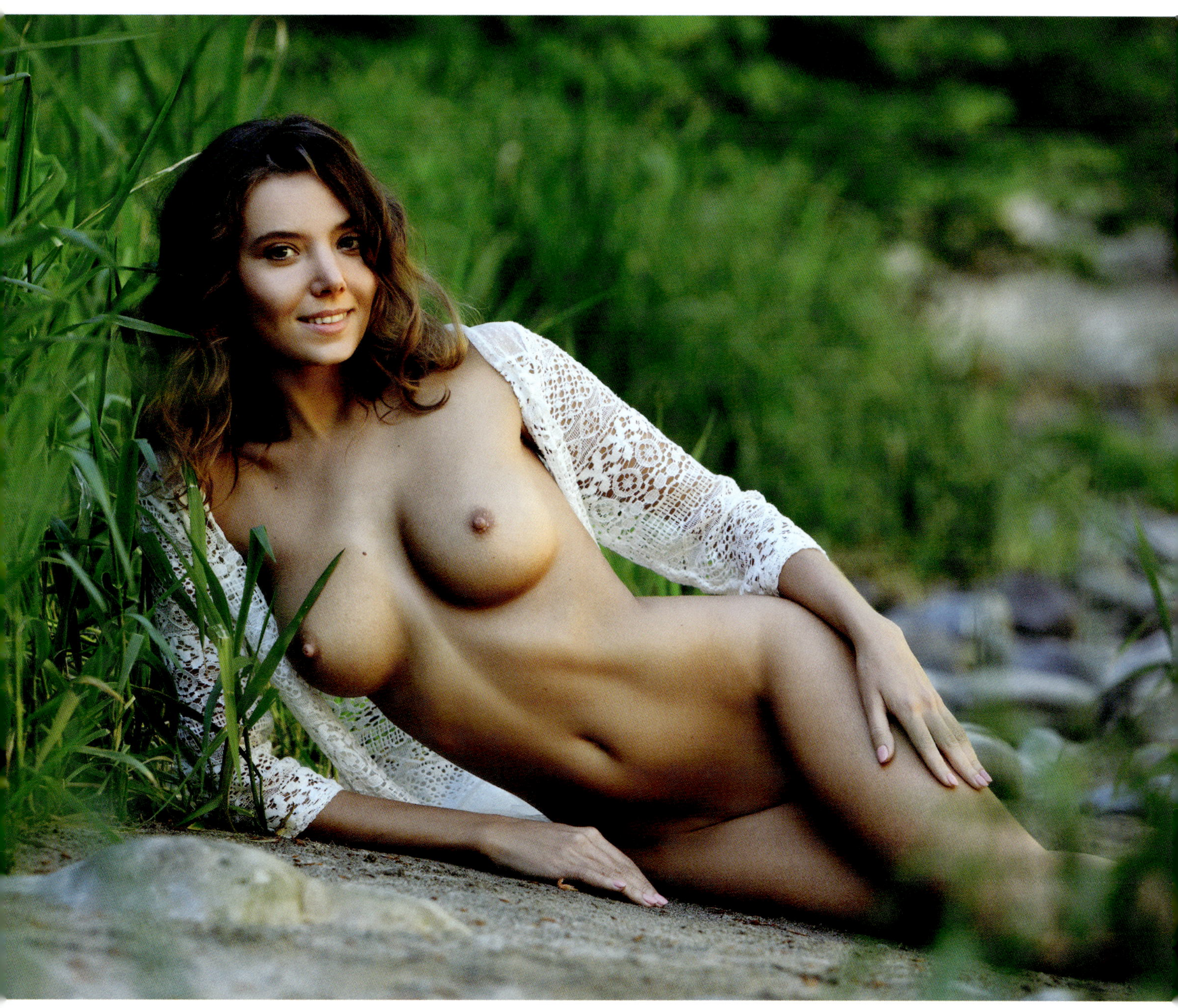

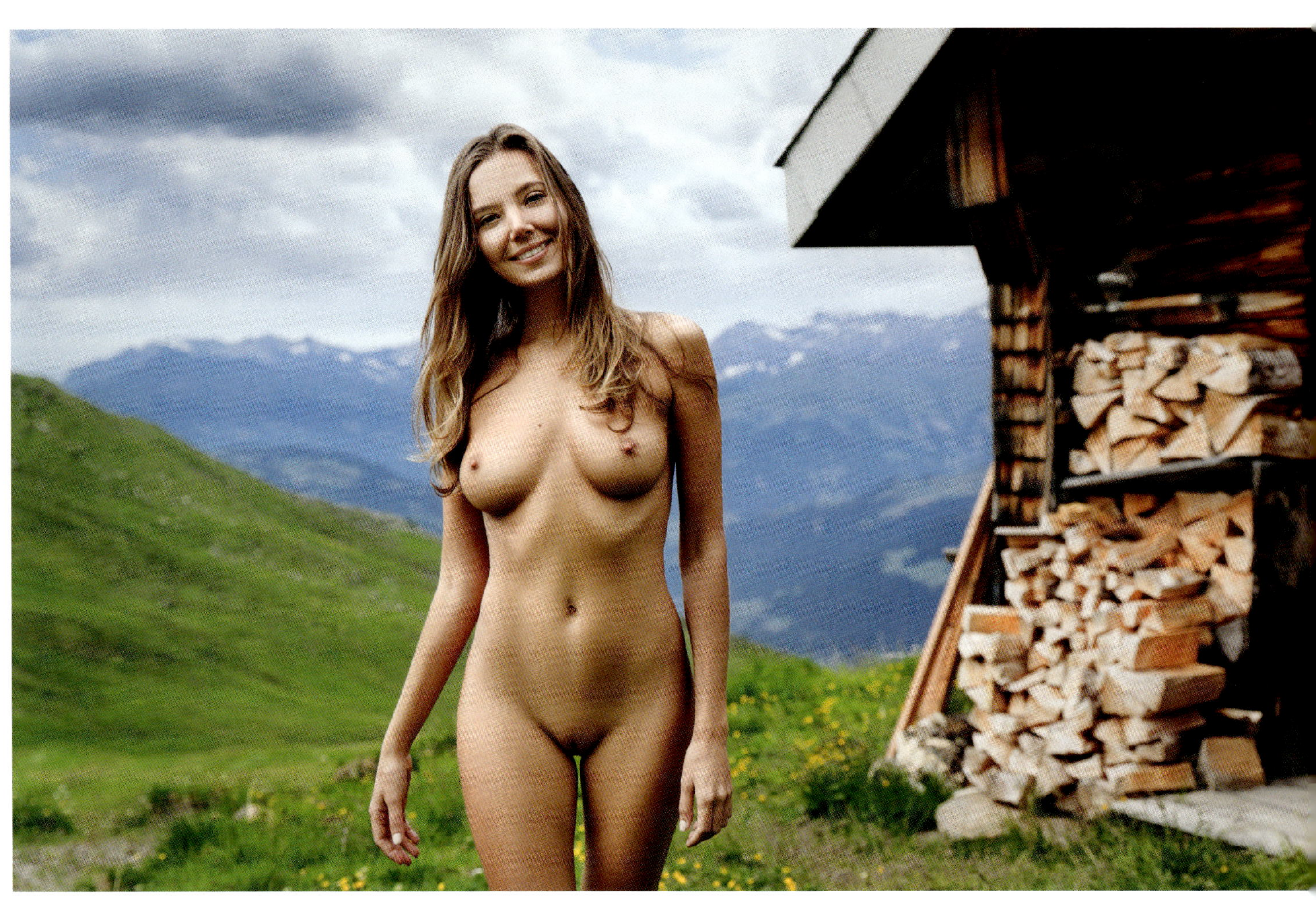

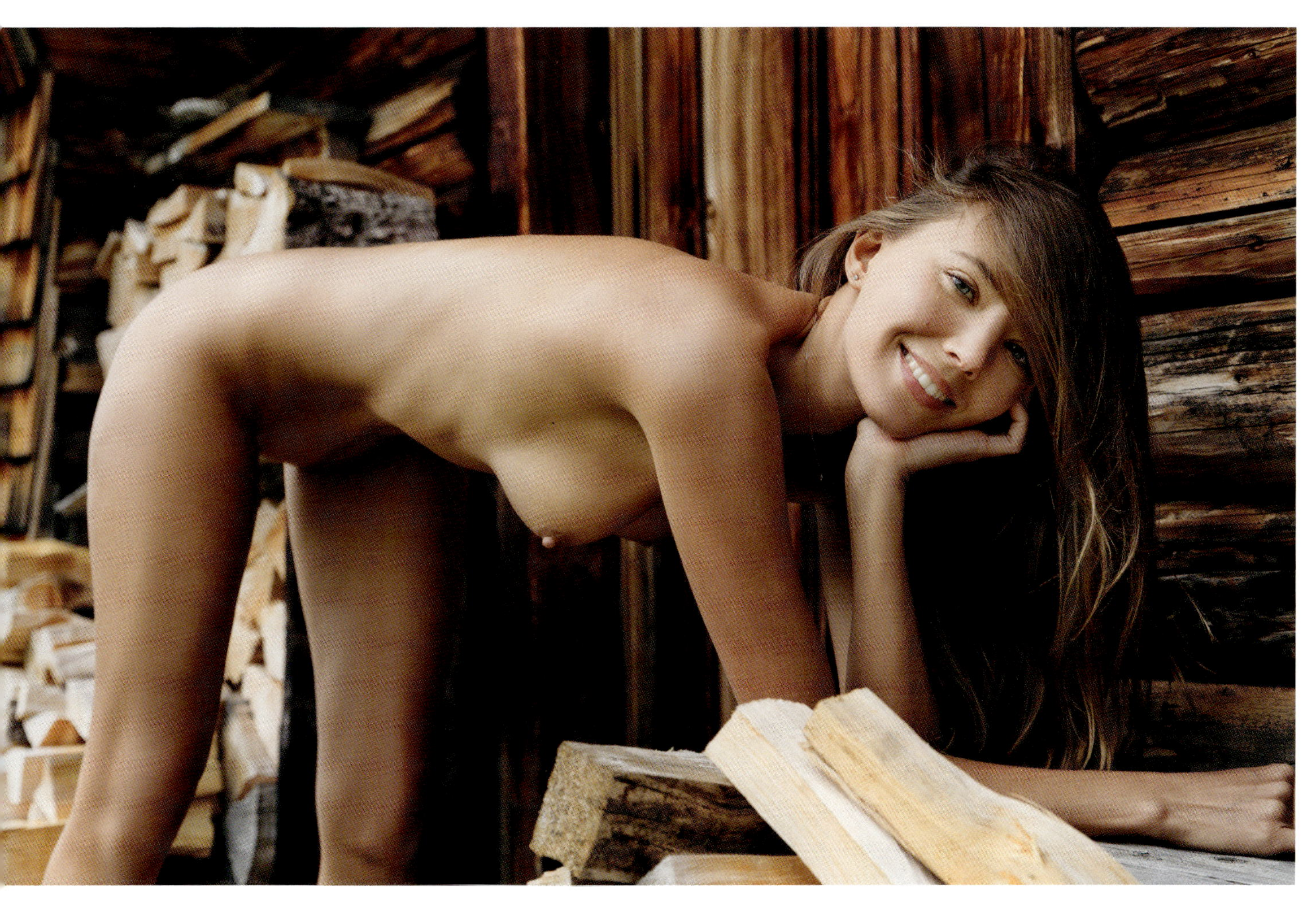

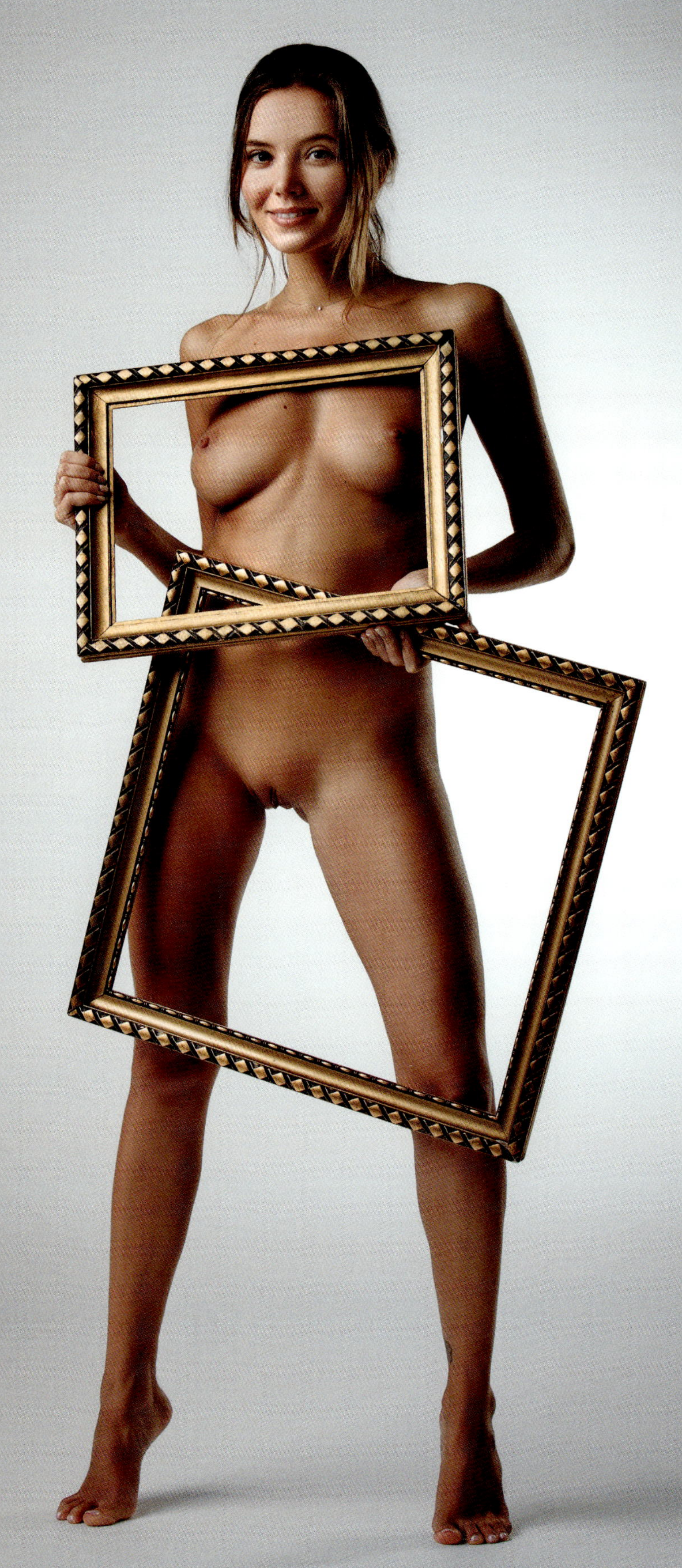

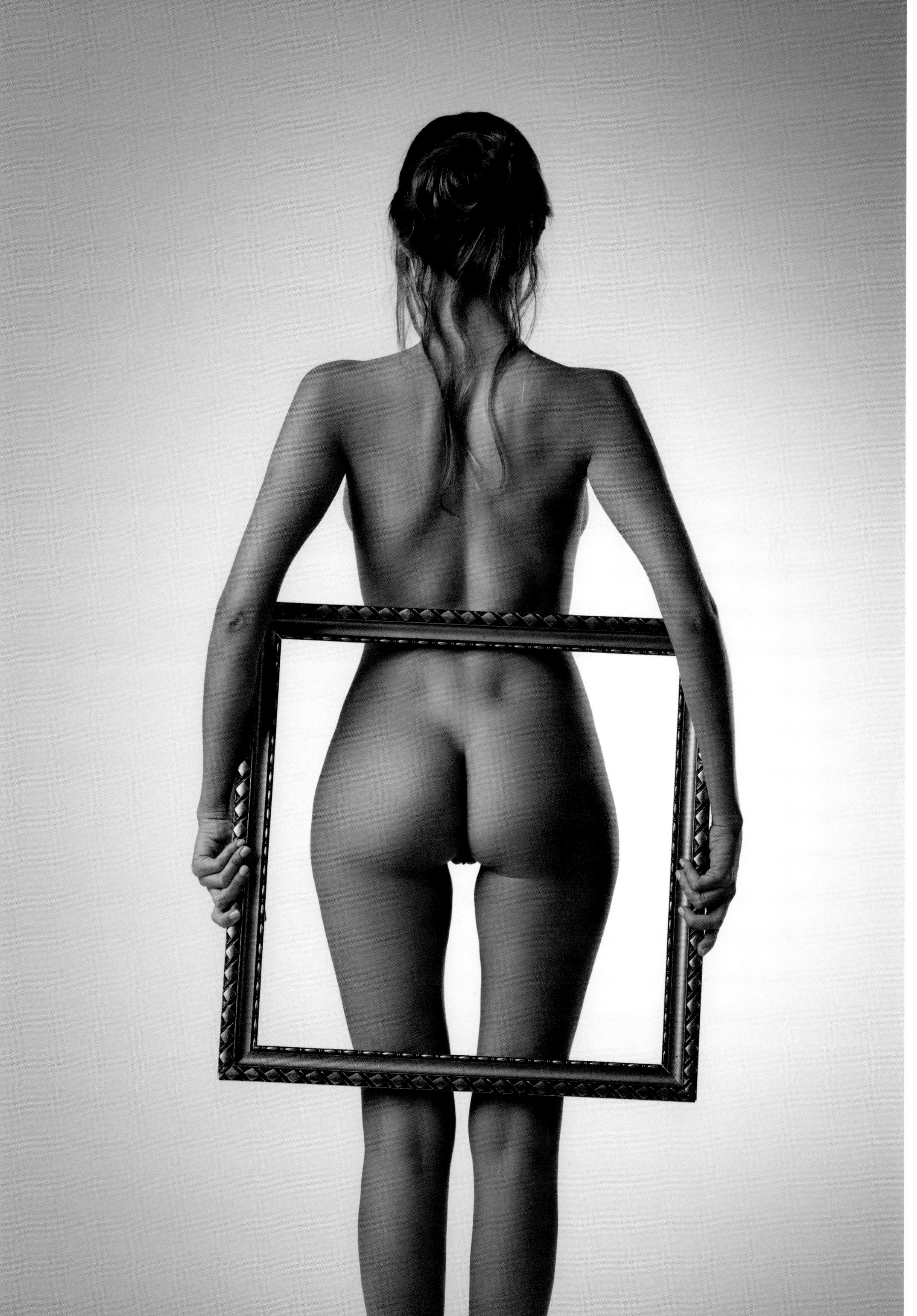

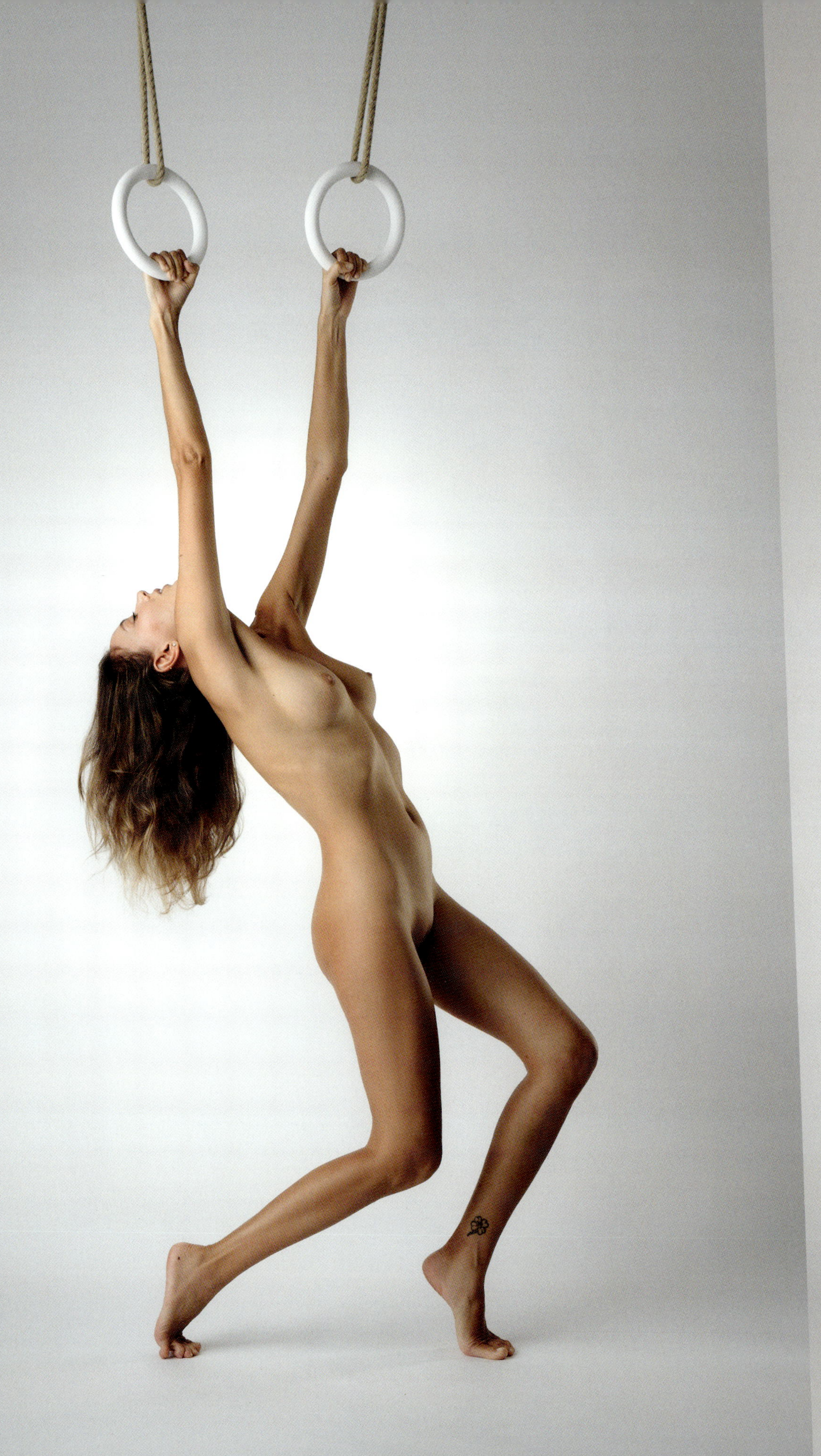

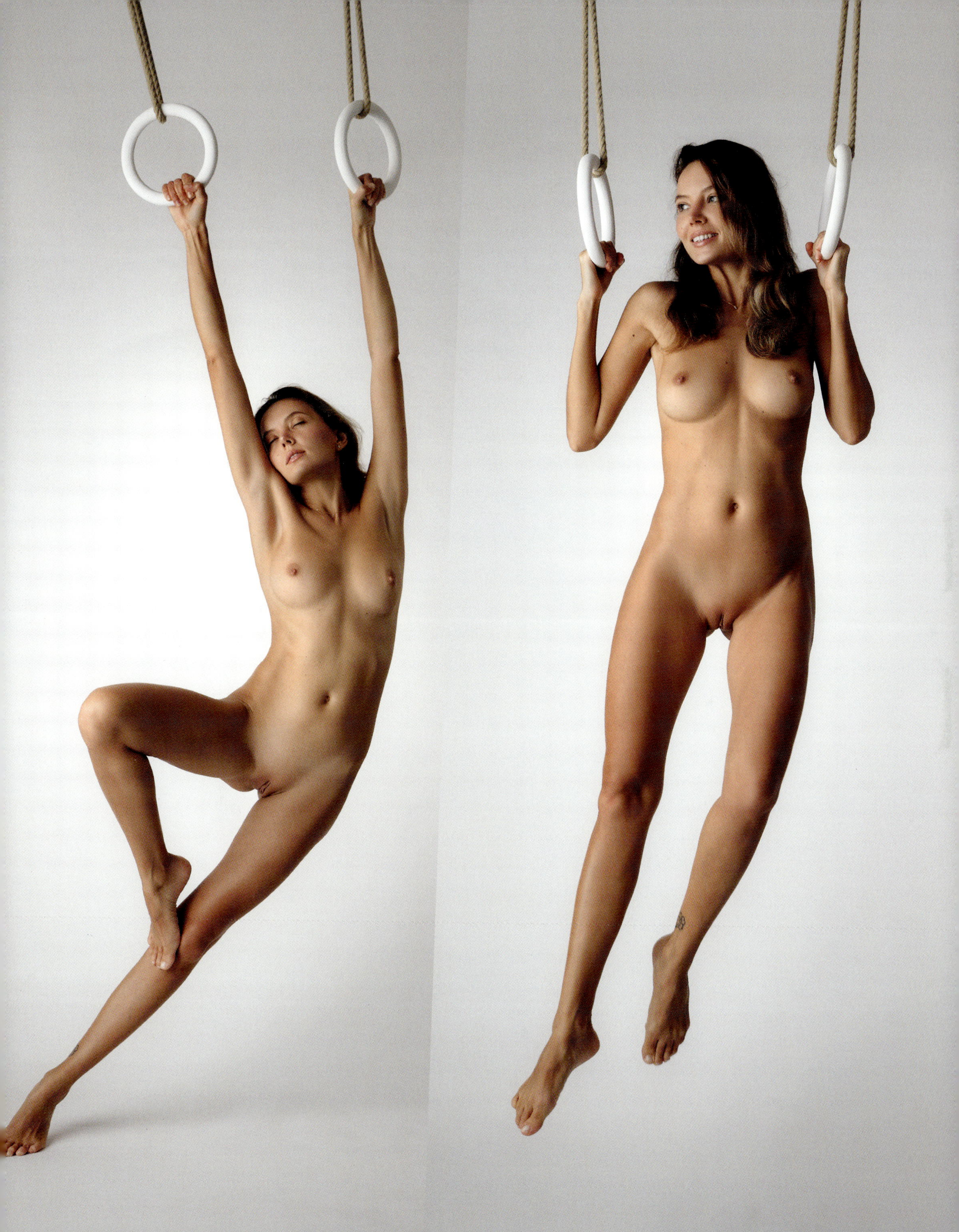

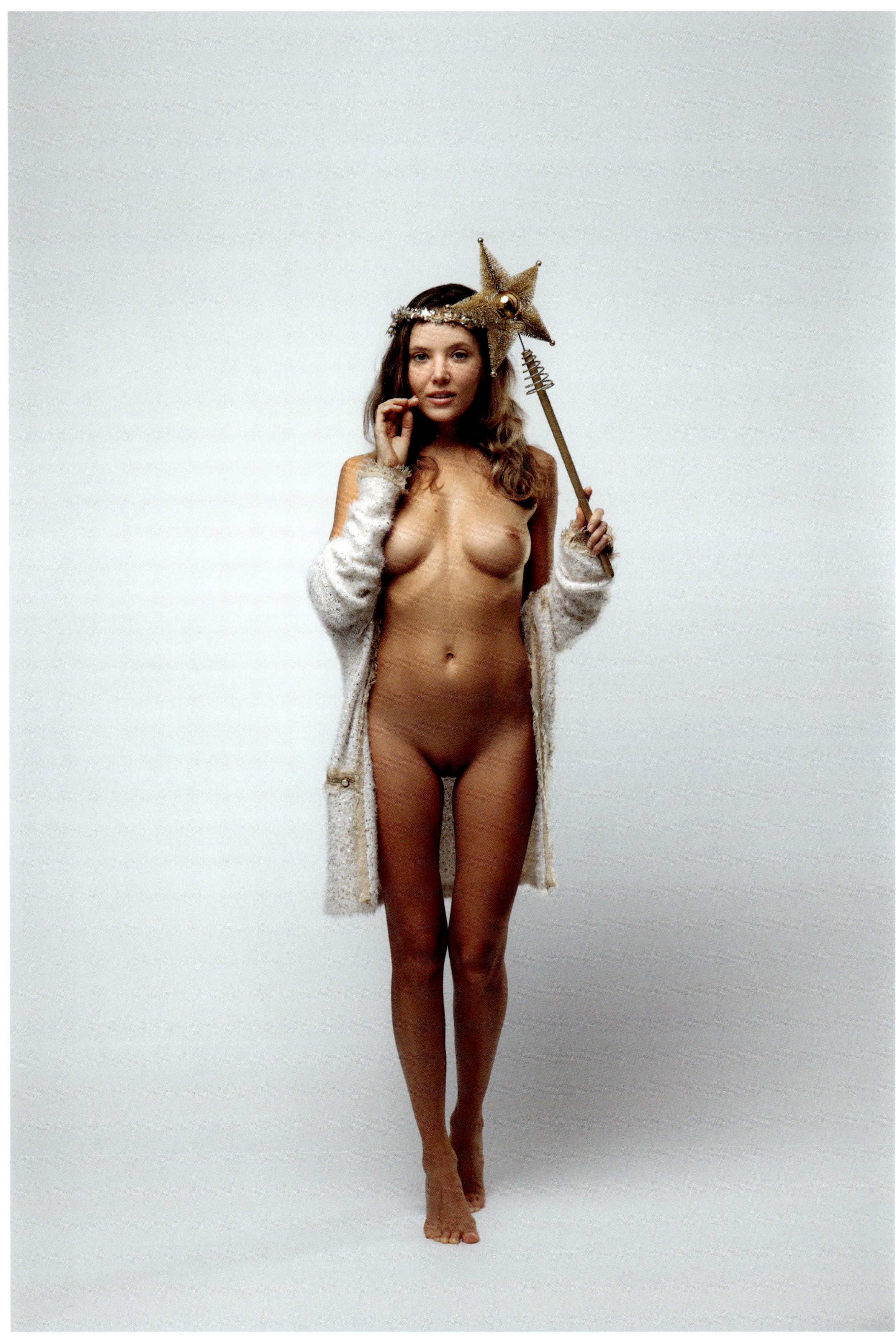

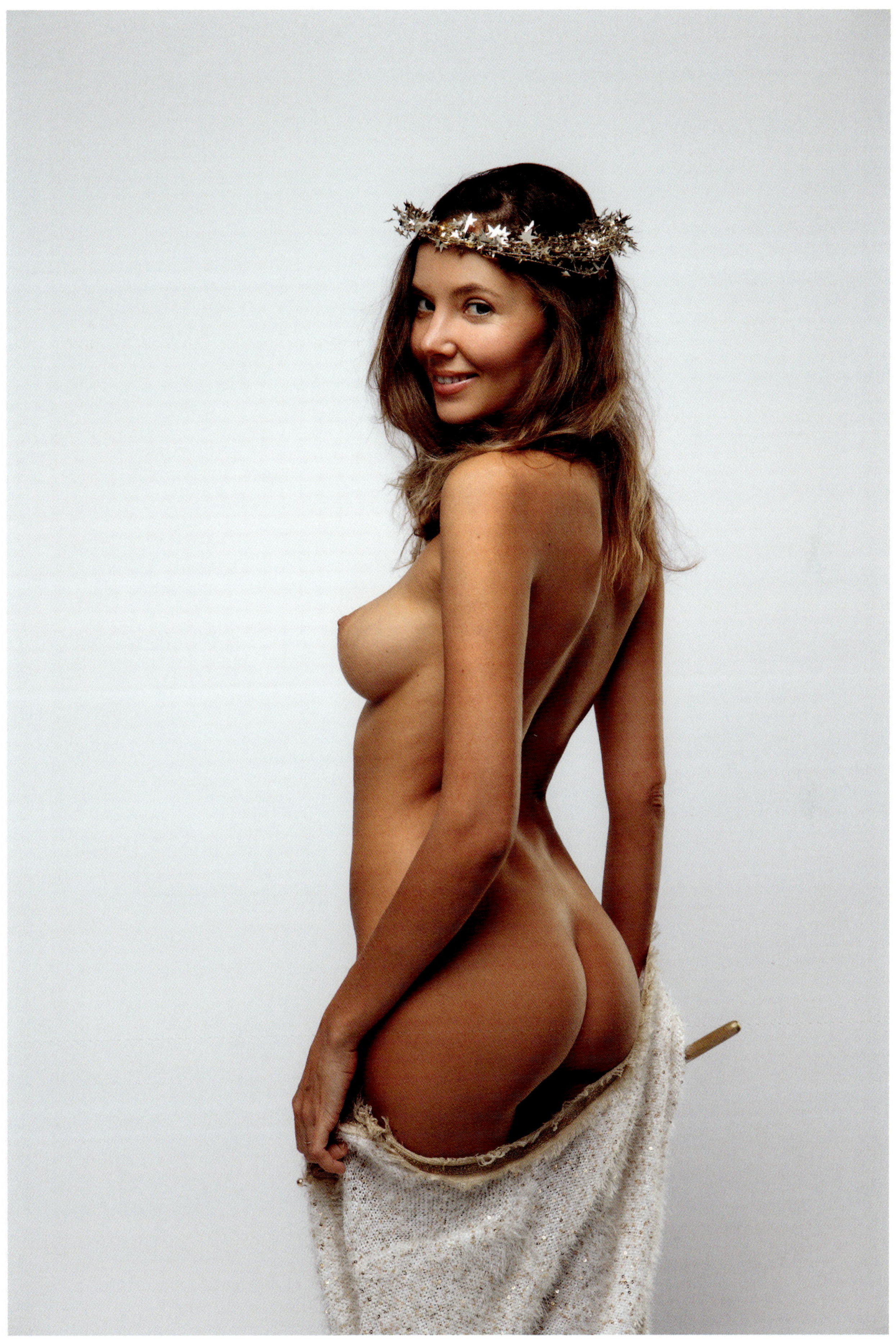

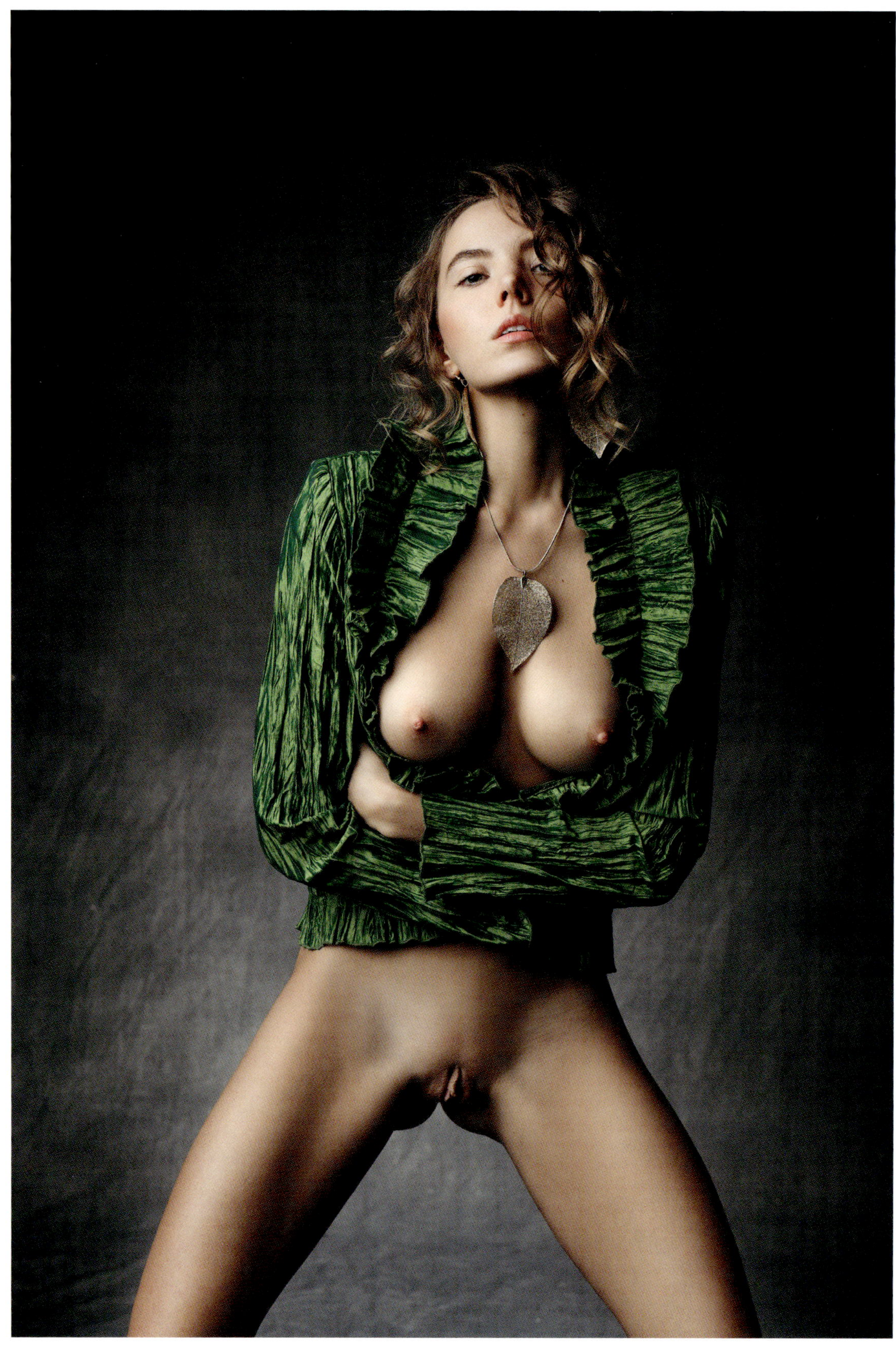

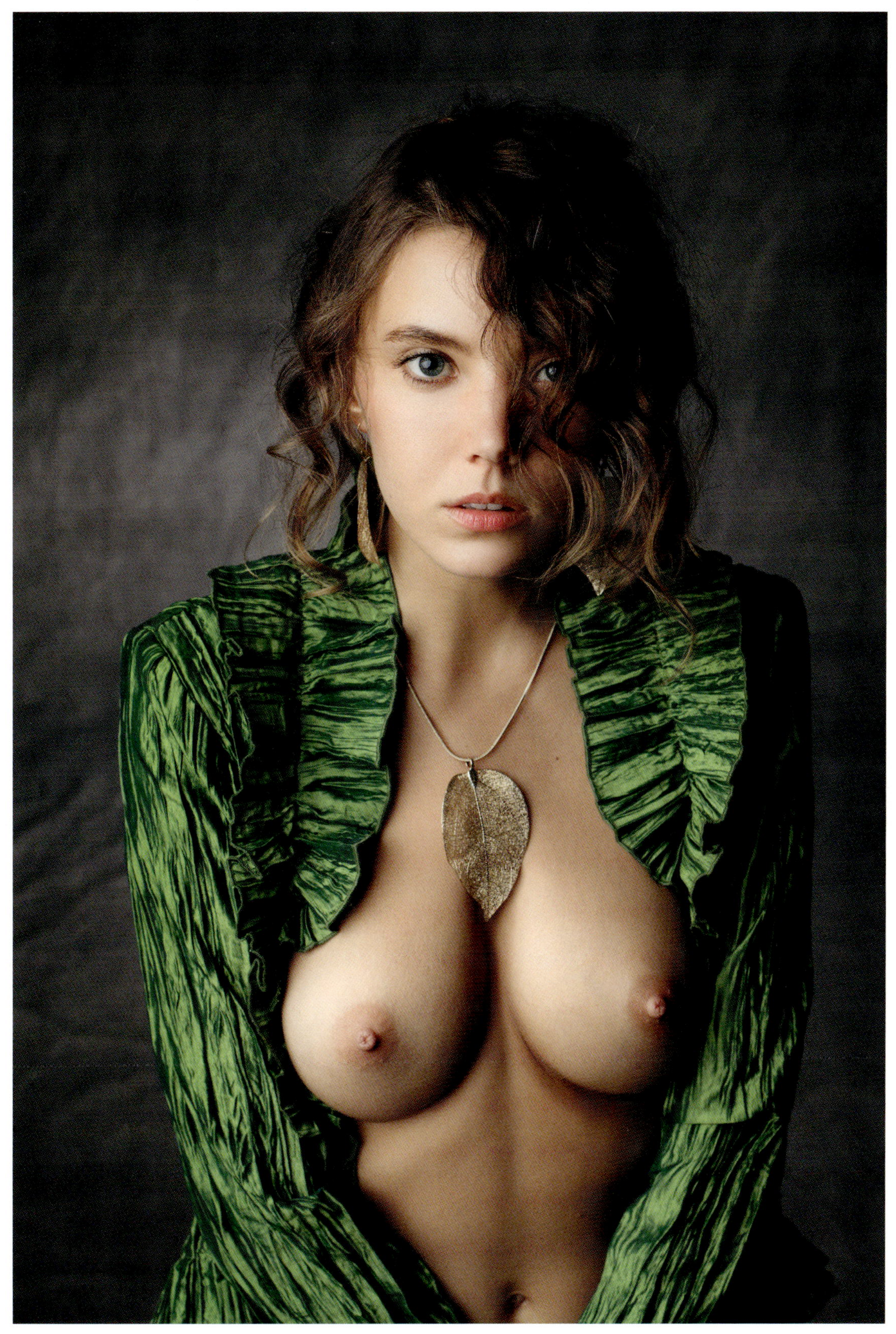

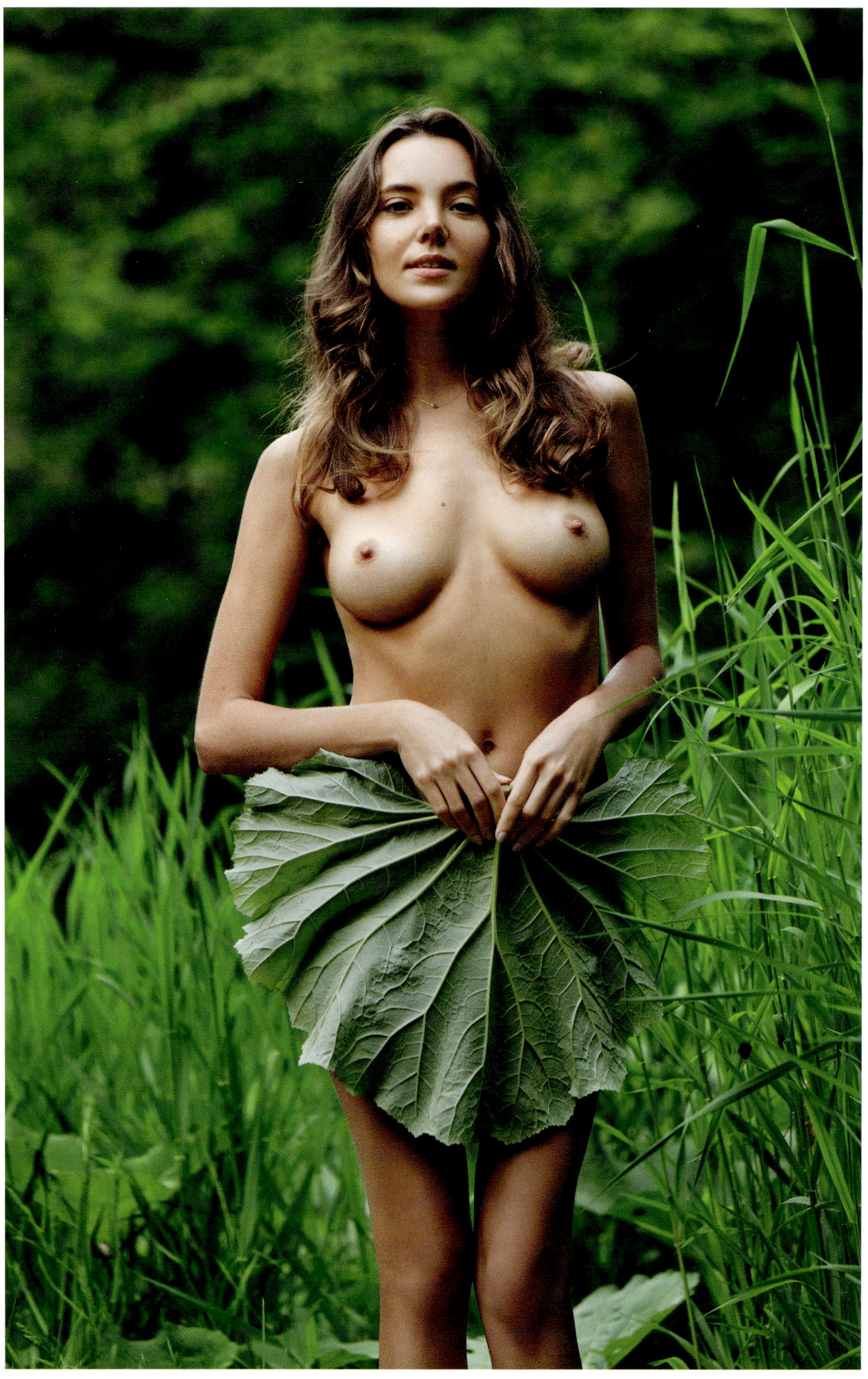

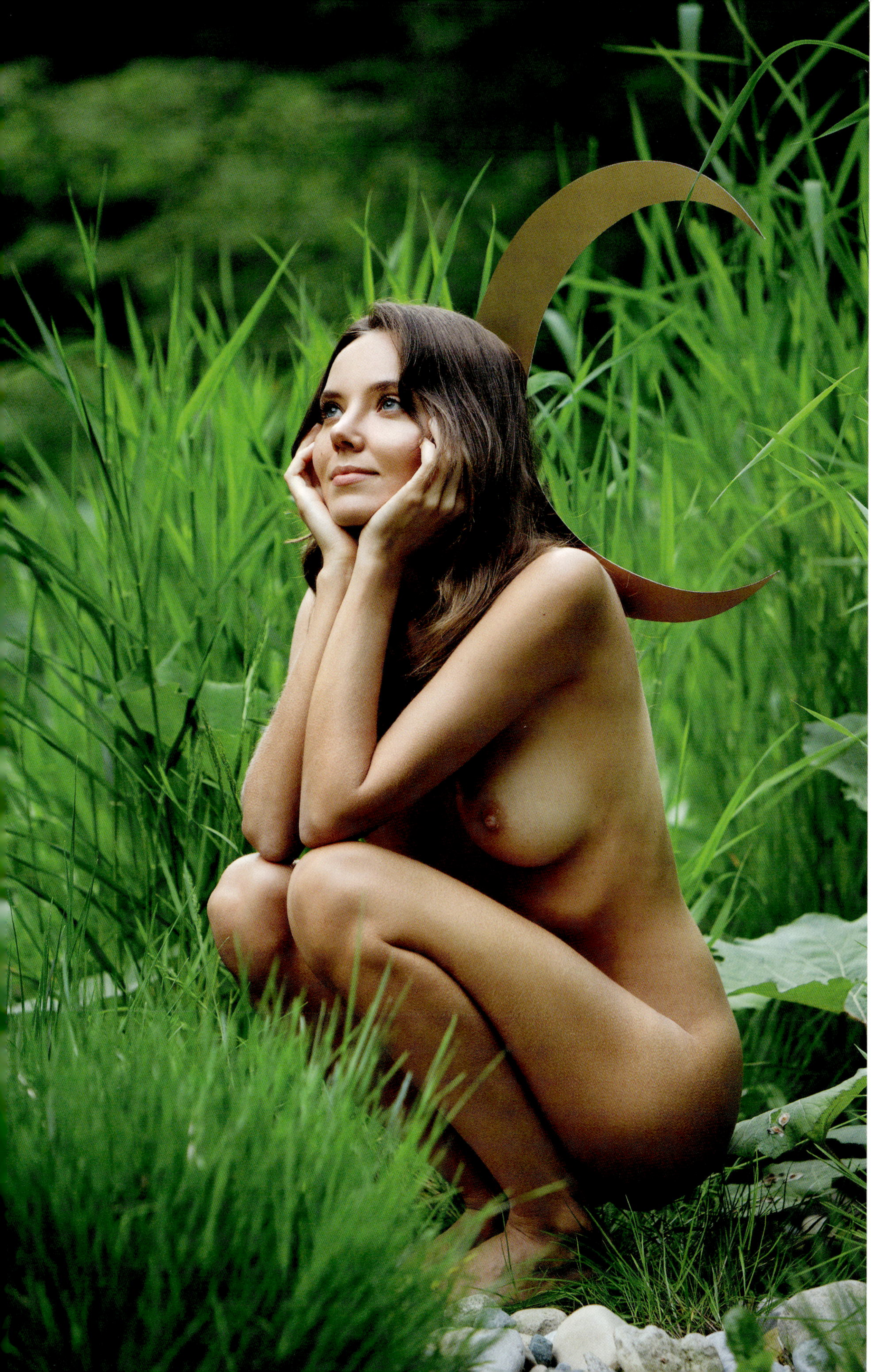

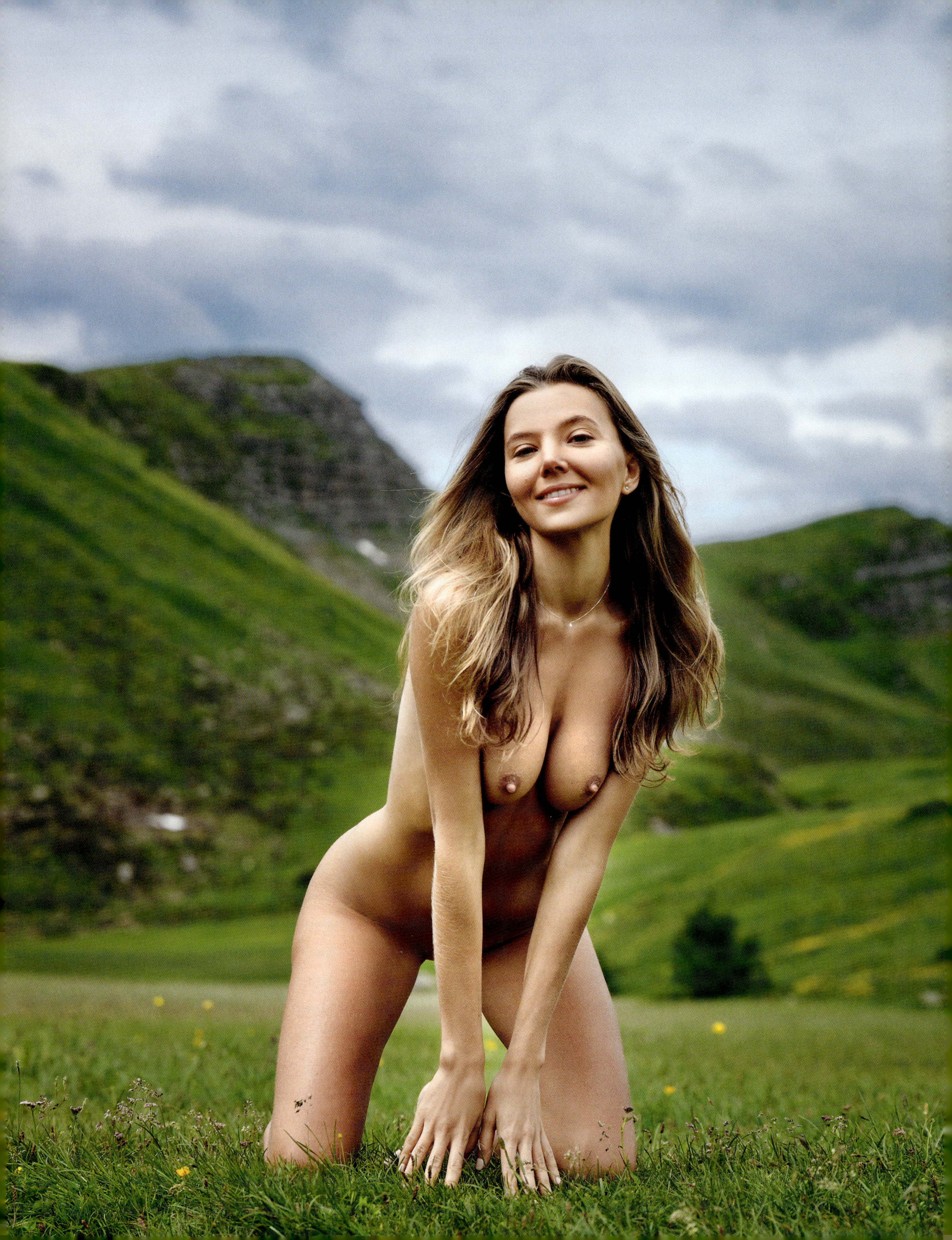

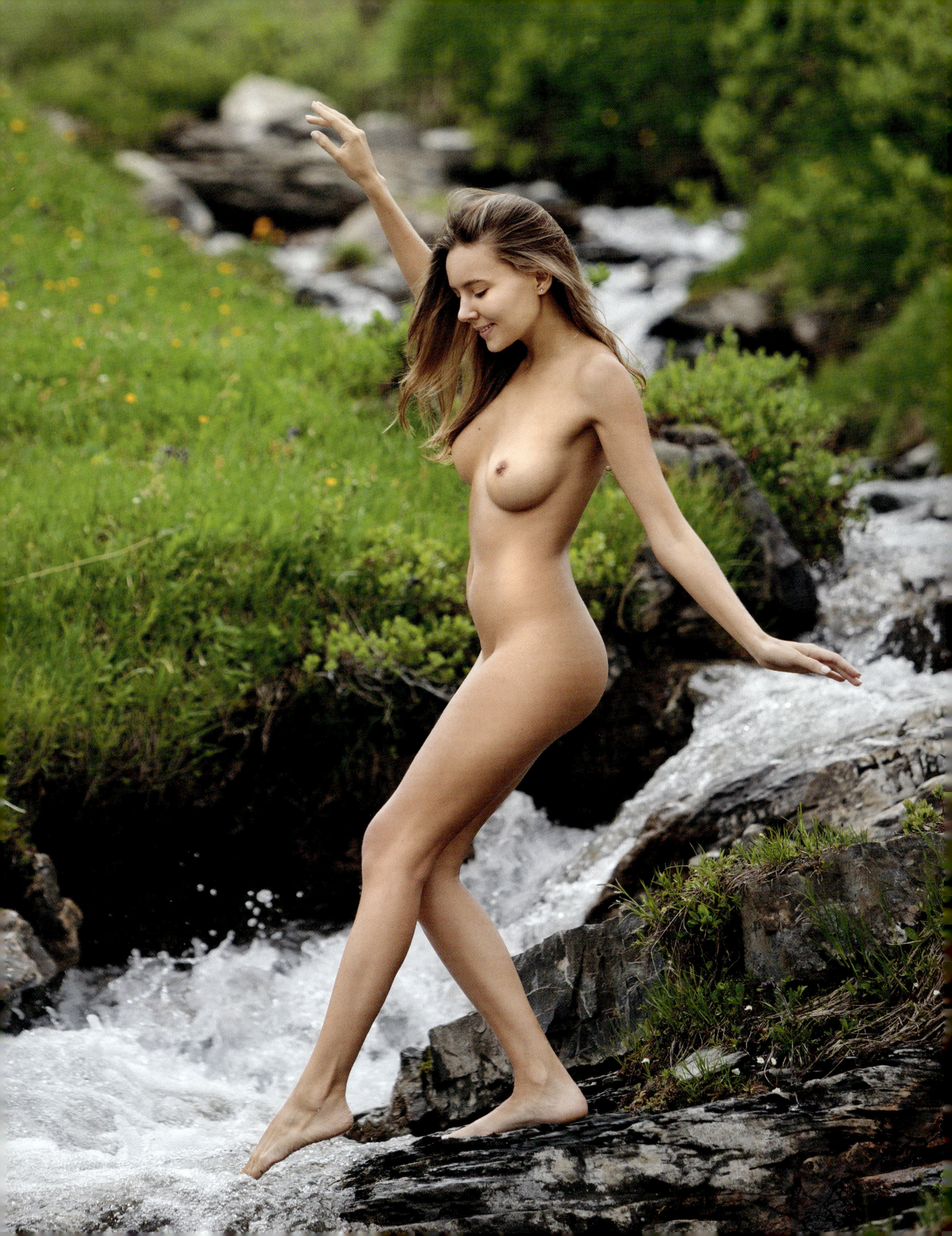

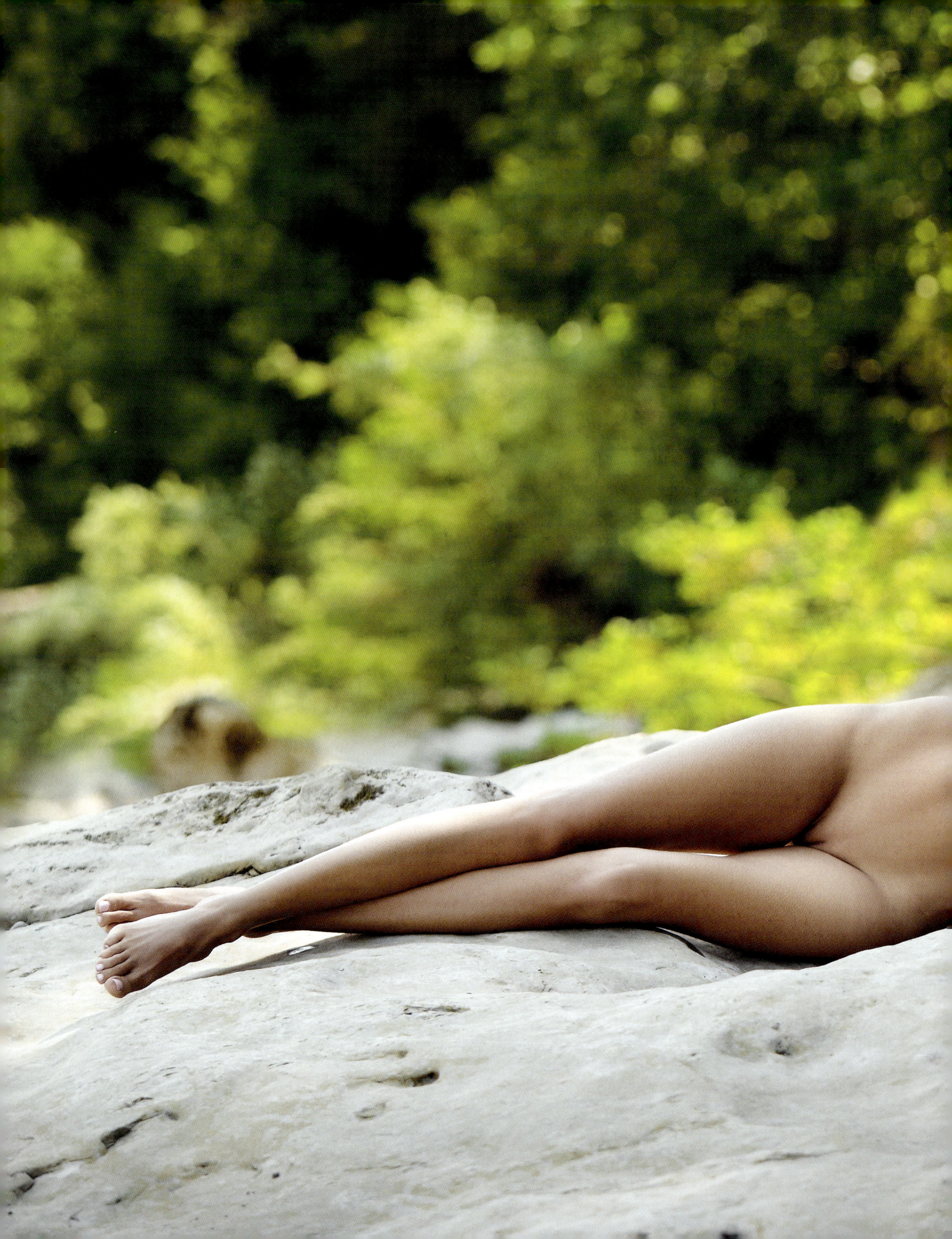

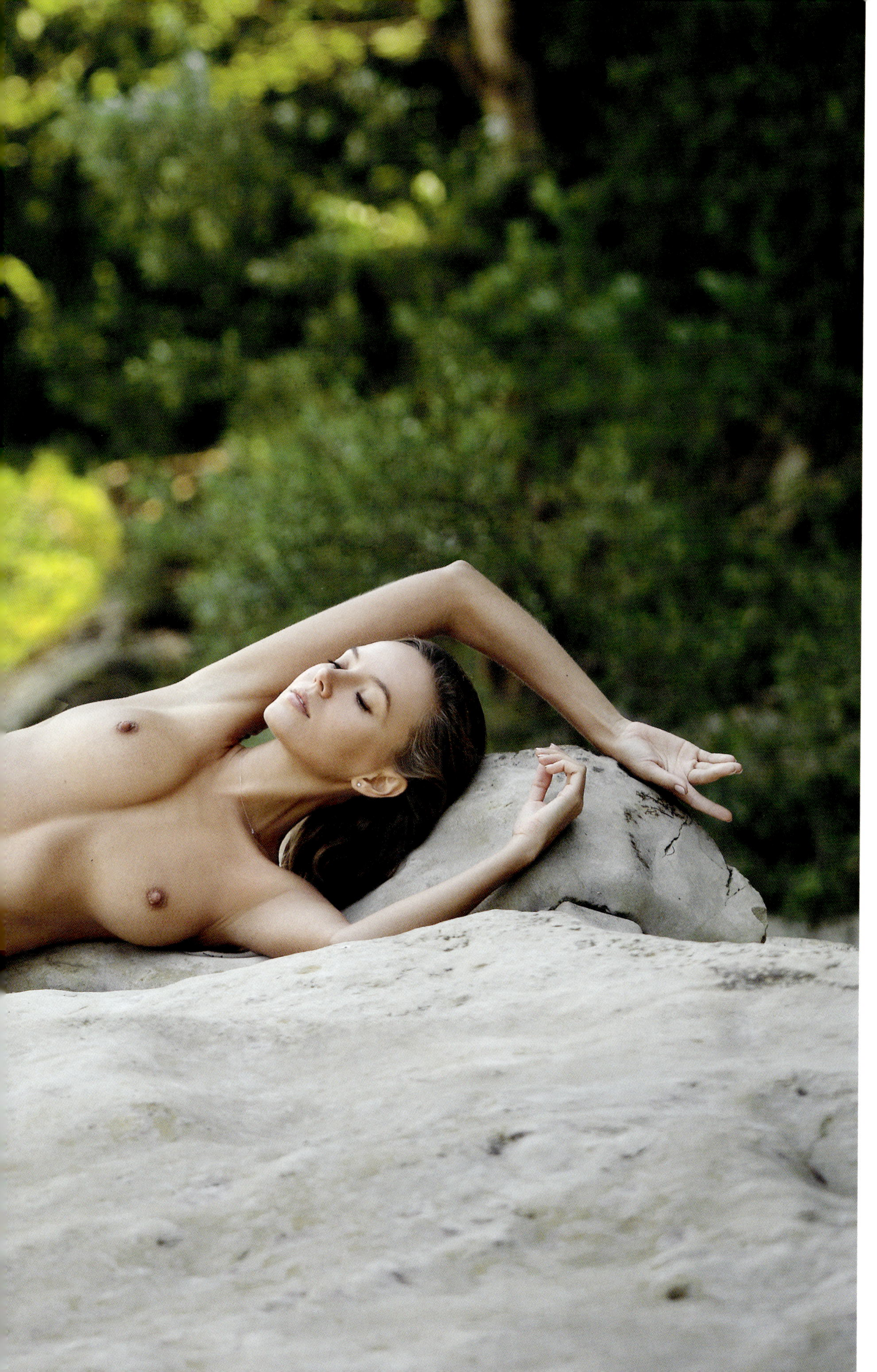

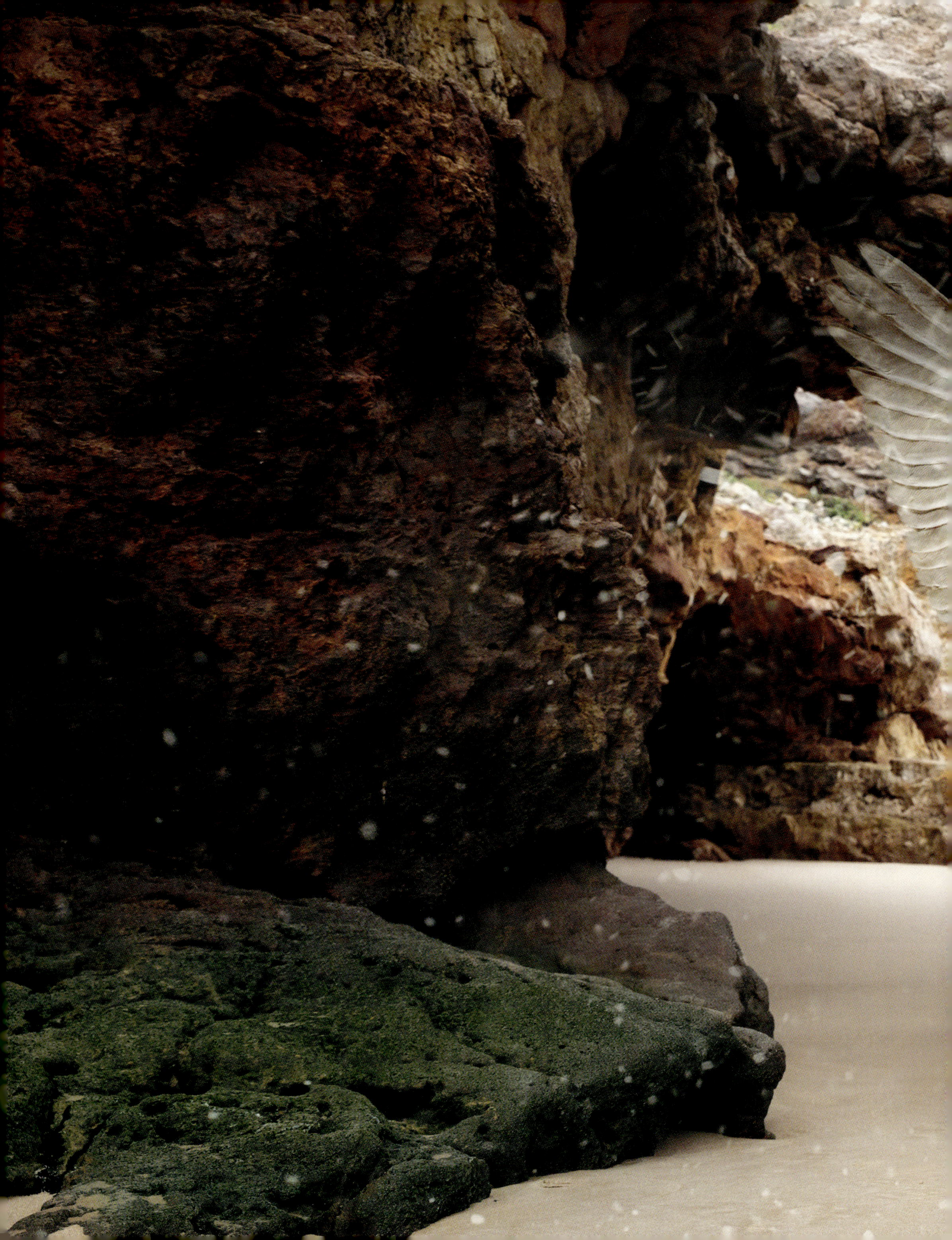

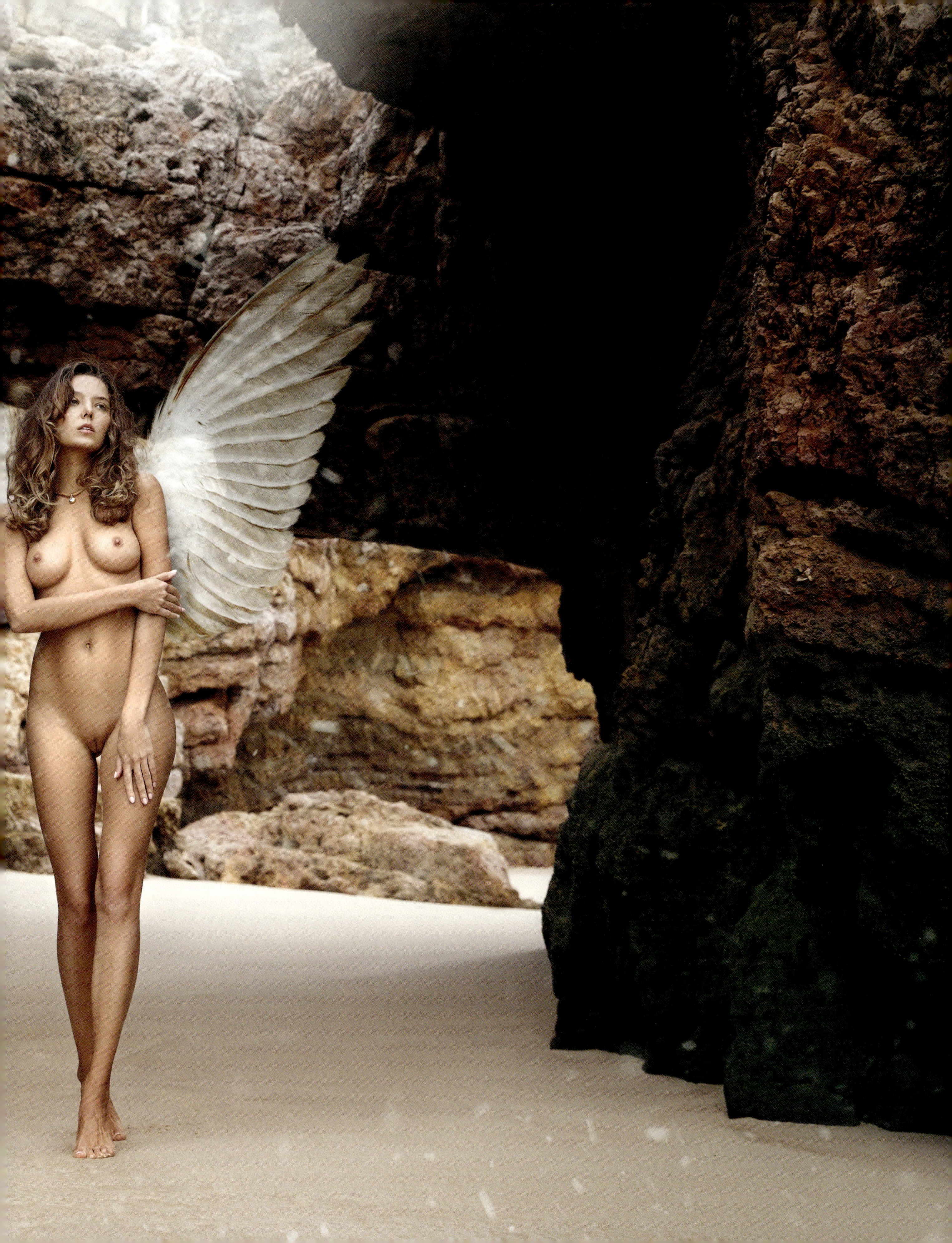

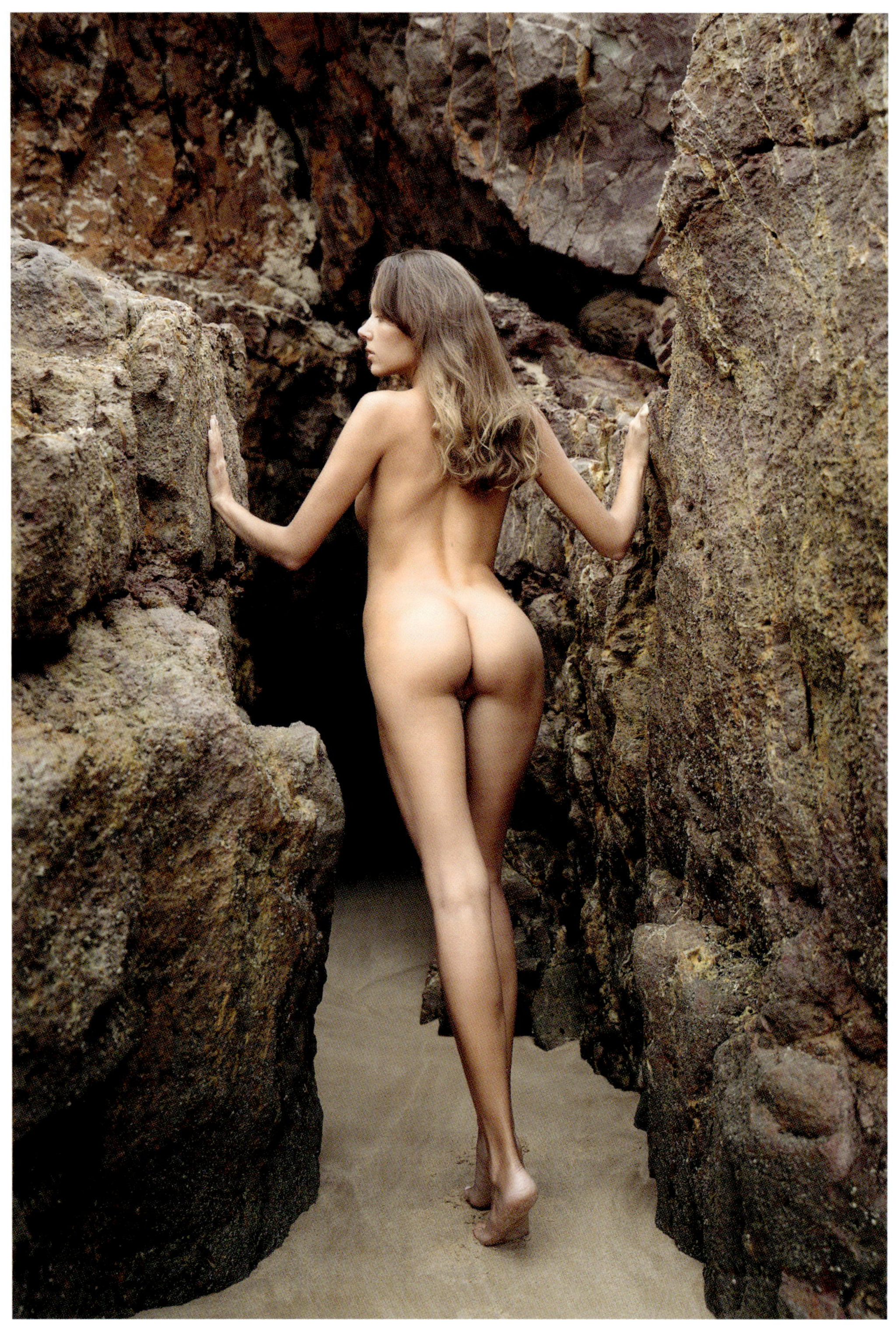

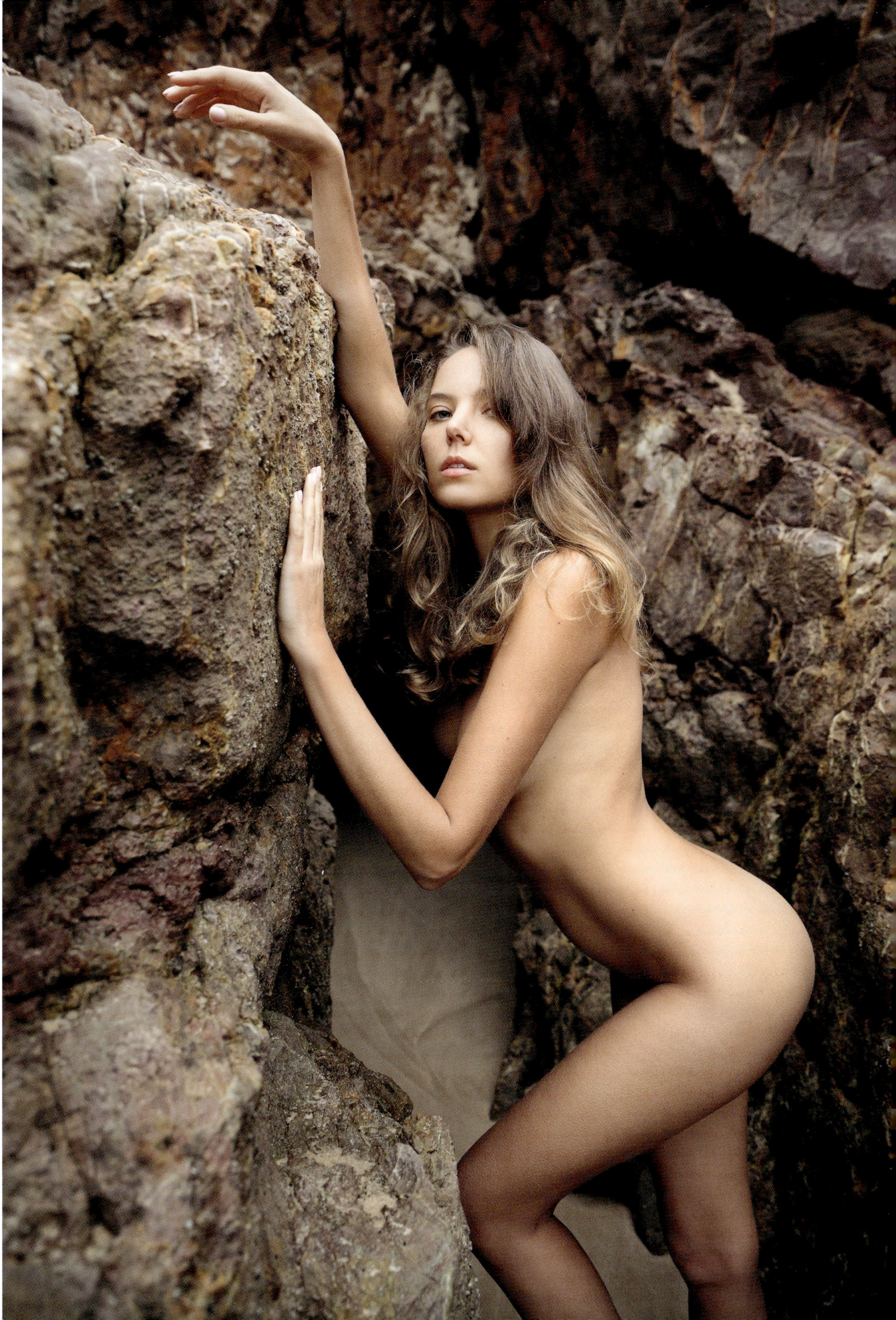

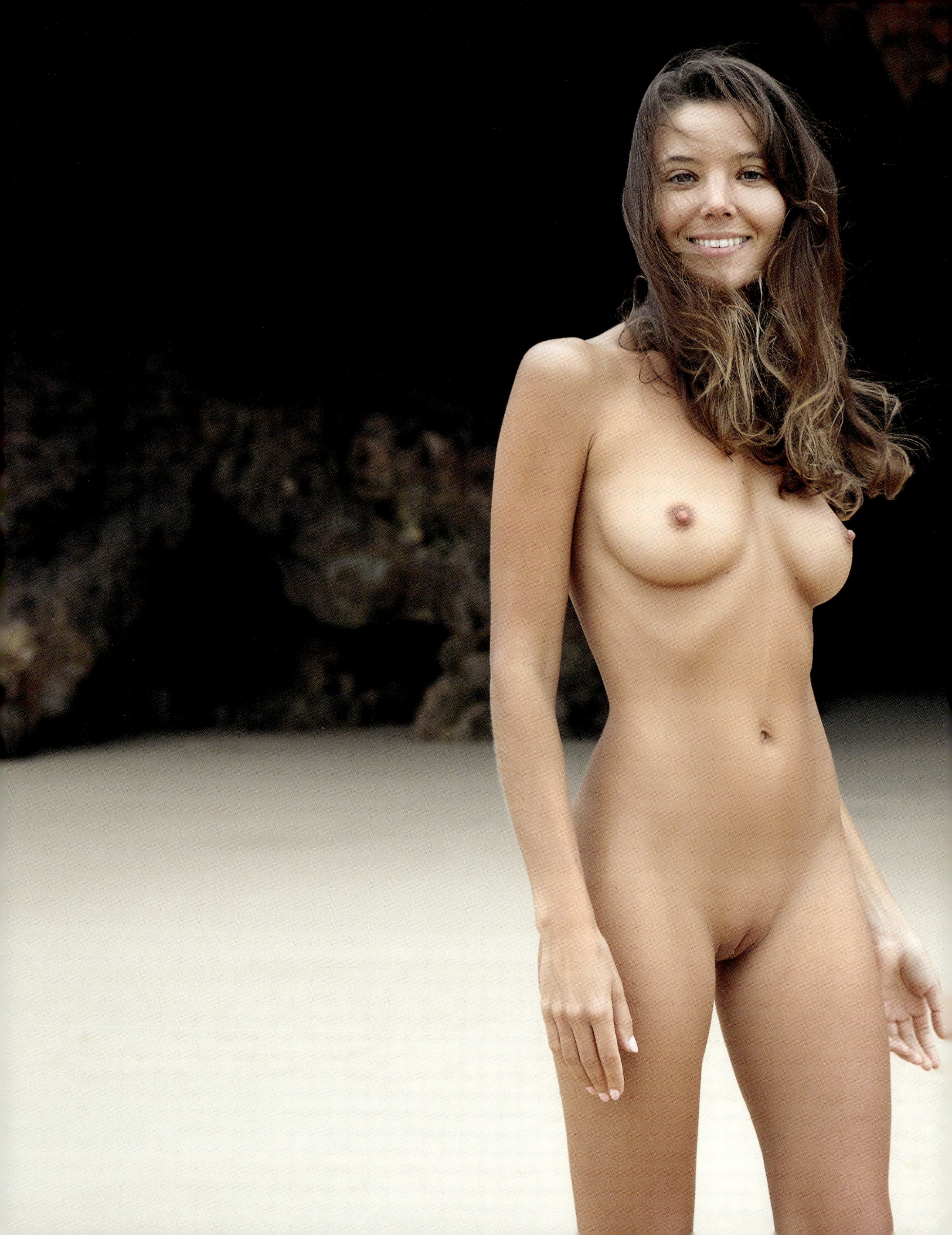

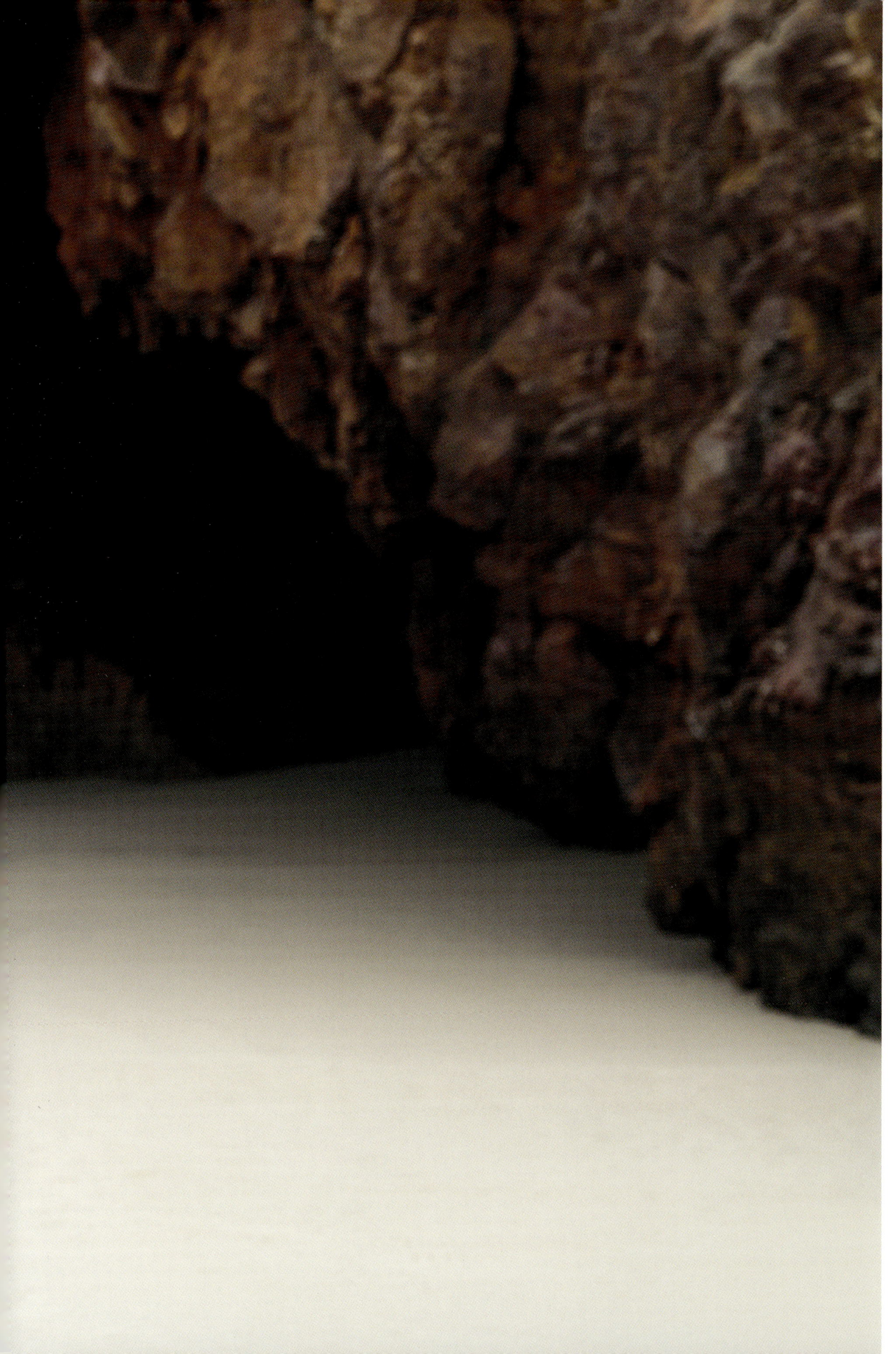

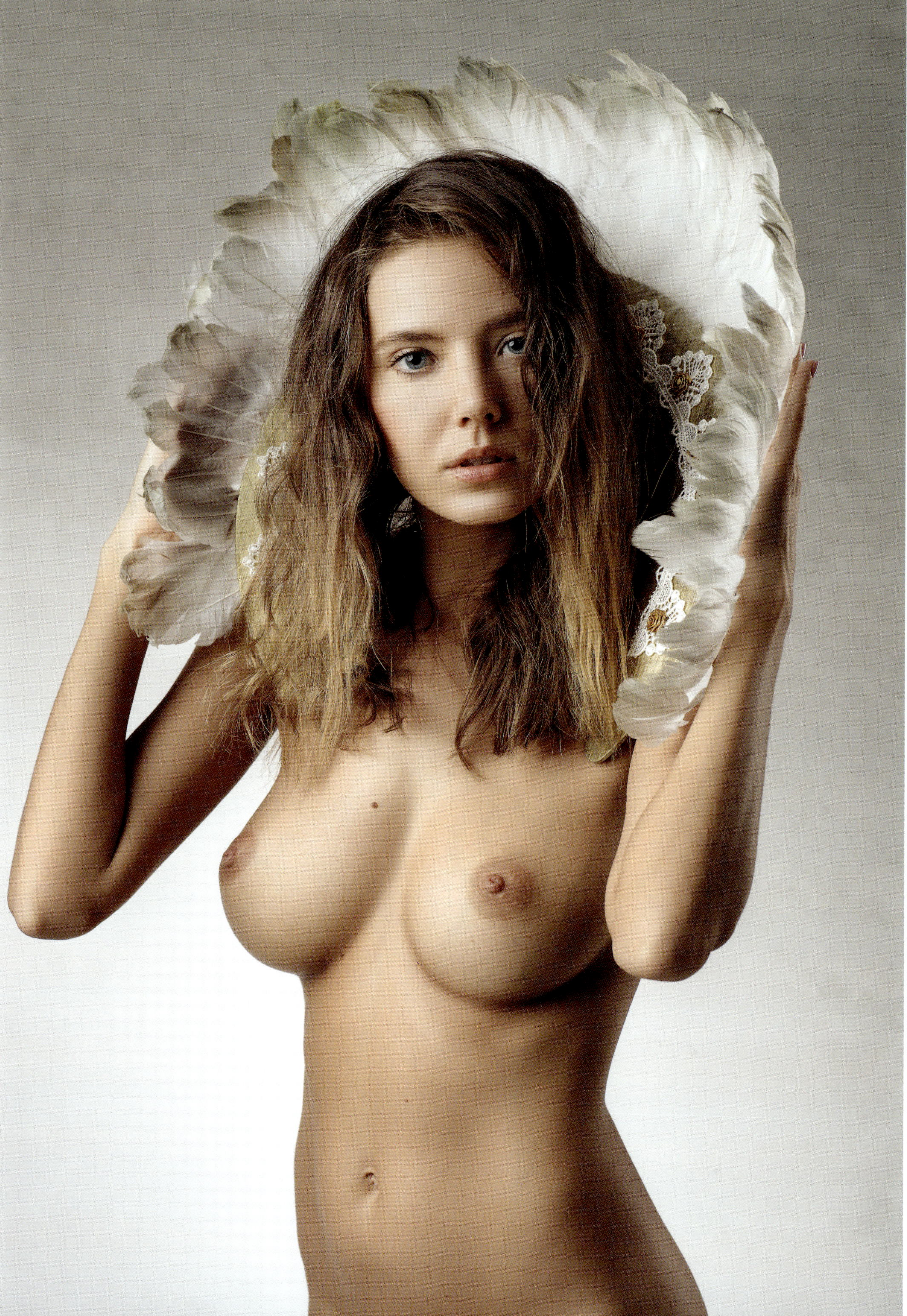

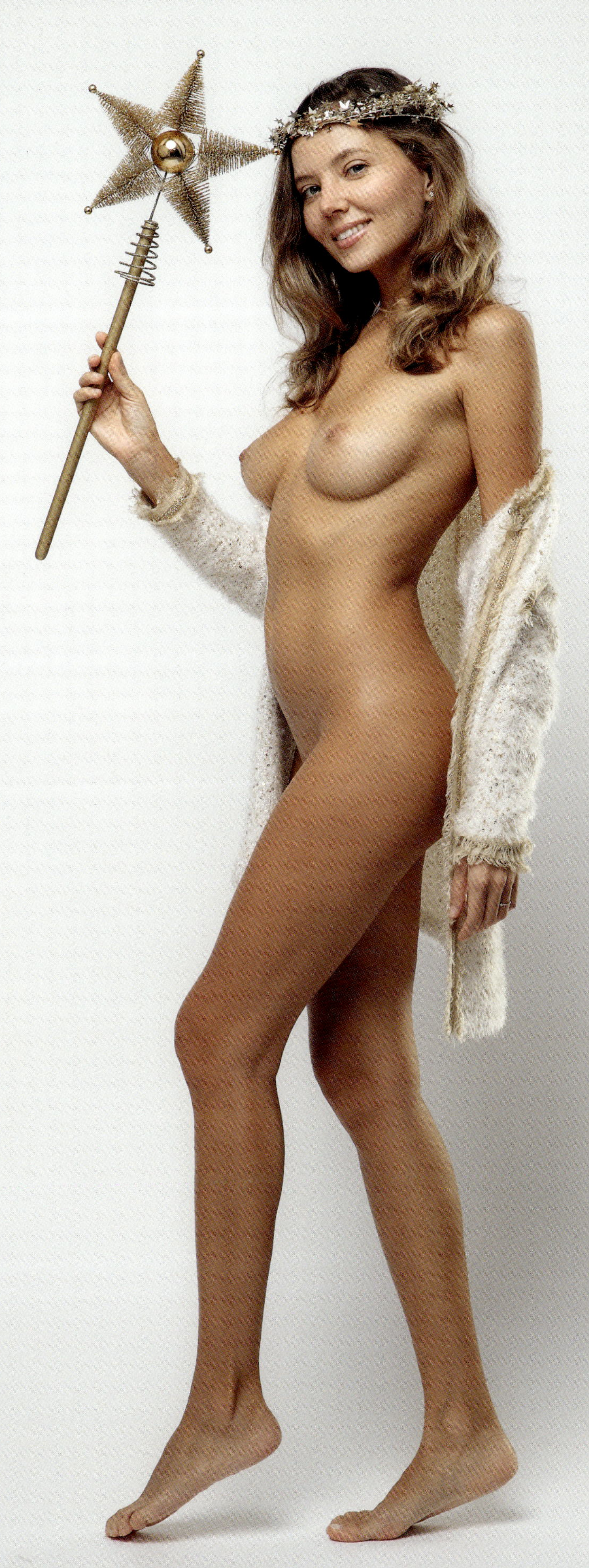

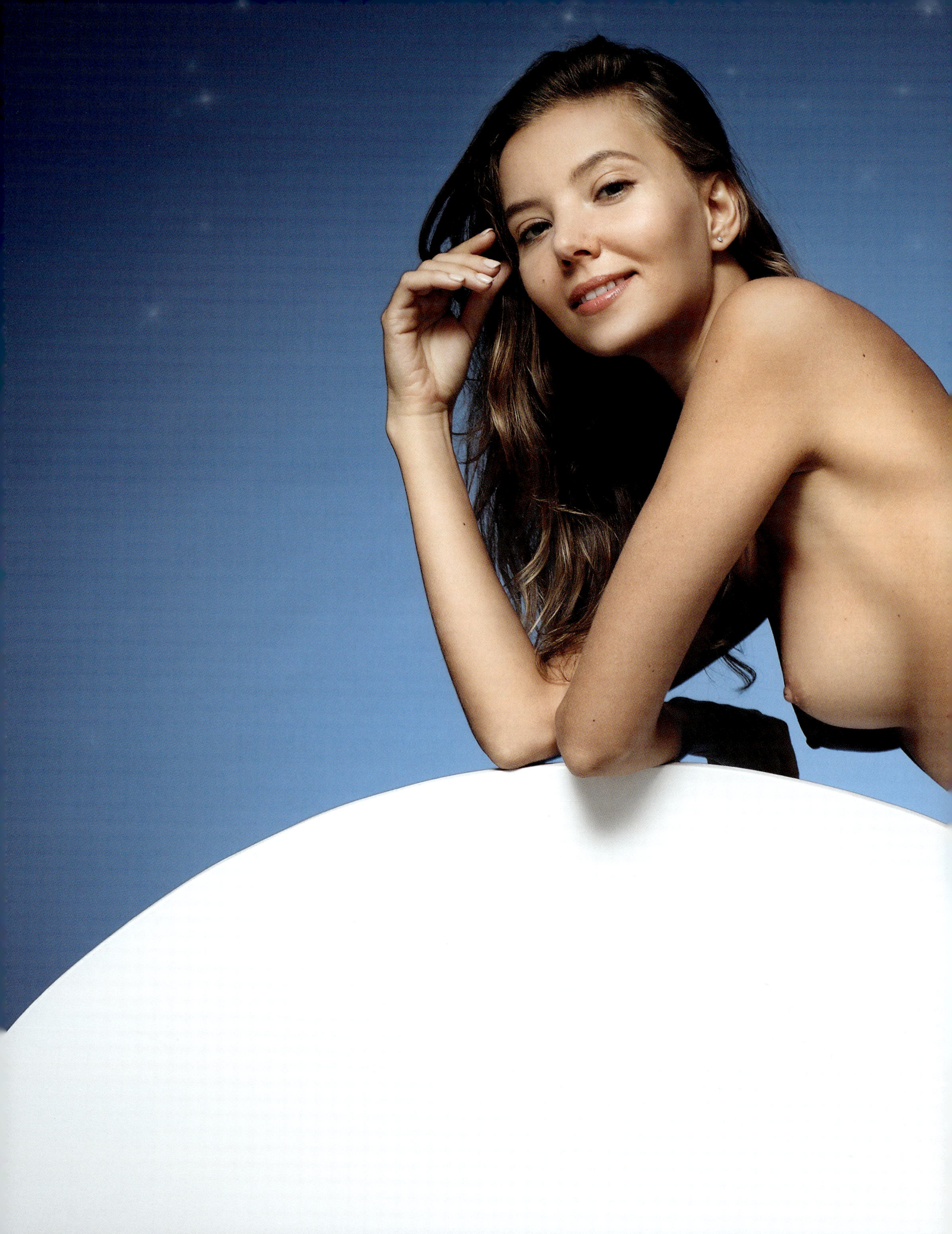

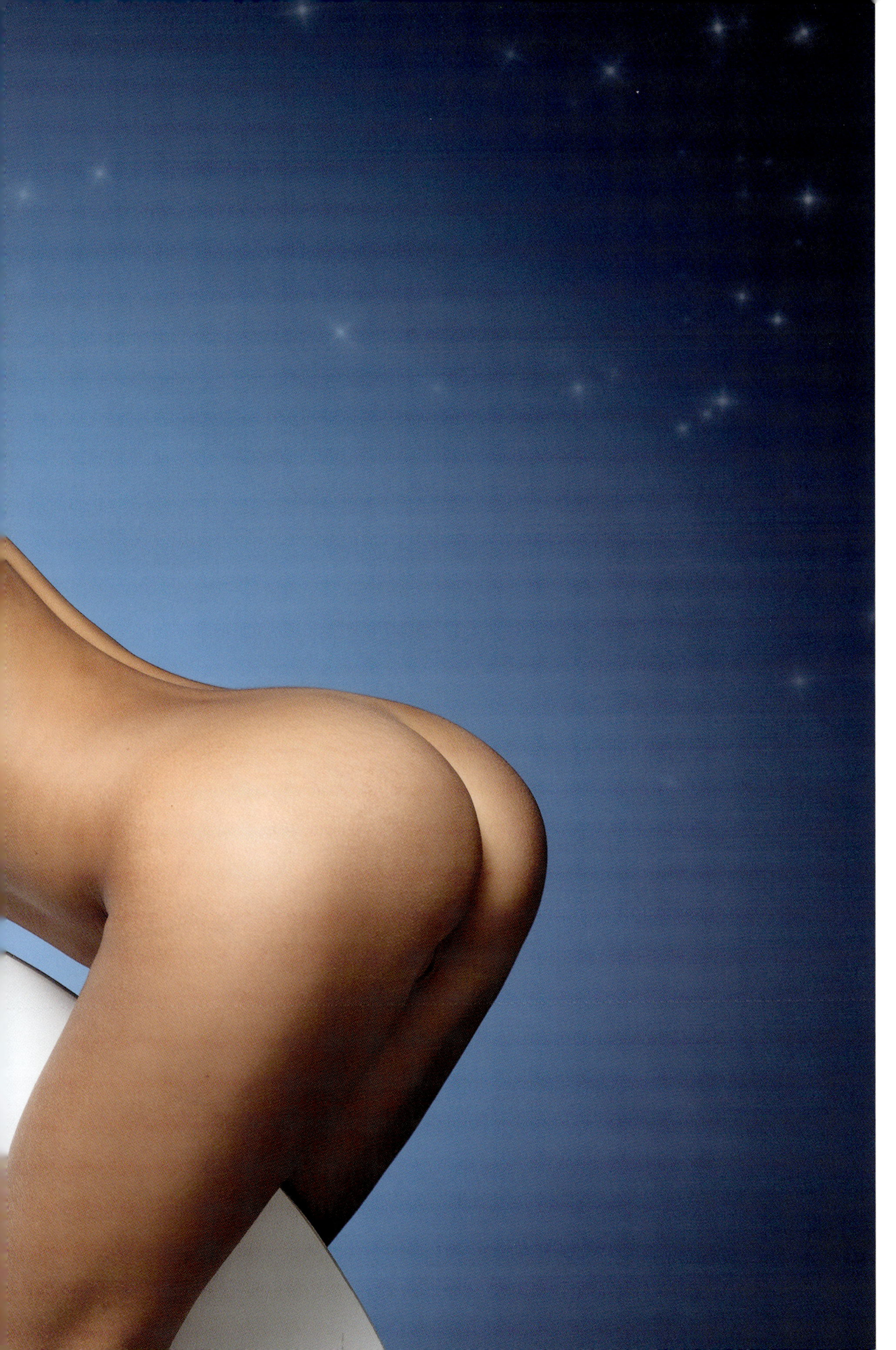

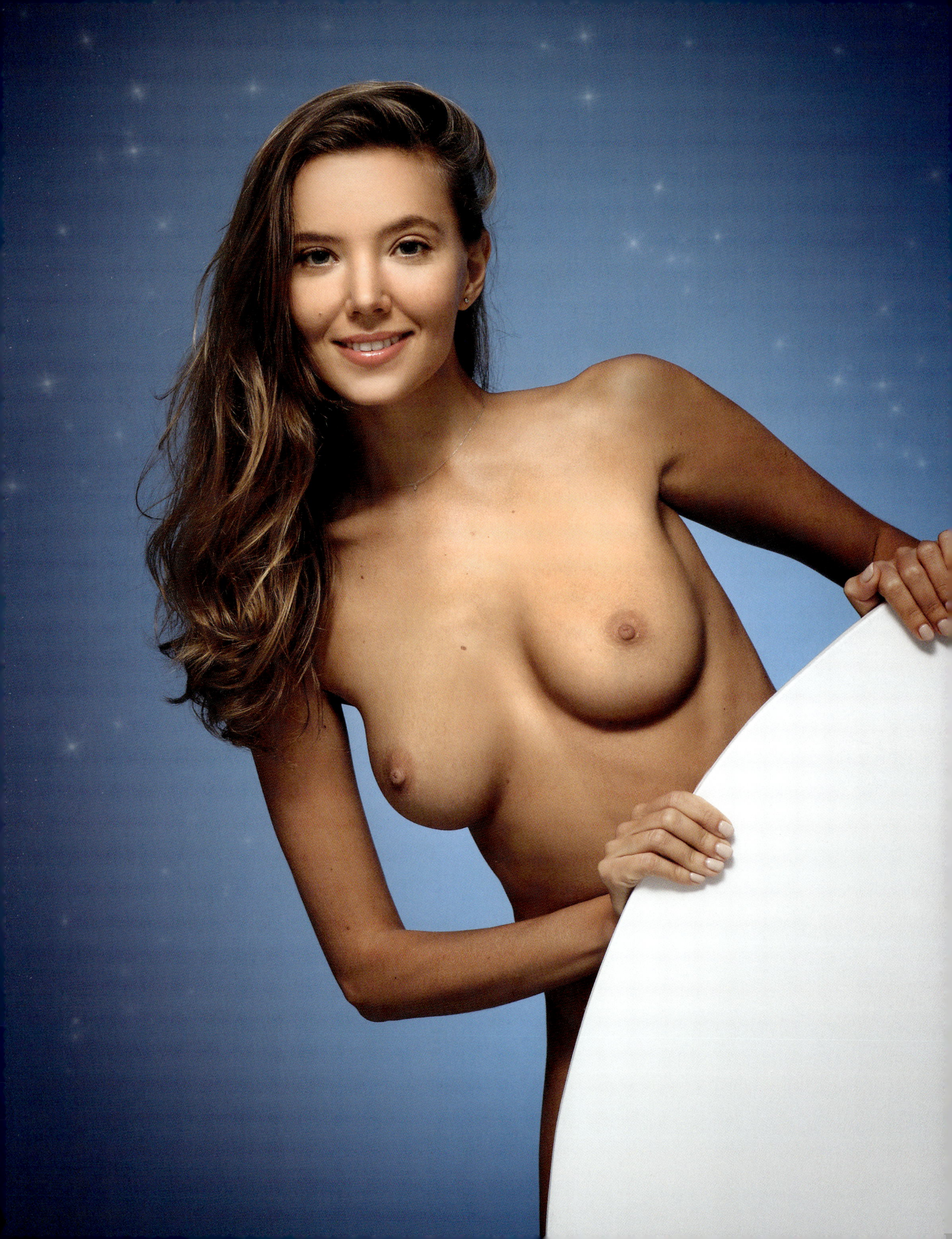

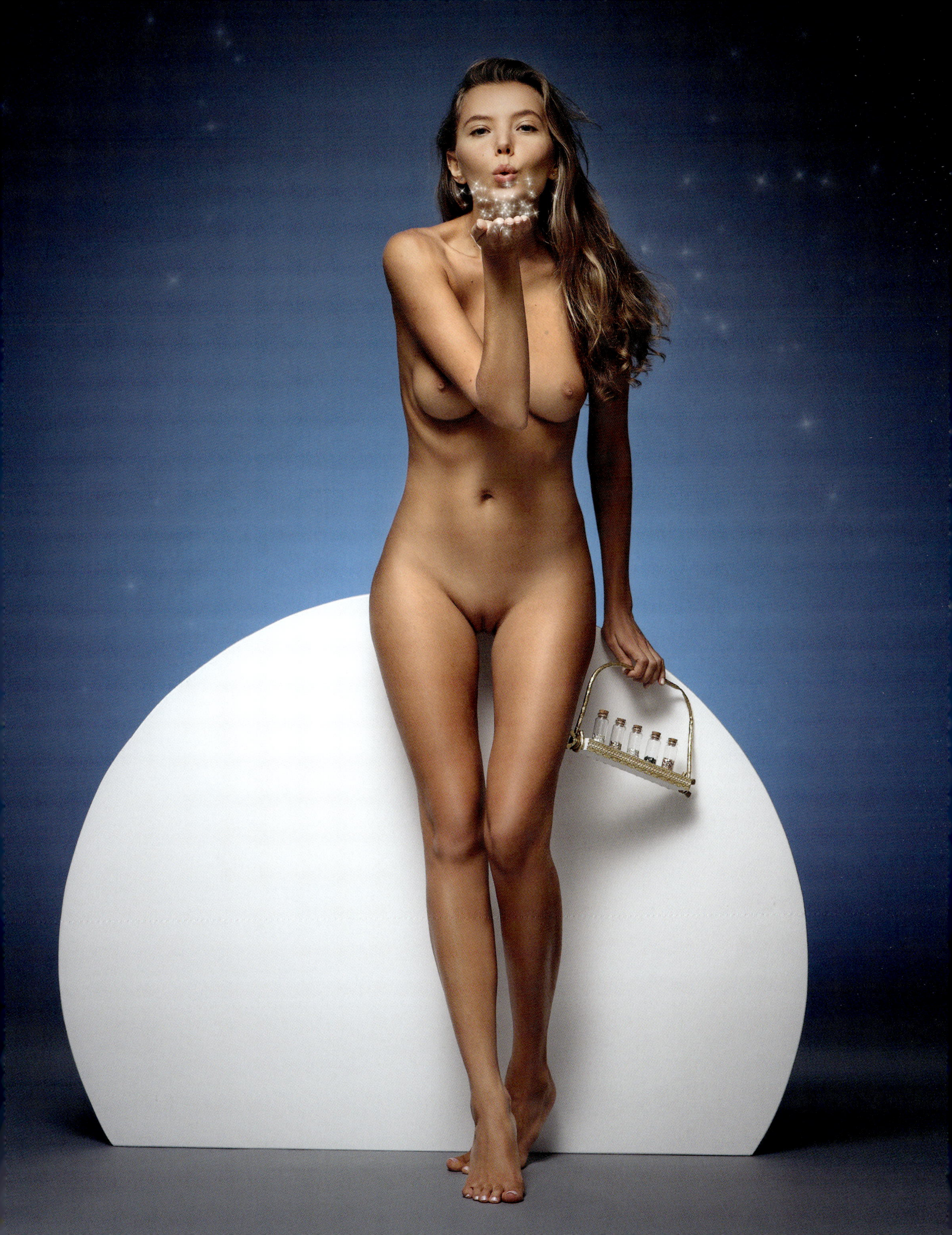

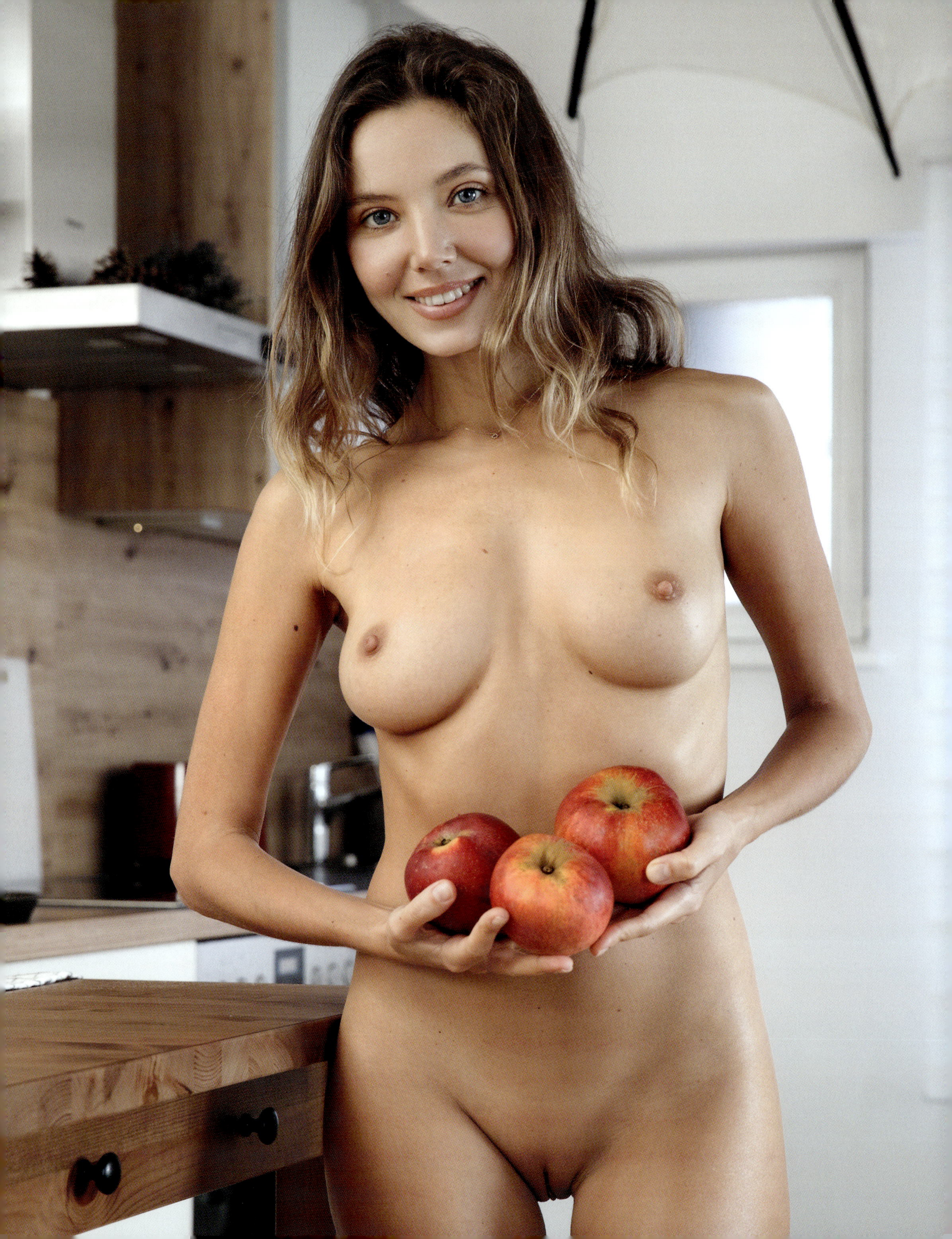

KATYA CLOVER'S FAVOURITE RECIPE FOR APPLE CAKE

KATYA CLOVERS LIEBLINGSREZEPT FÜR EINEN APFELKUCHEN

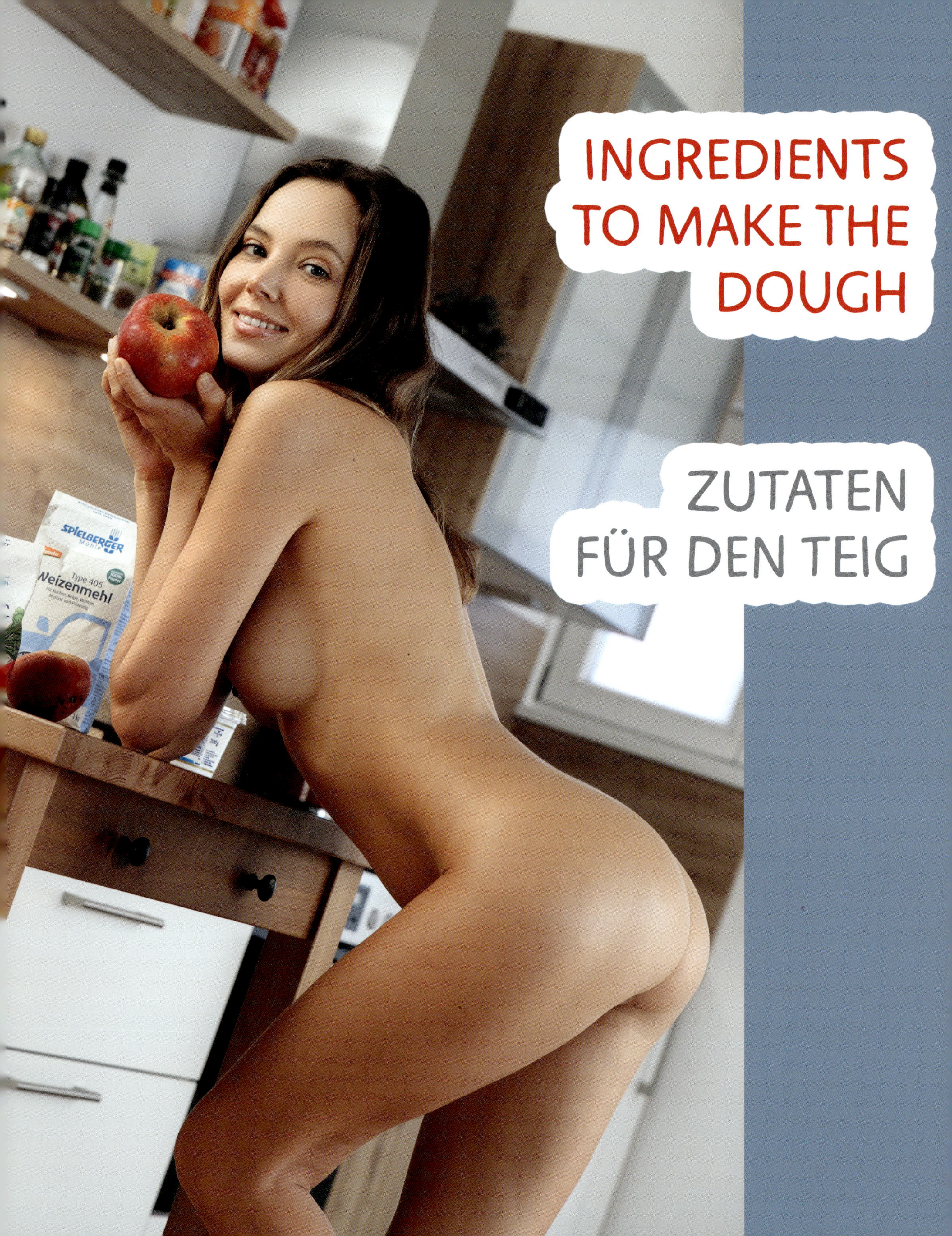
INGREDIENTS TO MAKE THE DOUGH
ZUTATEN FÜR DEN TEIG

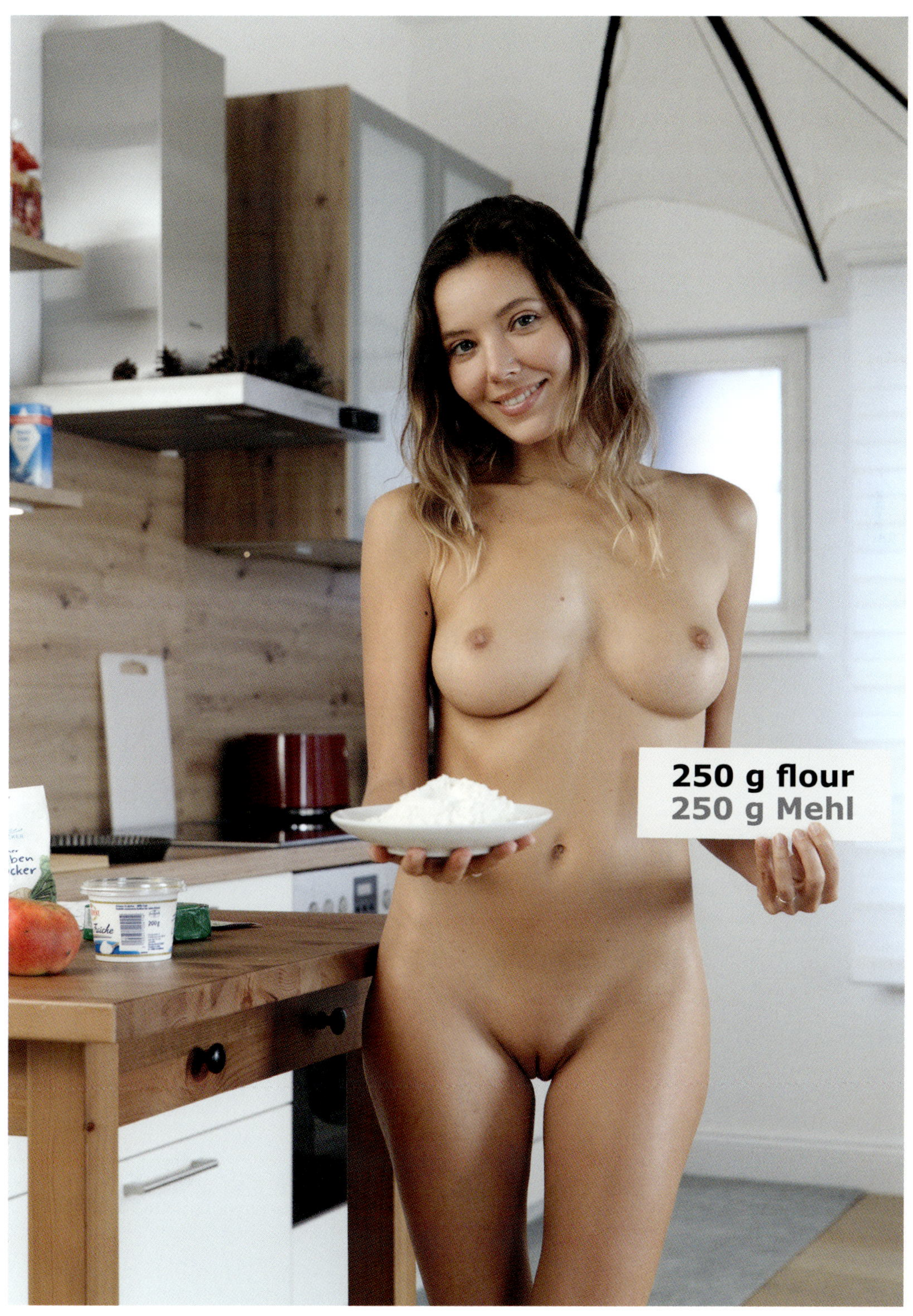

250 g flour
250 g Mehl

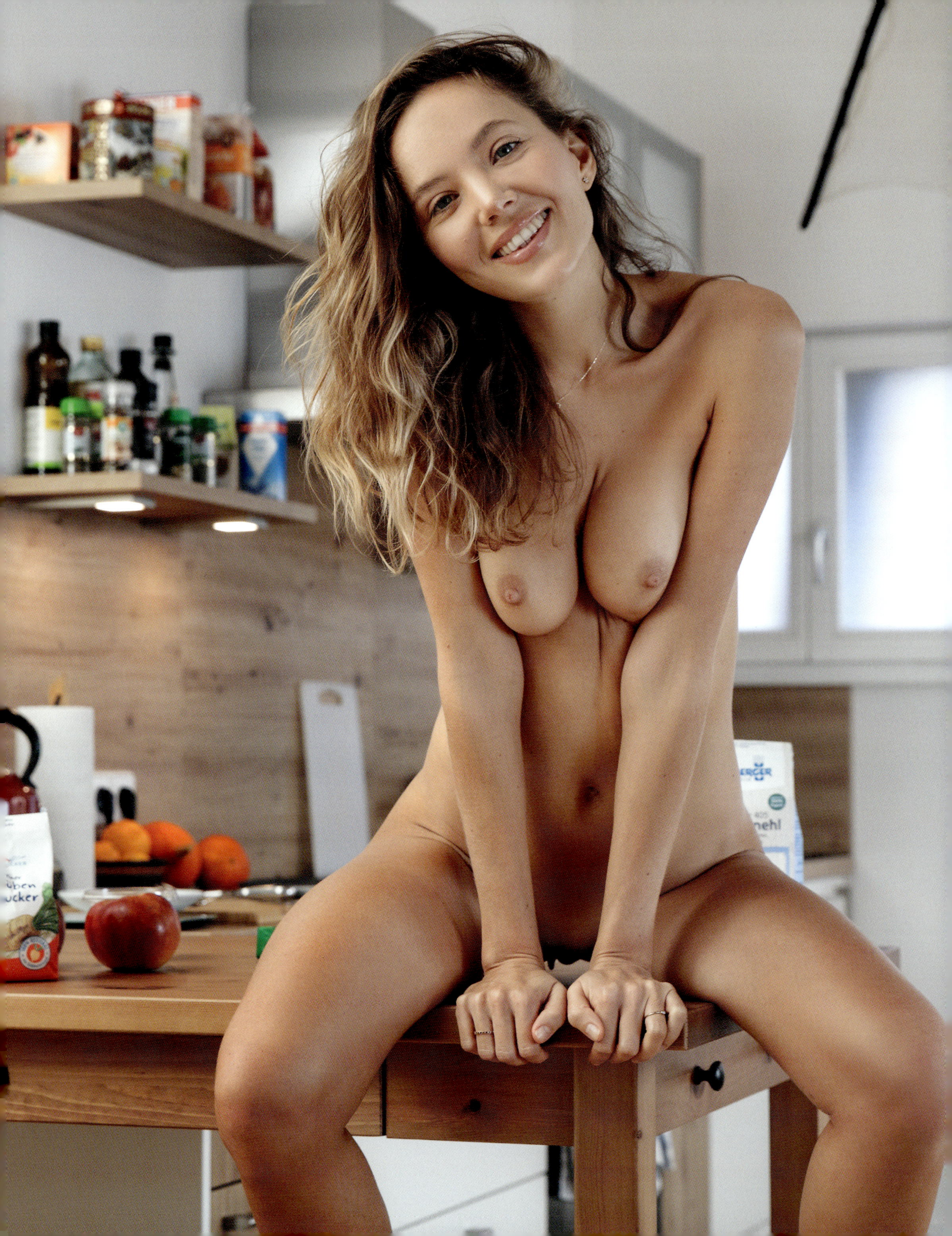

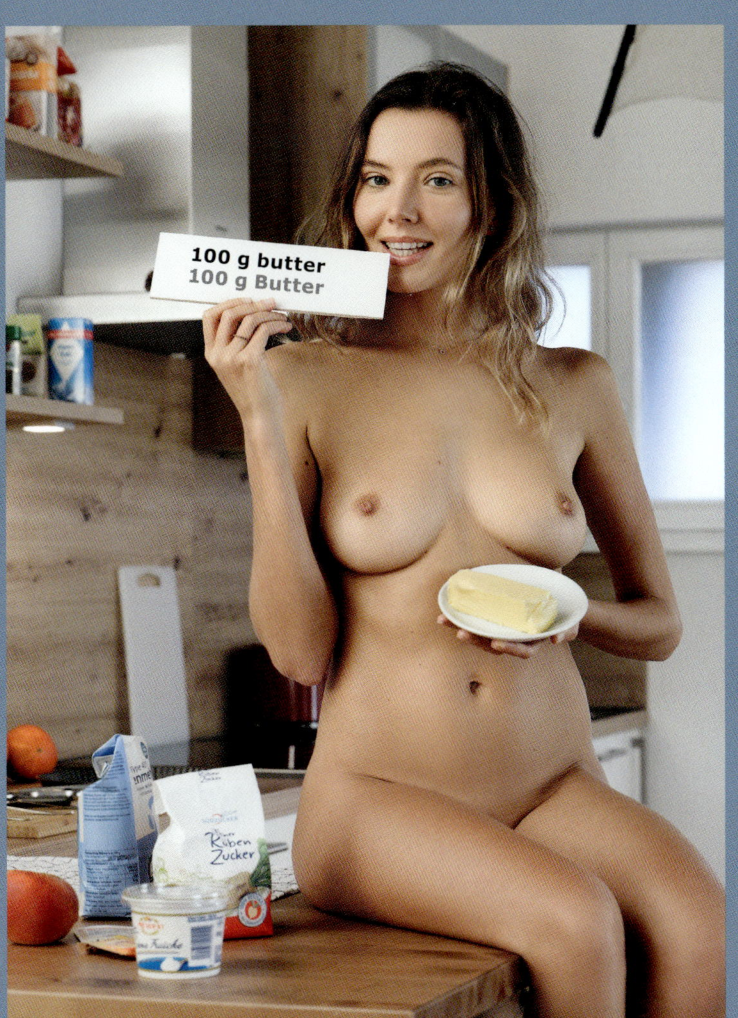

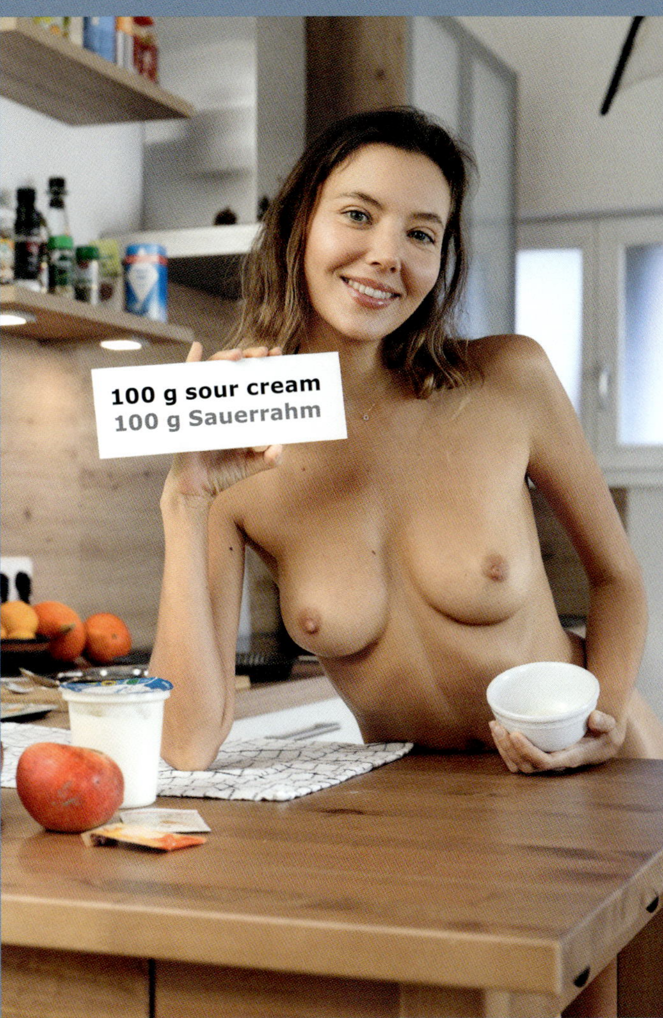

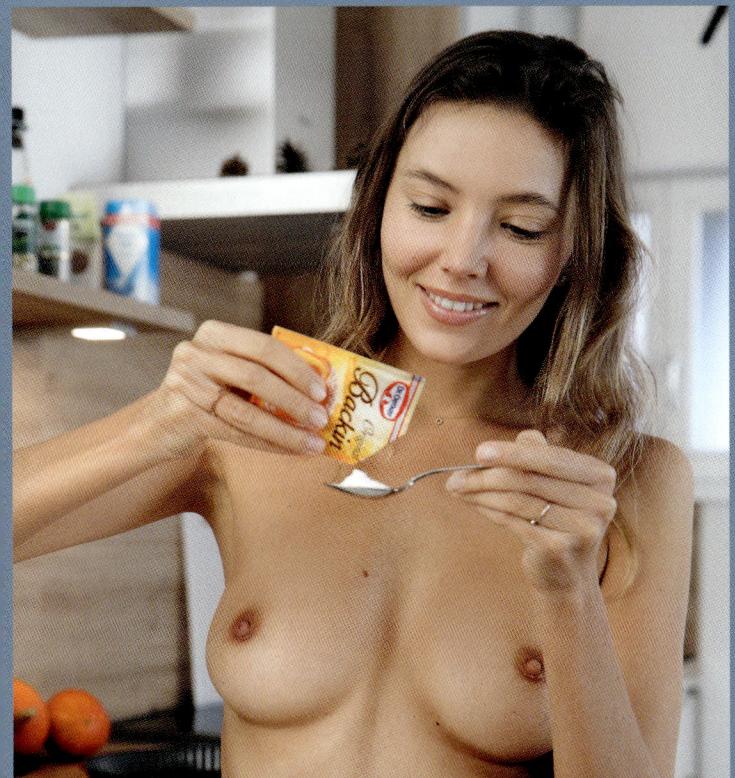

1 TEA SPOON
BAKING POWDER

1 TEELÖFFEL
BACKPULVER

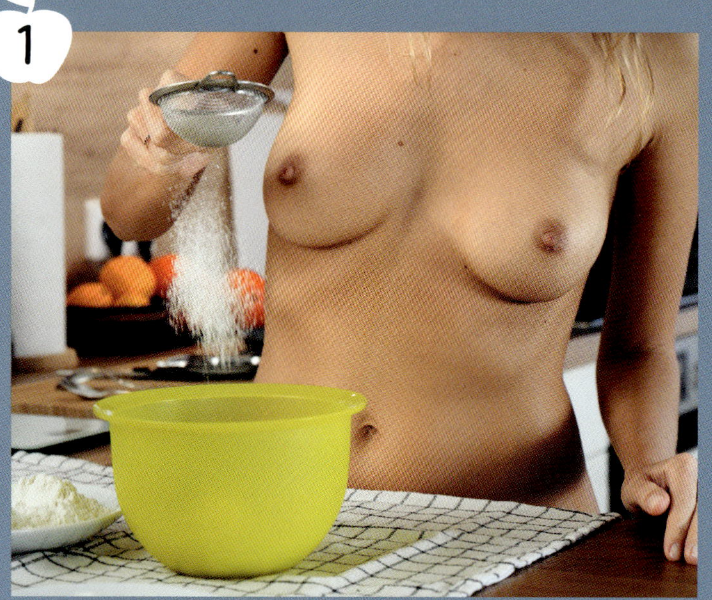

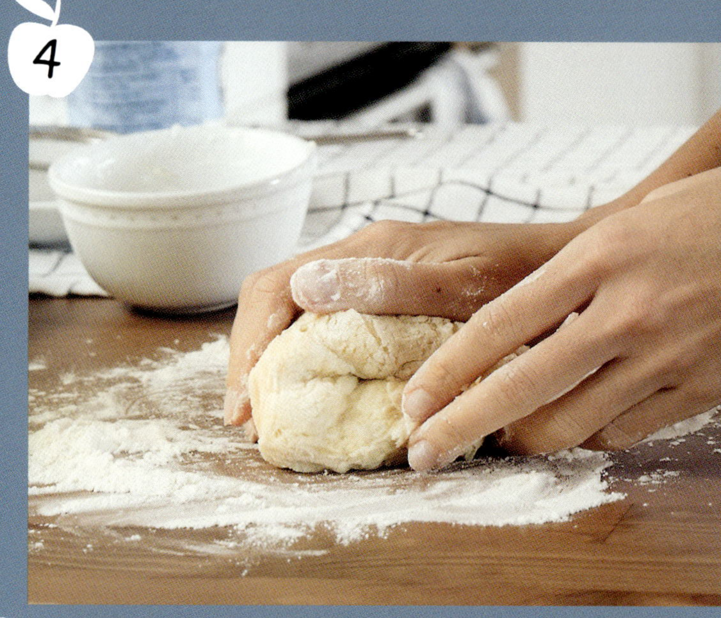

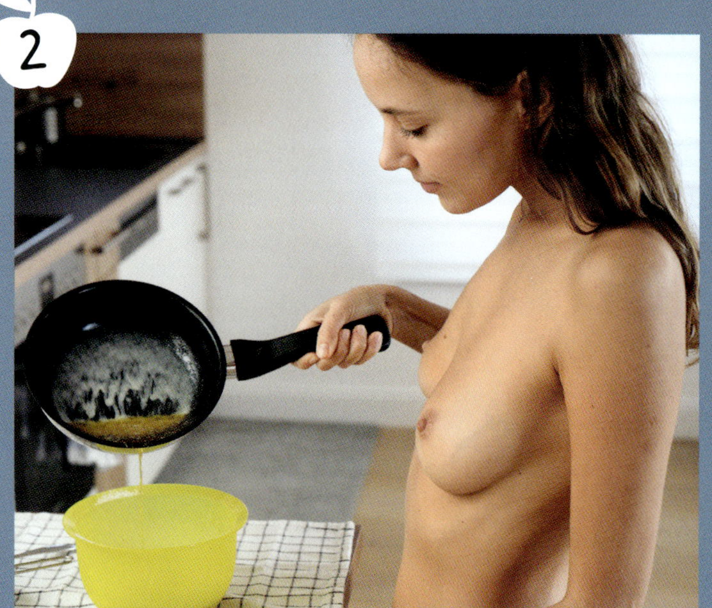

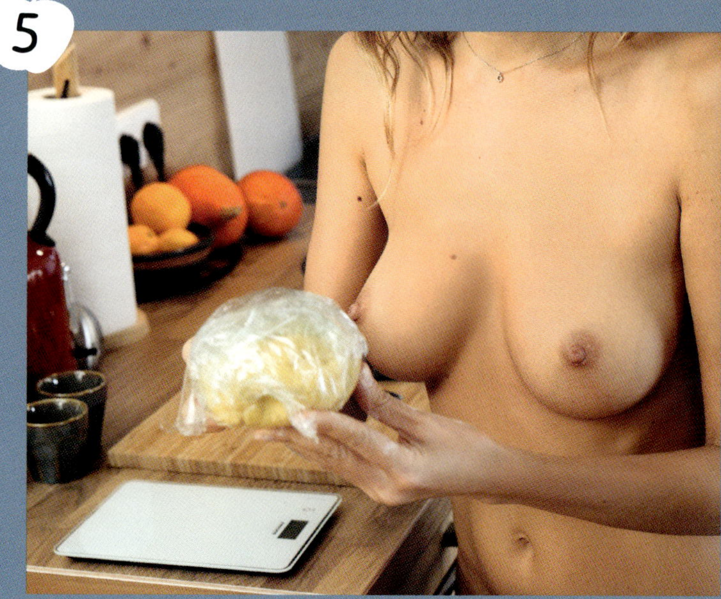

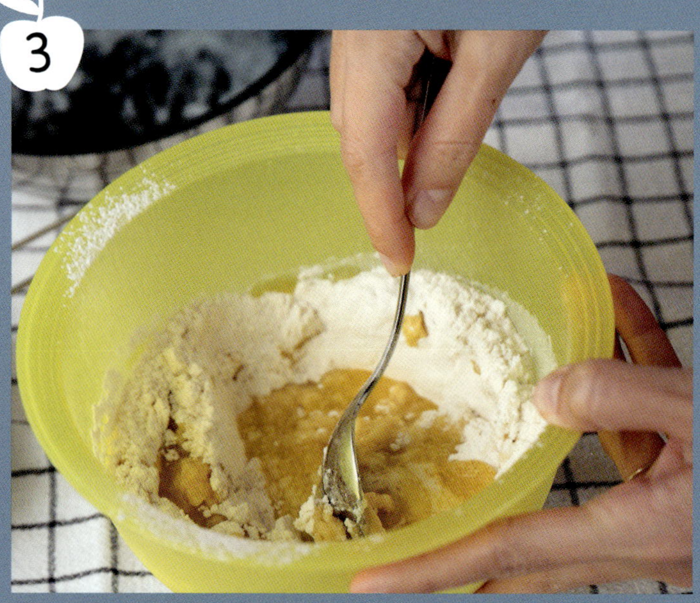

PREPARING THE DOUGH

1. In a small bowl, sift the flour through a sieve.
2. Add the baking powder and mix well using a whisk.
3. Then add soft, creamy butter and mix.
4. Add the sour cream and knead the dough vigorously.
5. Wrap the dough in cling film and put in the fridge to cool for at least 30 minutes.

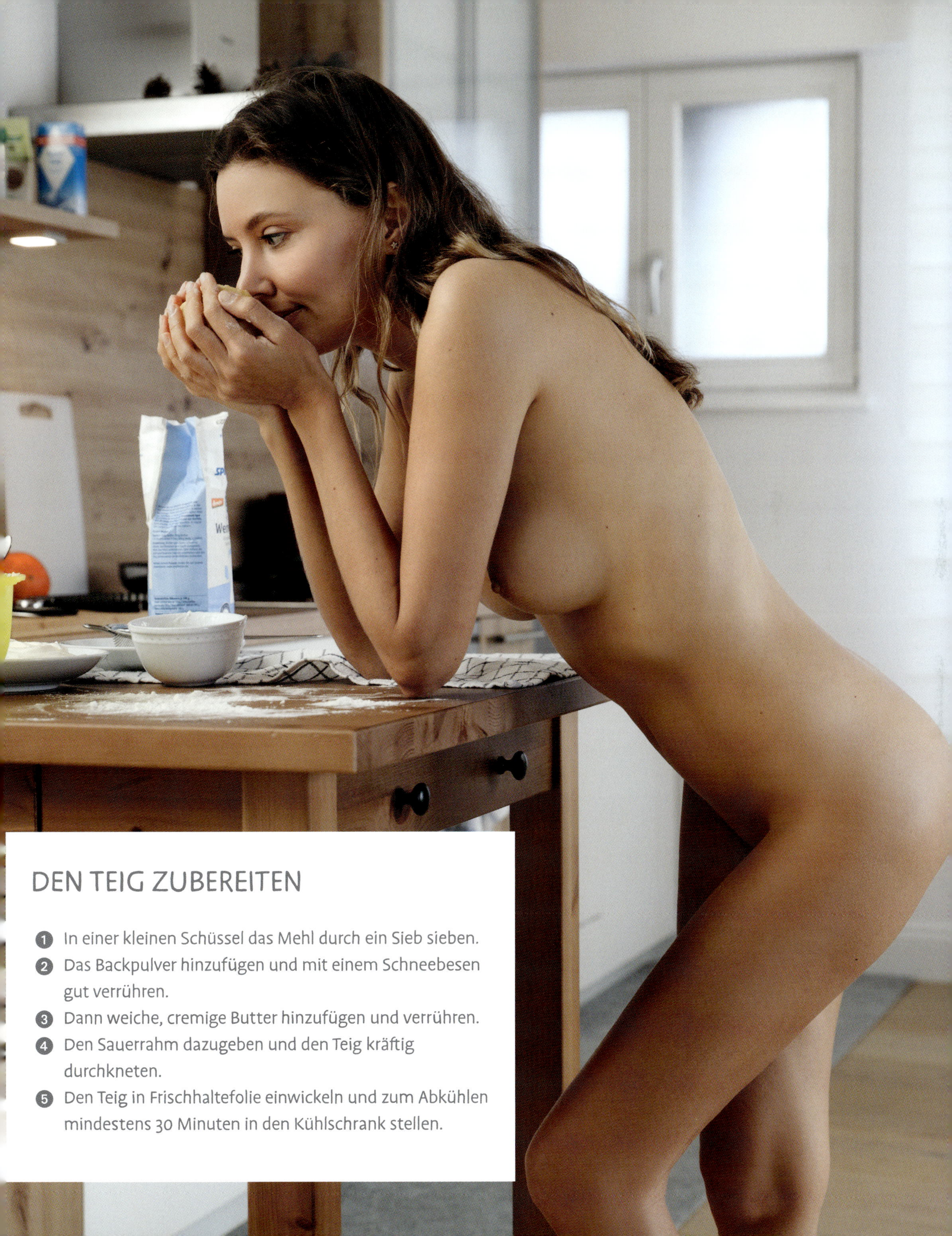

DEN TEIG ZUBEREITEN

1 In einer kleinen Schüssel das Mehl durch ein Sieb sieben.
2 Das Backpulver hinzufügen und mit einem Schneebesen
gut verrühren.
3 Dann weiche, cremige Butter hinzufügen und verrühren.
4 Den Sauerrahm dazugeben und den Teig kräftig
durchkneten.
5 Den Teig in Frischhaltefolie einwickeln und zum Abkühlen
mindestens 30 Minuten in den Kühlschrank stellen.

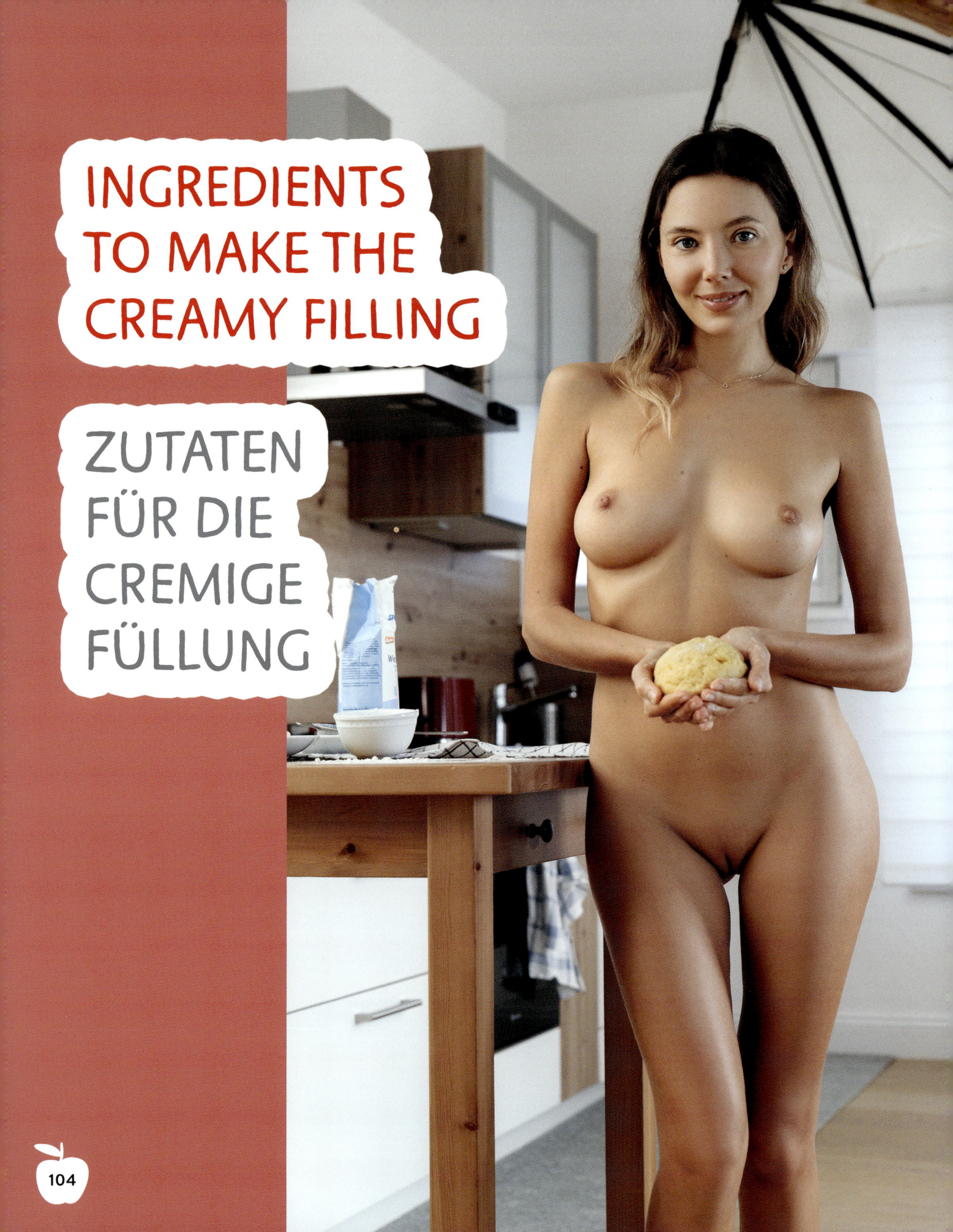

INGREDIENTS
TO MAKE THE
CREAMY FILLING

ZUTATEN
FÜR DIE
CREMIGE
FÜLLUNG

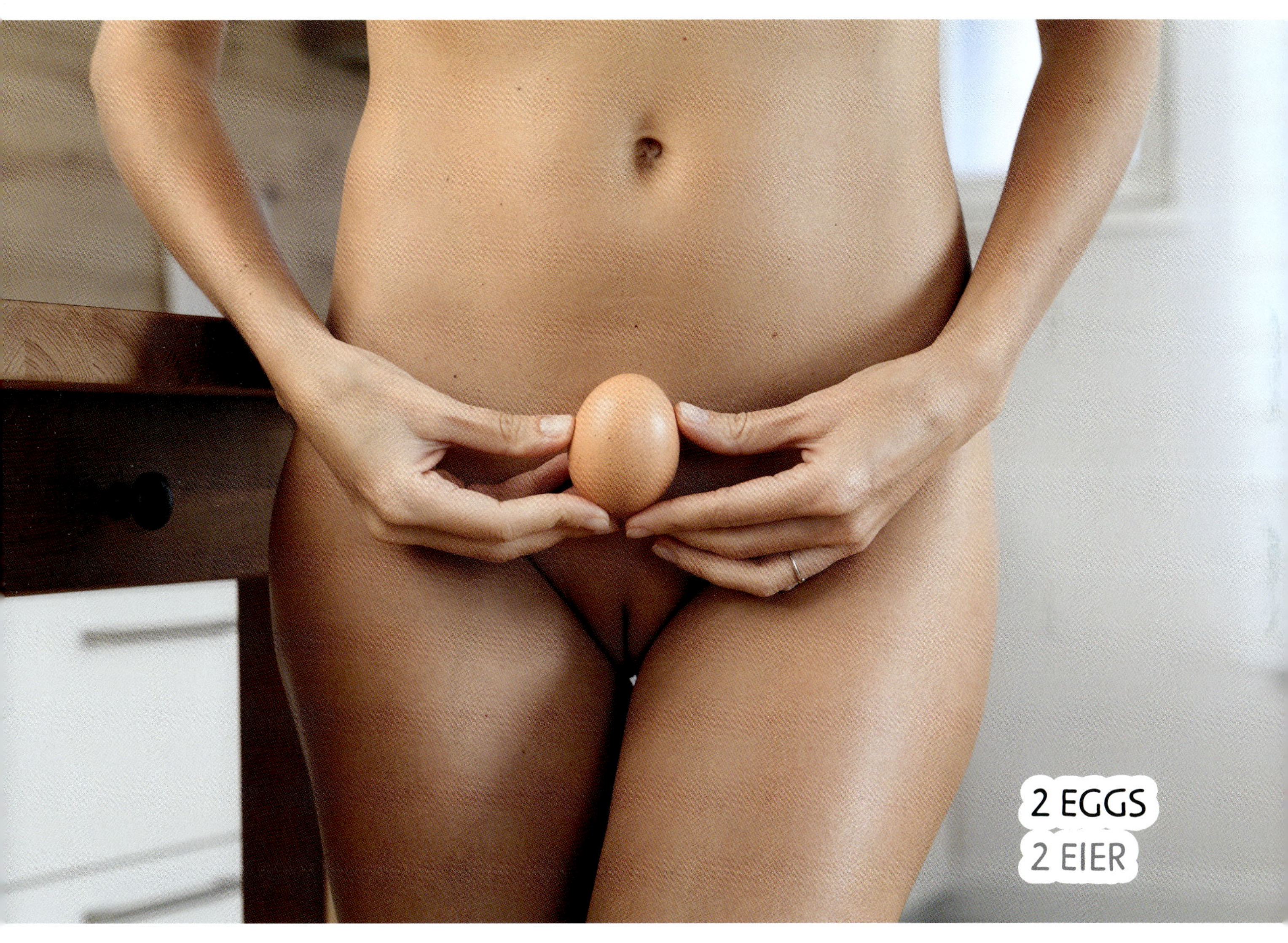

2 EGGS
2 EIER

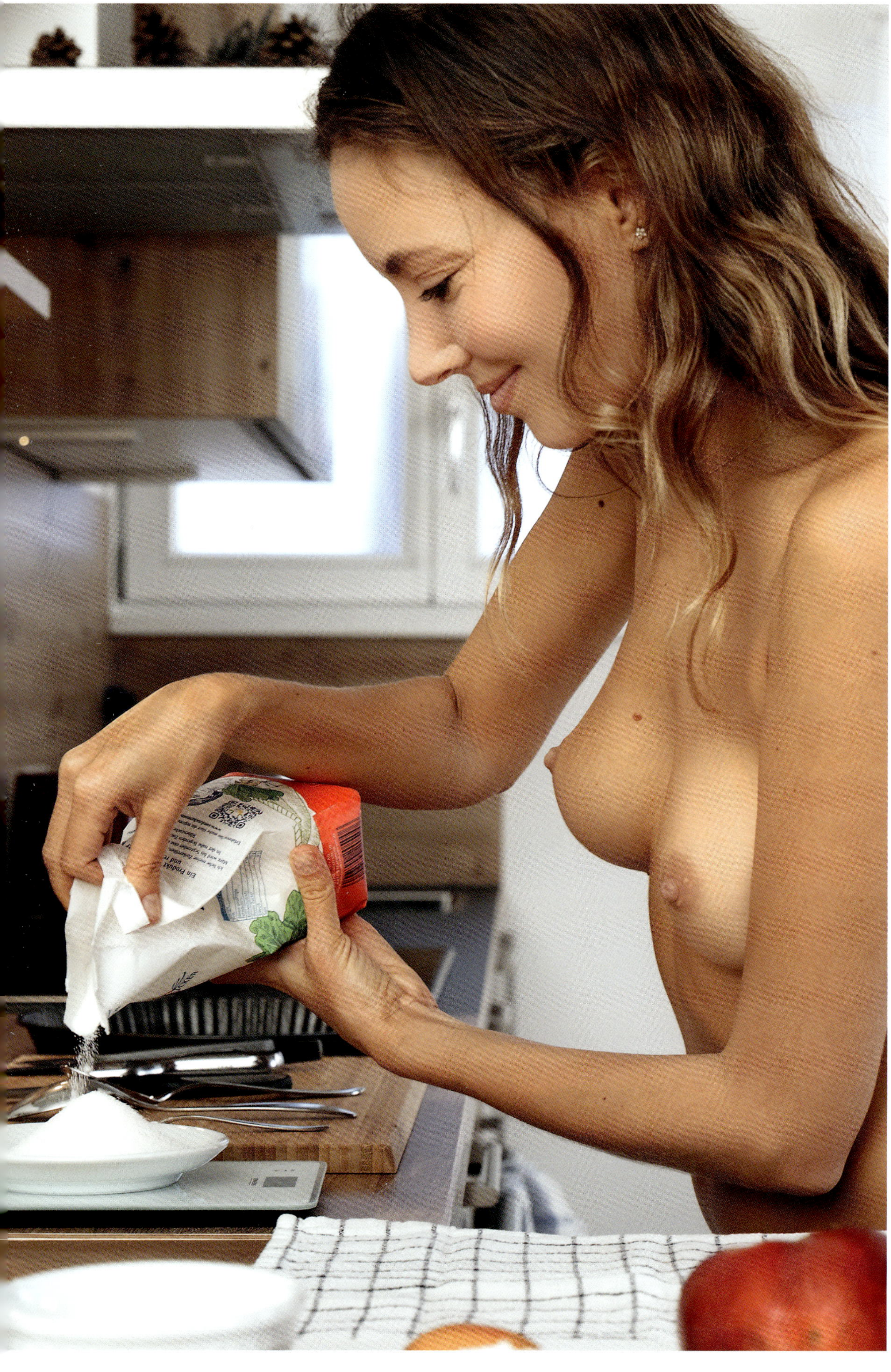

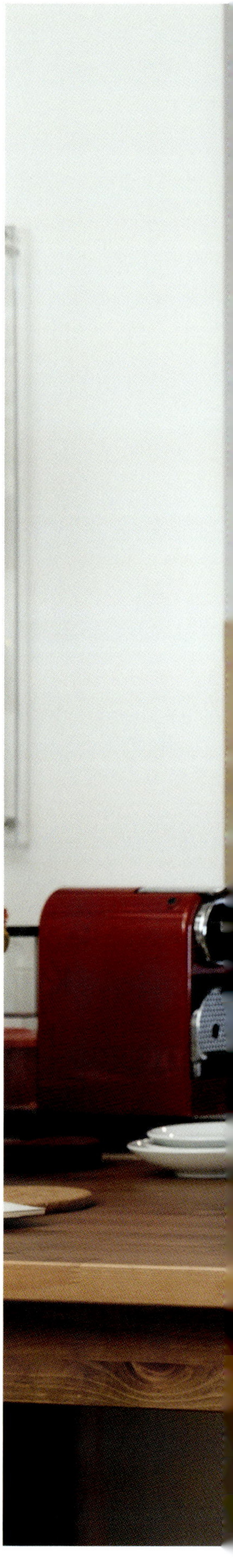

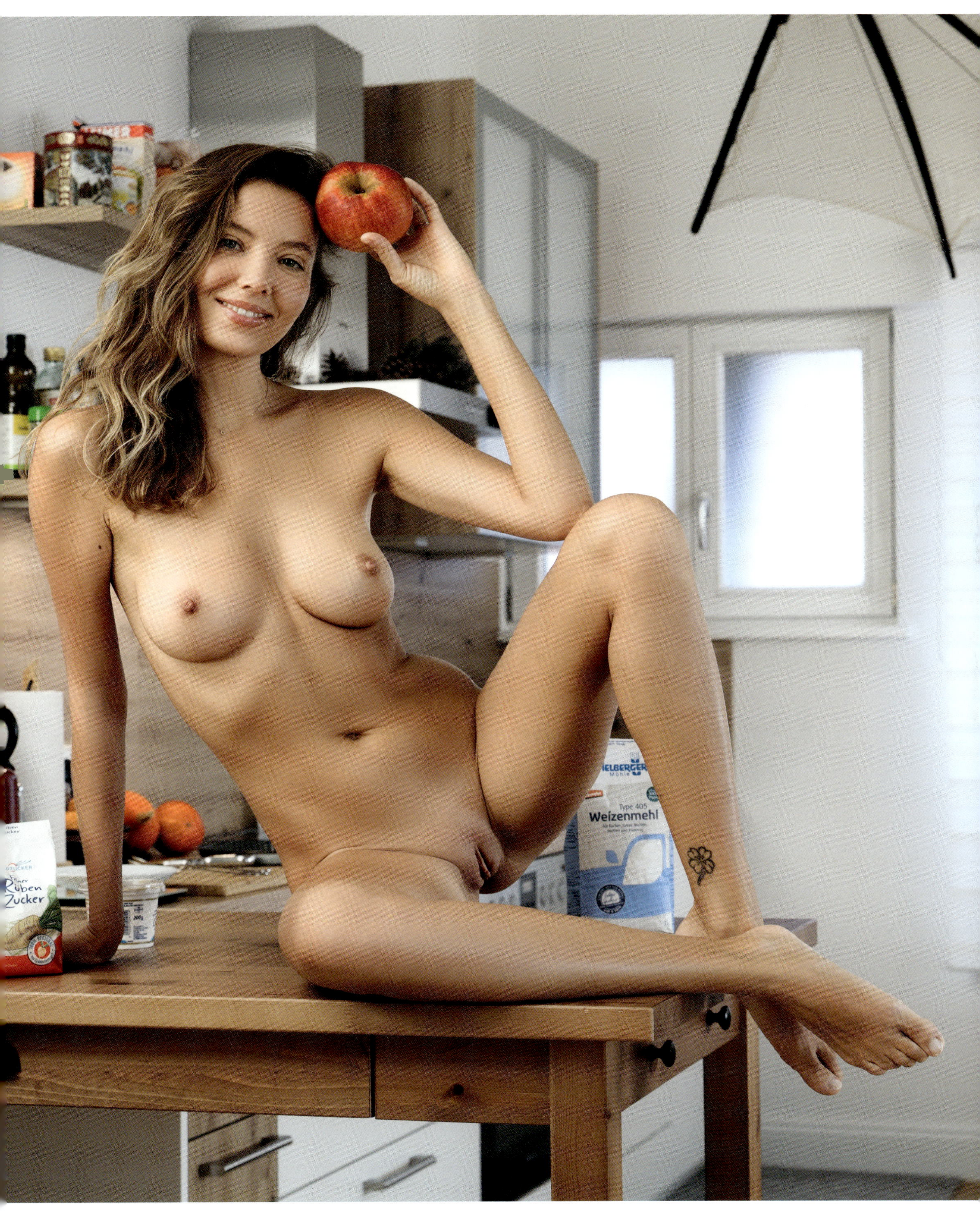

Type 405
Weizenmehl
Rüben
Zucker

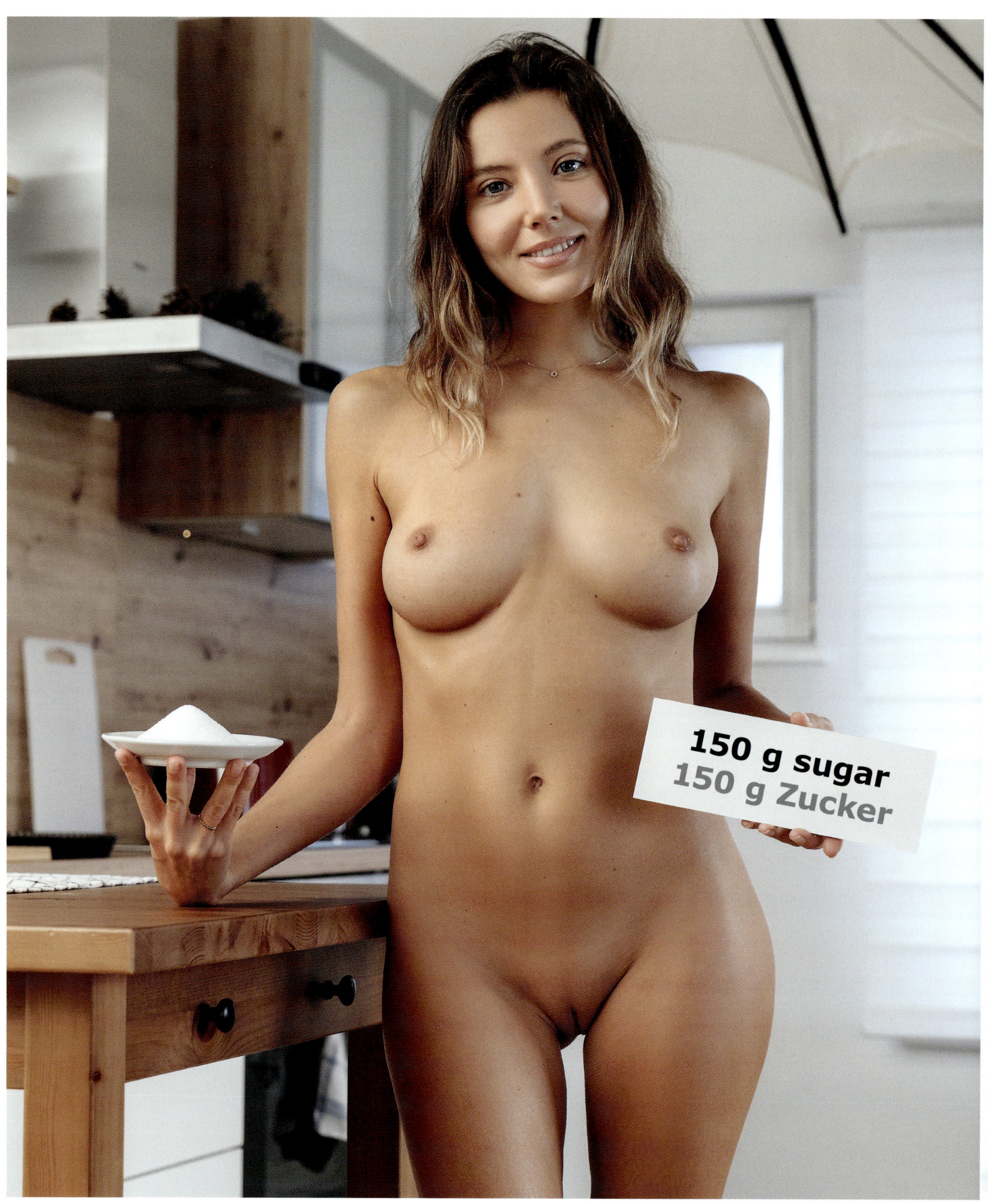150 g sugar
150 g Zucker

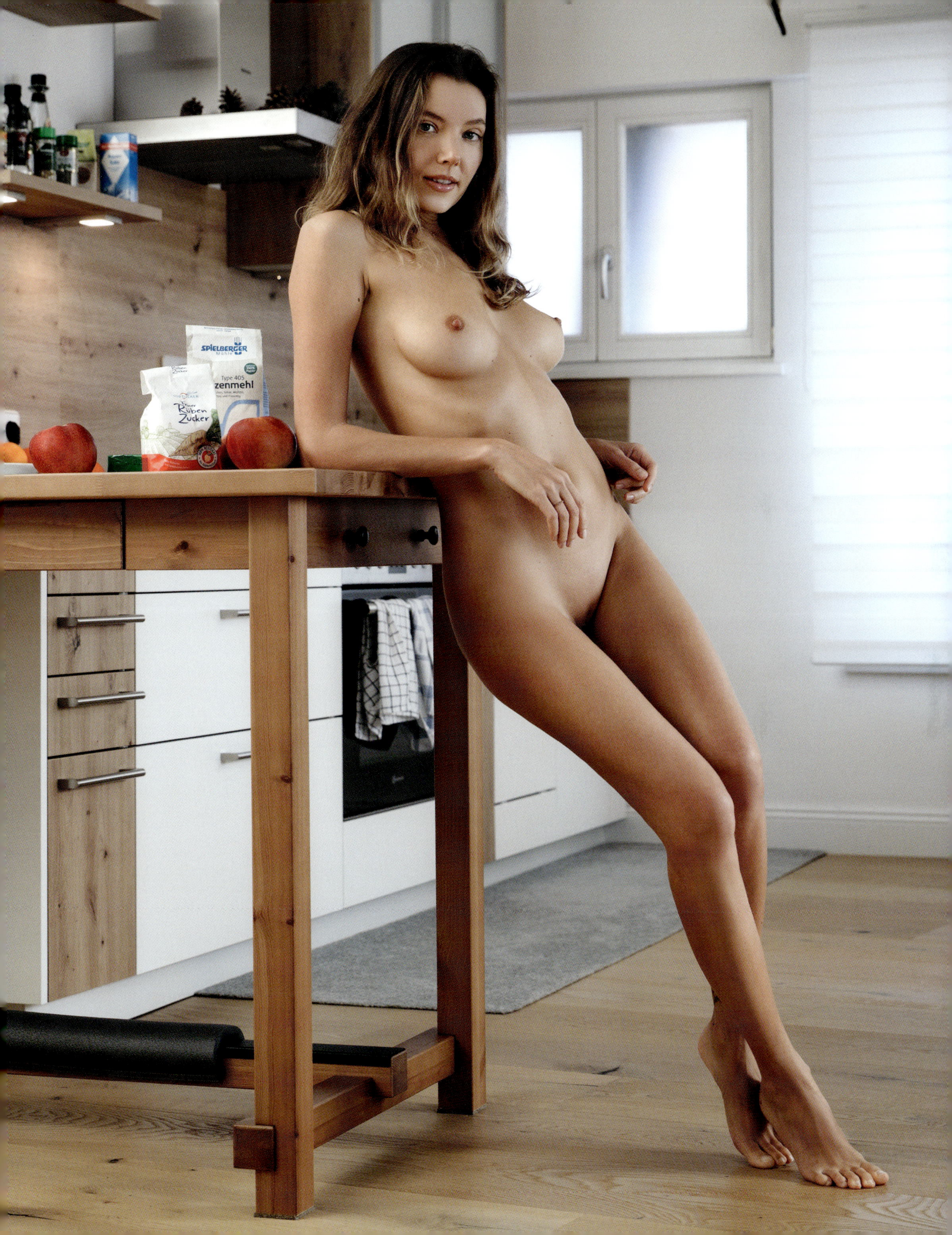

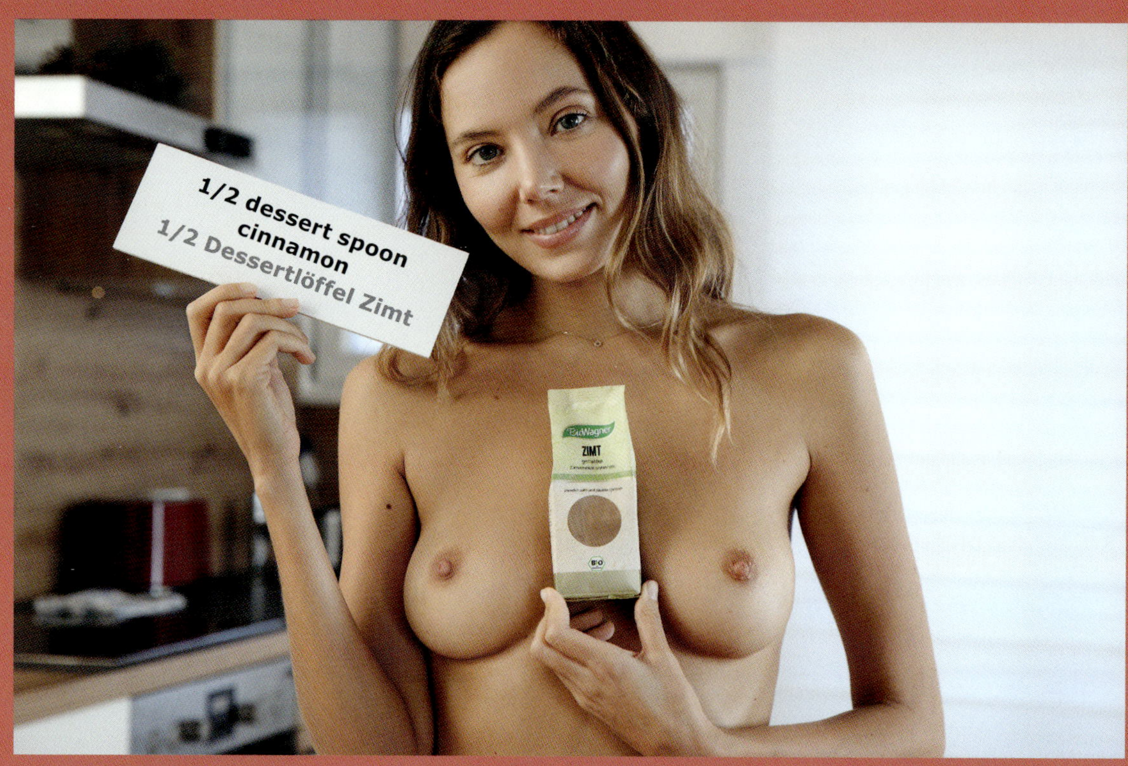

1/2 dessert spoon
cinnamon
1/2 Dessertlöffel Zimt

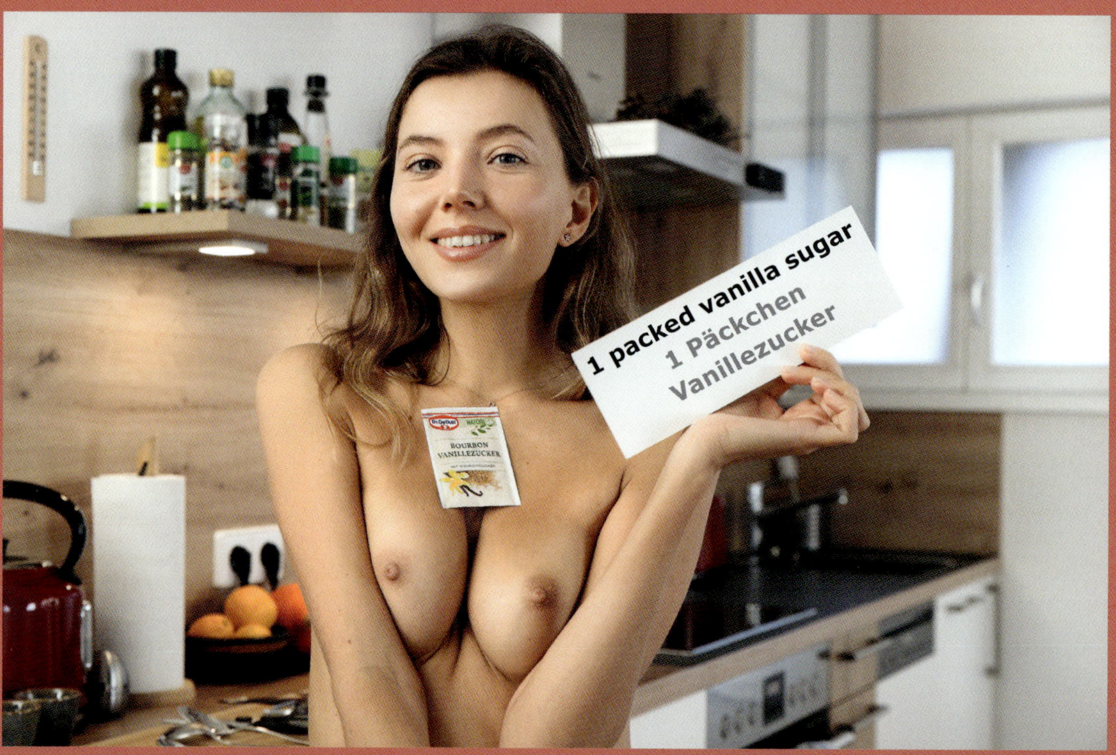

1 packed vanilla sugar
1 Päckchen
Vanillezucker

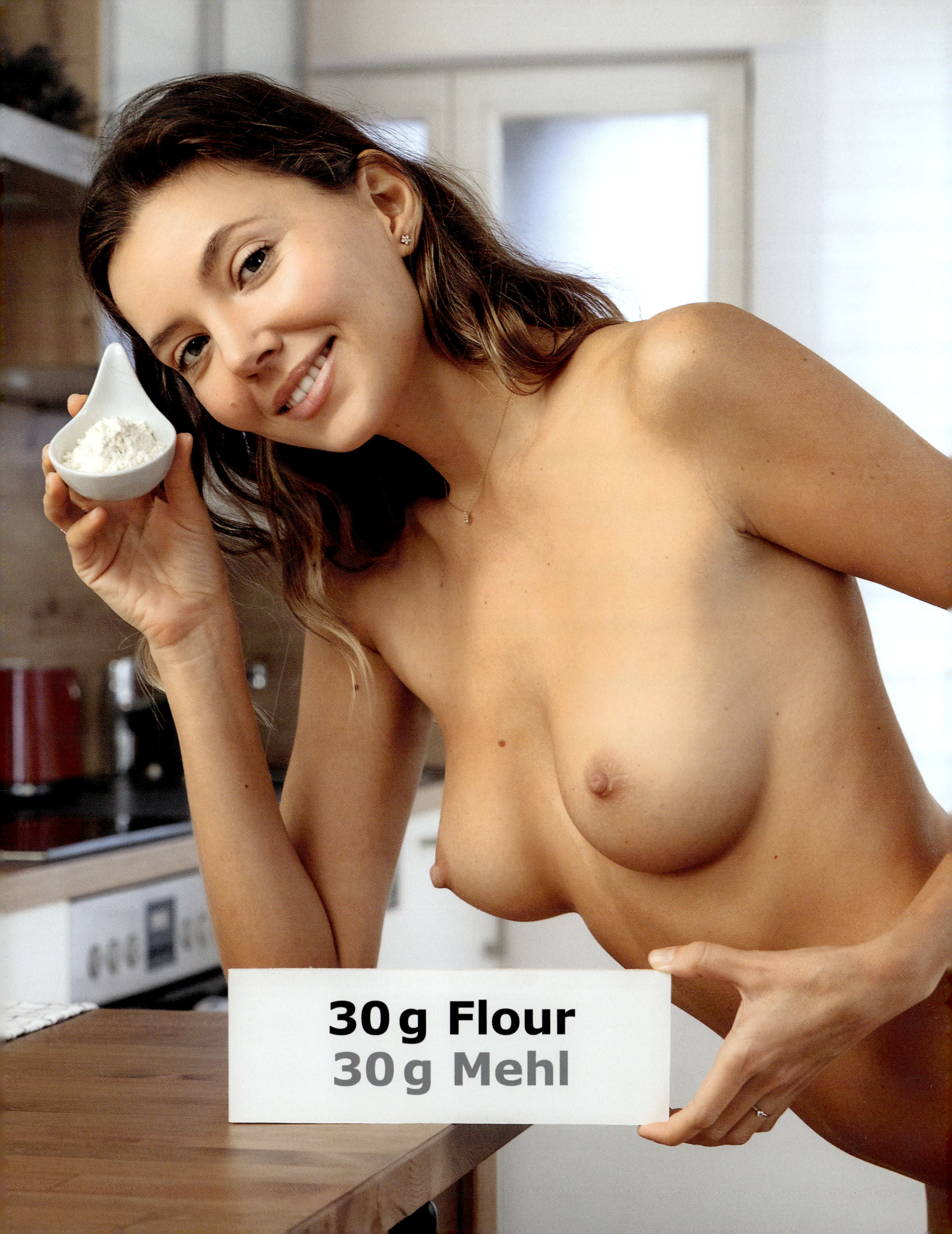

30 g Flour
30 g Mehl

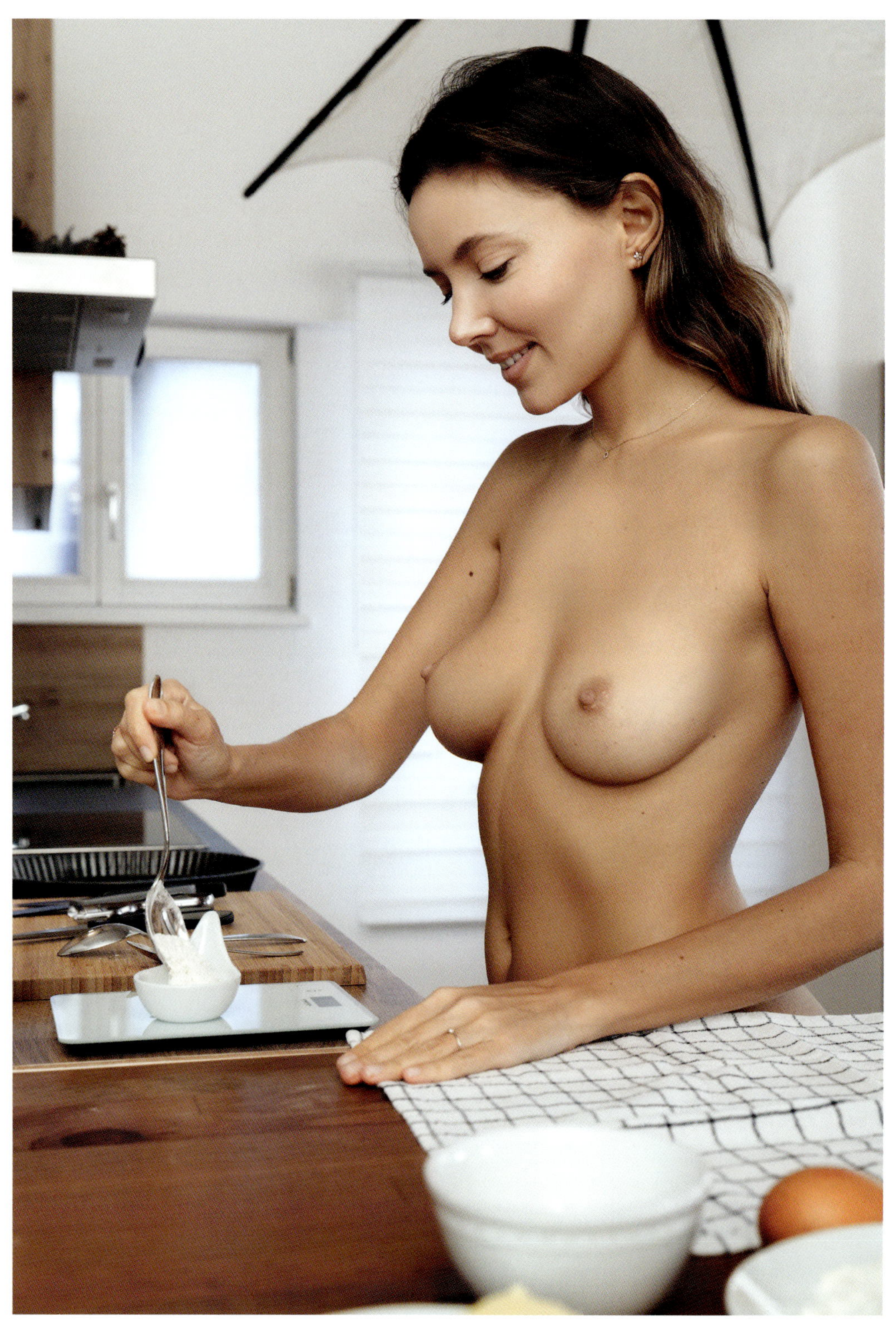

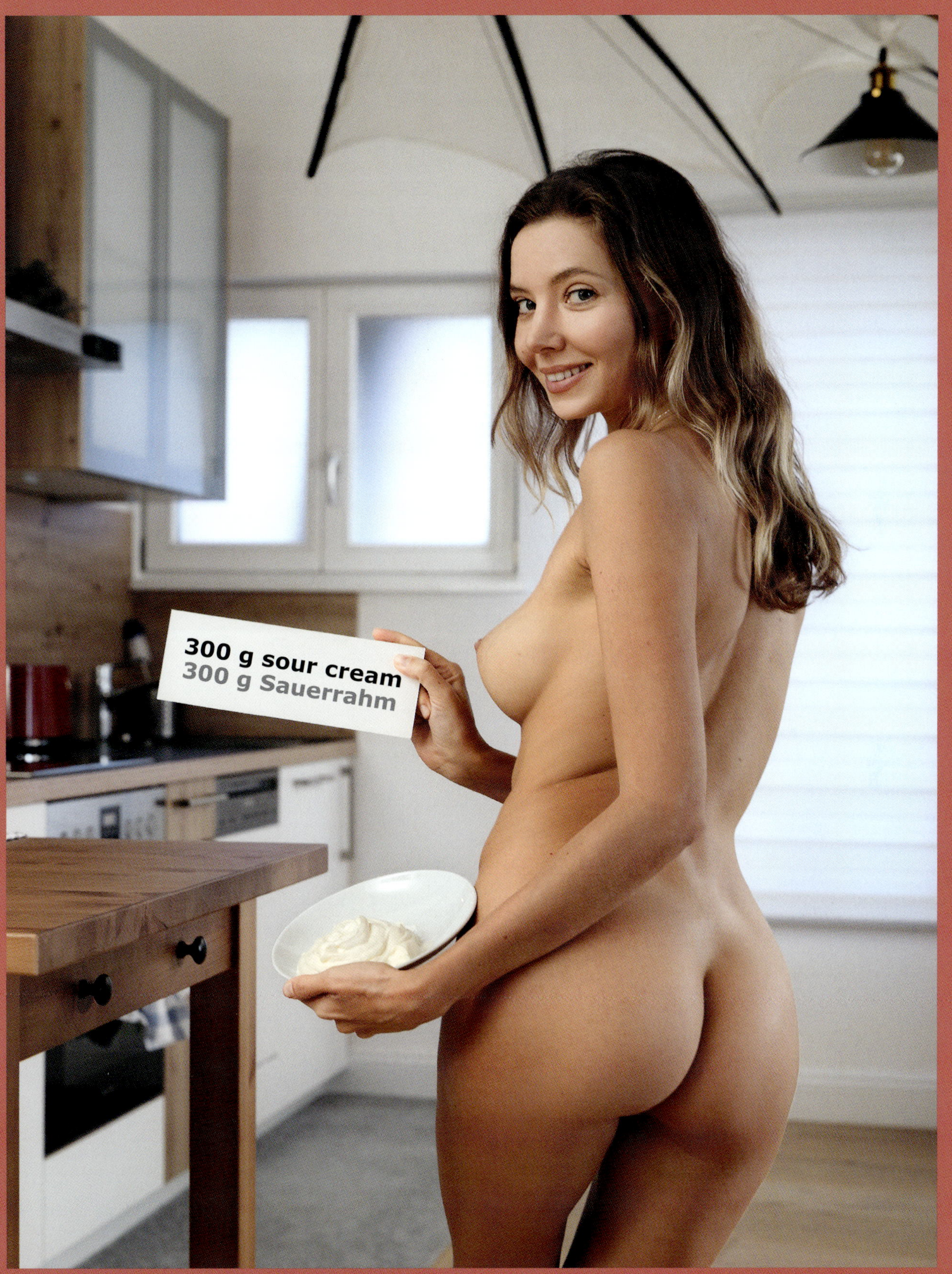
300 g sour cream
300 g Sauerrahm

PREPARING THE FILLING

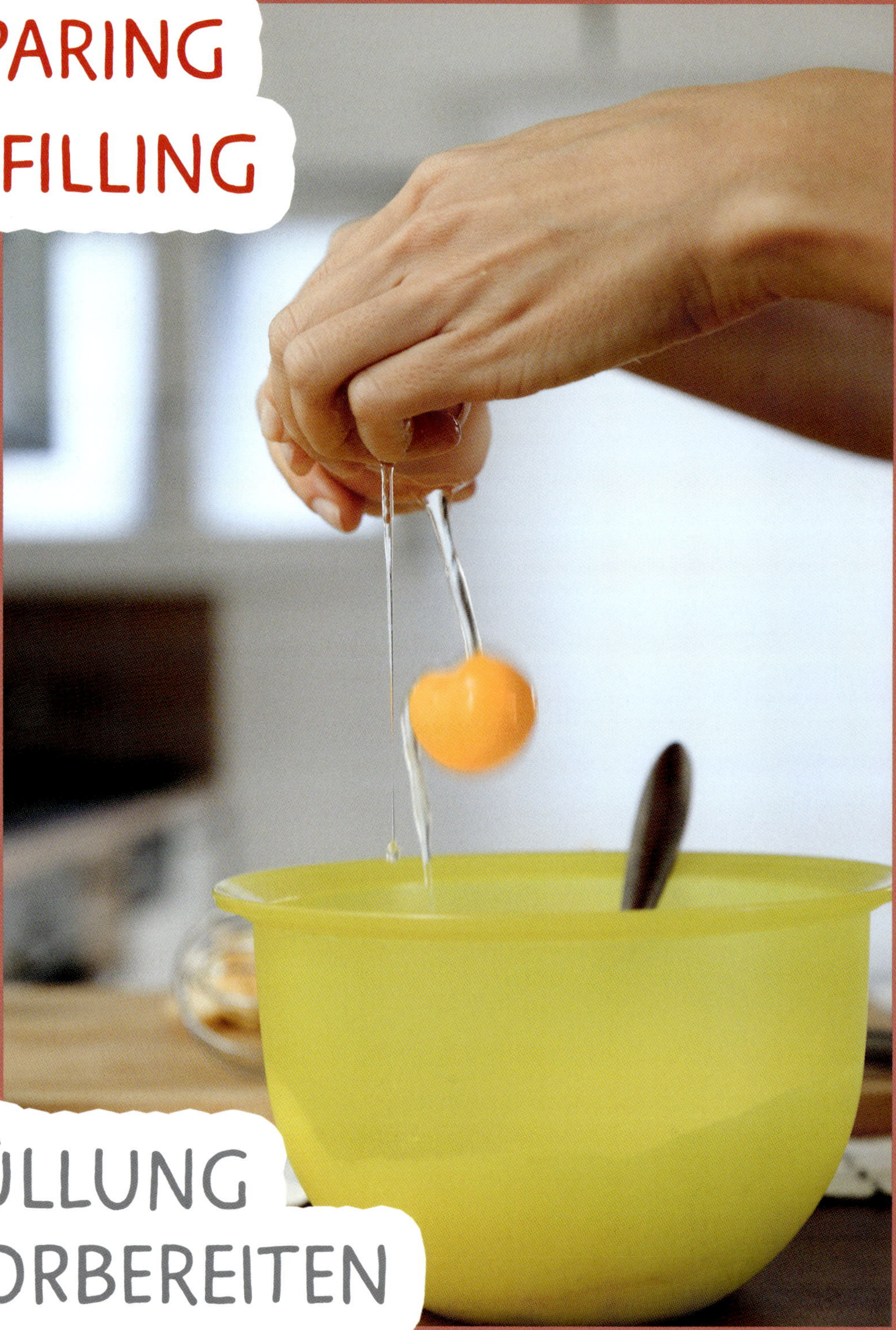

FÜLLUNG VORBEREITEN

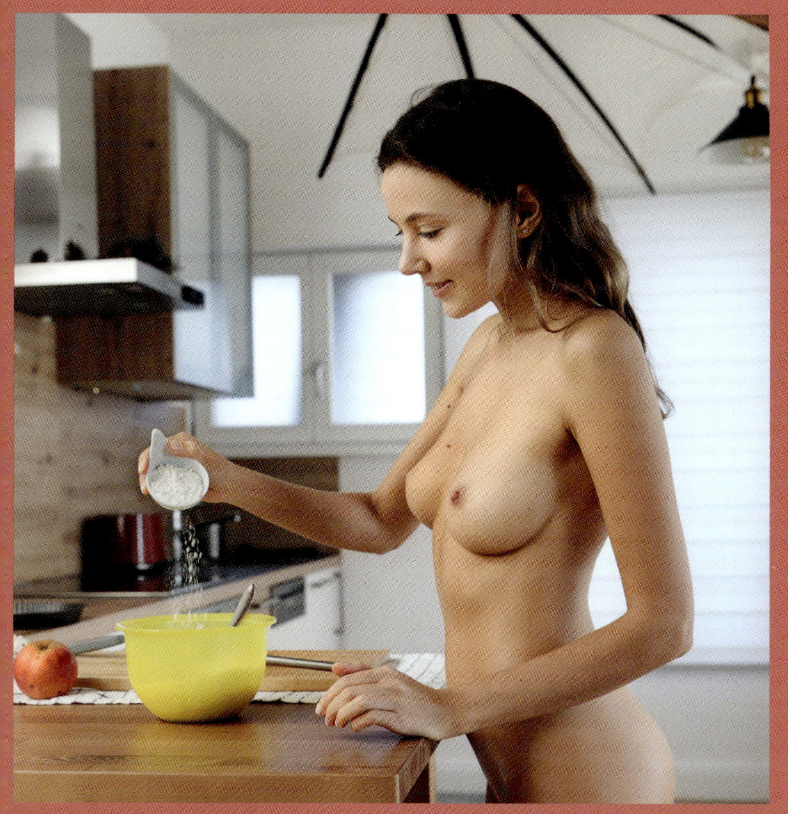

PUT THE EGGS, SUGAR AND VANILLA SUGAR INTO A BOWL TOGETHER

BEAT EVERYTHING FOR ABOUT FOUR TO FIVE MINUTES UNTIL THE EGGS BECOME FLUFFY

ADD SOUR CREAM AND FLOUR AND WHISK TOGETHER THOROUGHLY FOR ABOUT FIVE MINUTES

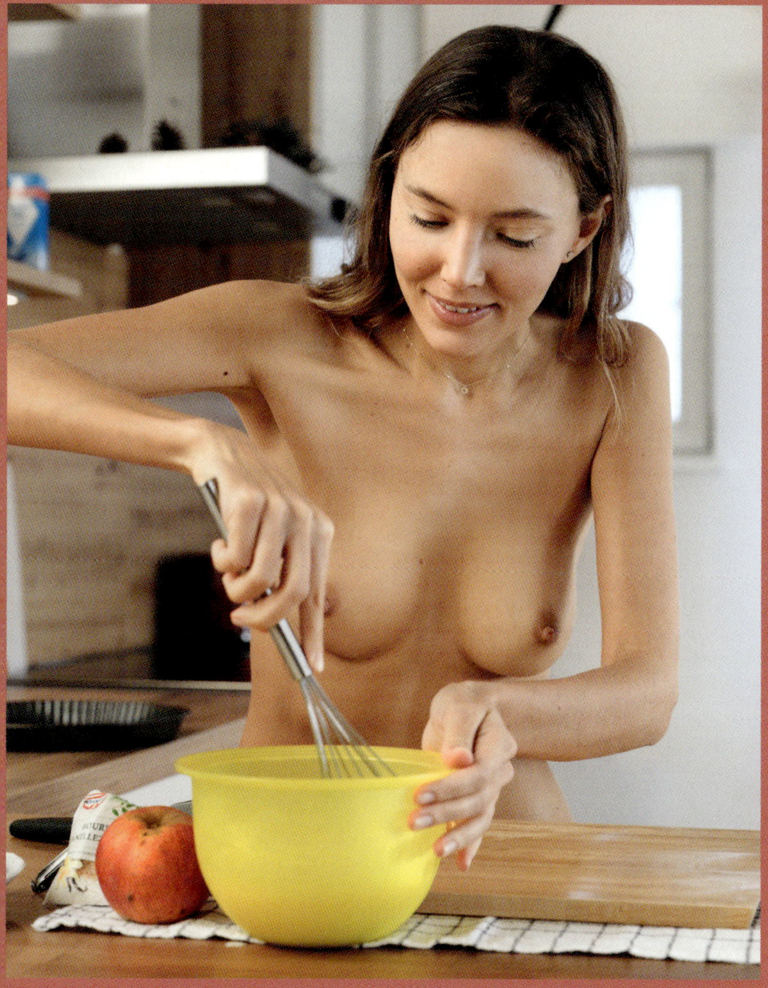

EIER, ZUCKER UND VANILLEZUCKER ZUSAMMEN IN EINE SCHÜSSEL GEBEN

ALLES ETWA VIER BIS FÜNF MINUTEN LANG SCHLAGEN, BIS DIE EIER SCHAUMIG WERDEN

SAUERRAHM UND MEHL HINZUFÜGEN UND ETWA FÜNF MINUTEN LANG GRÜNDLICH VERRÜHREN

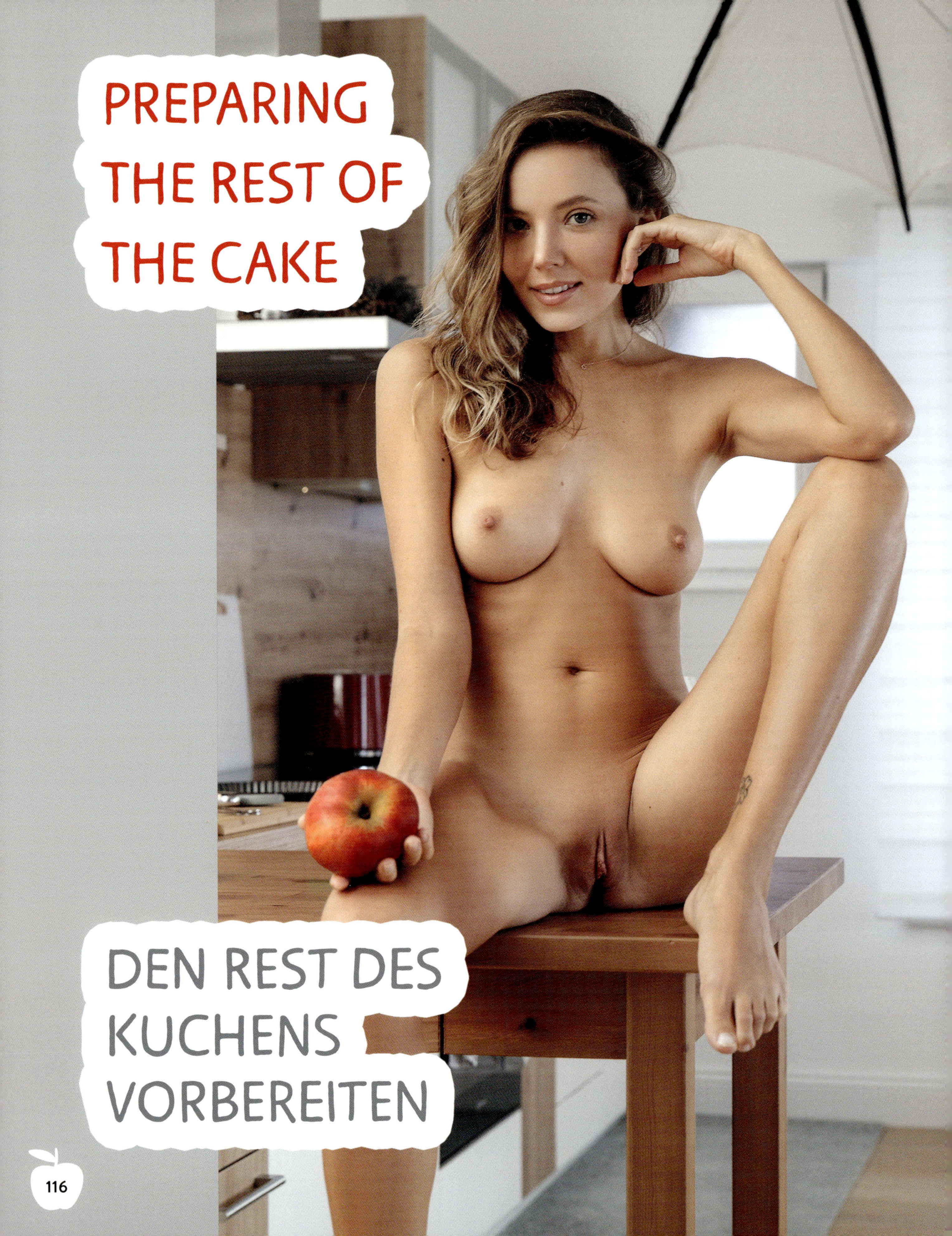PREPARING
THE REST OF
THE CAKE

DEN REST DES
KUCHENS
VORBEREITEN

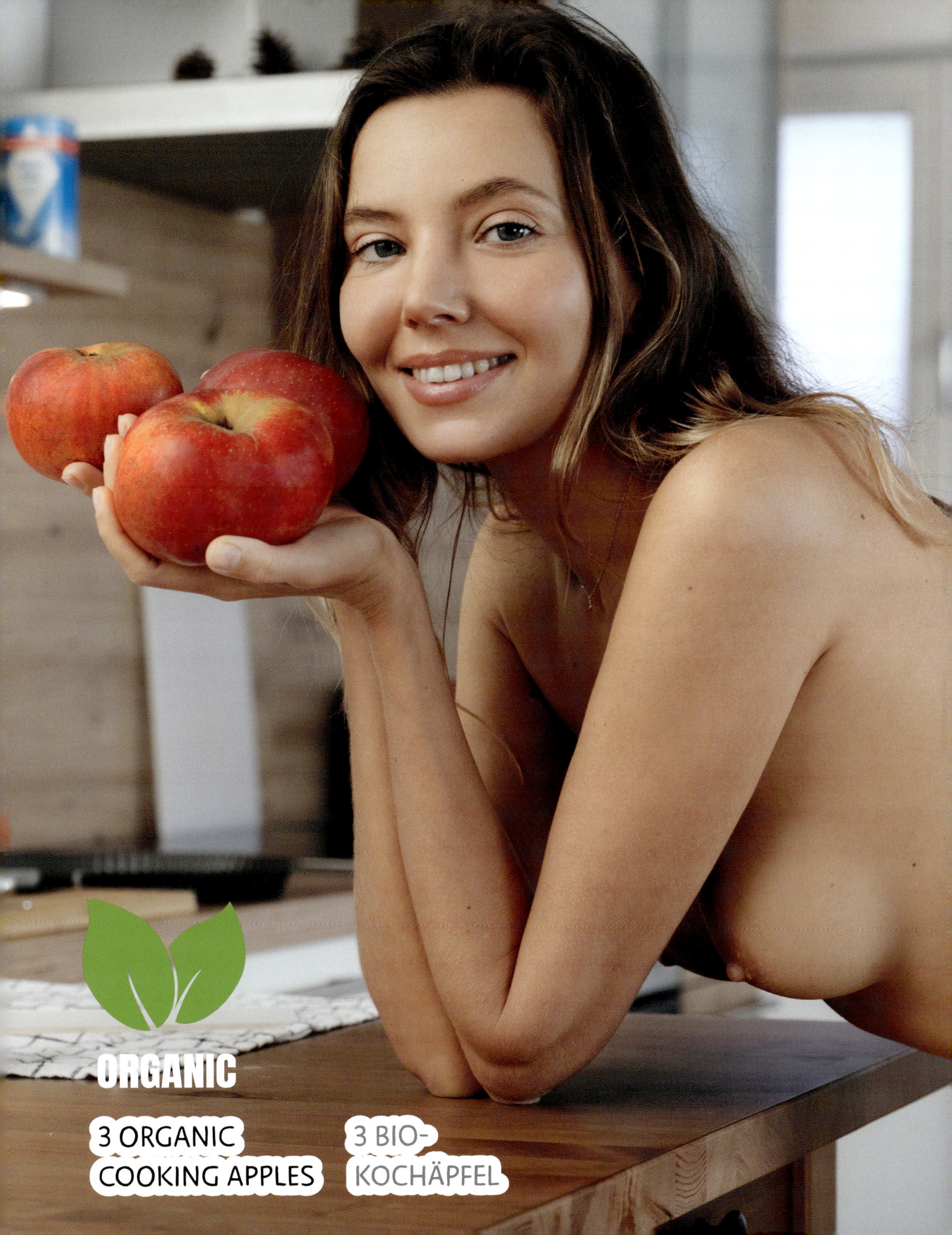

ORGANIC
3 ORGANIC COOKING APPLES
3 BIO-KOCHÄPFEL

CUT INTO QUARTERS AND
REMOVE THE CORES AND SKINS

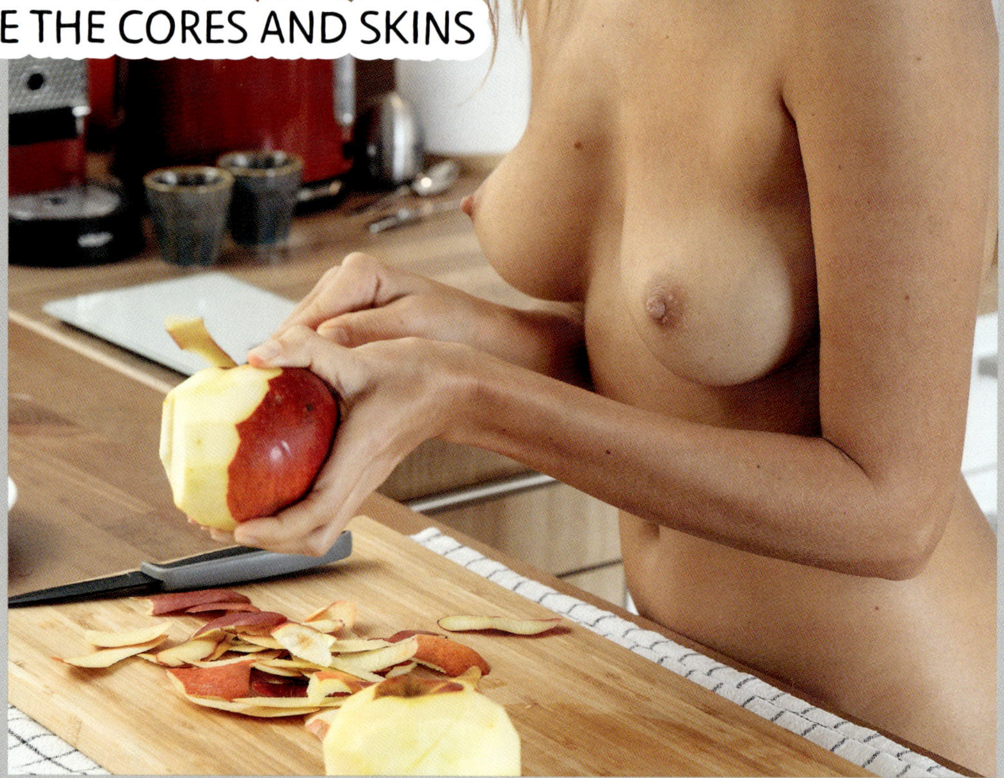

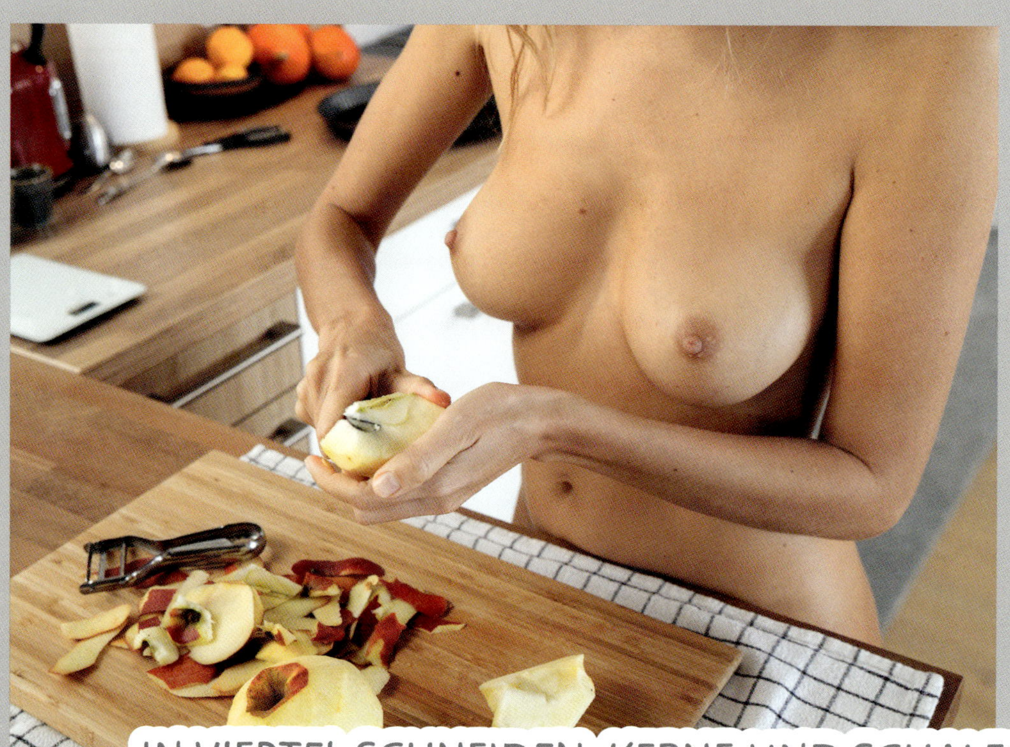

IN VIERTEL SCHNEIDEN, KERNE UND SCHALEN
ENTFERNEN

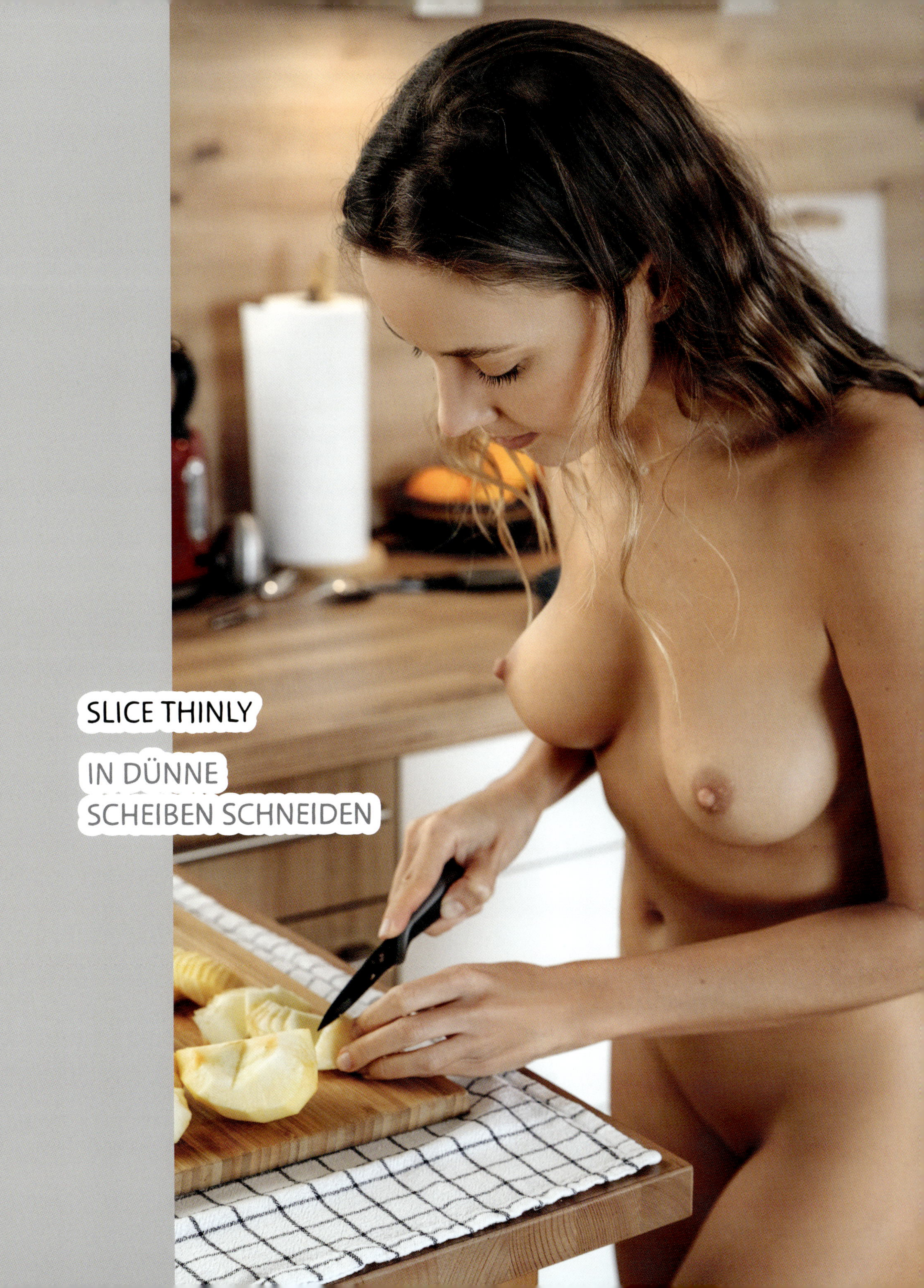
SLICE THINLY
IN DÜNNE
SCHEIBEN SCHNEIDEN

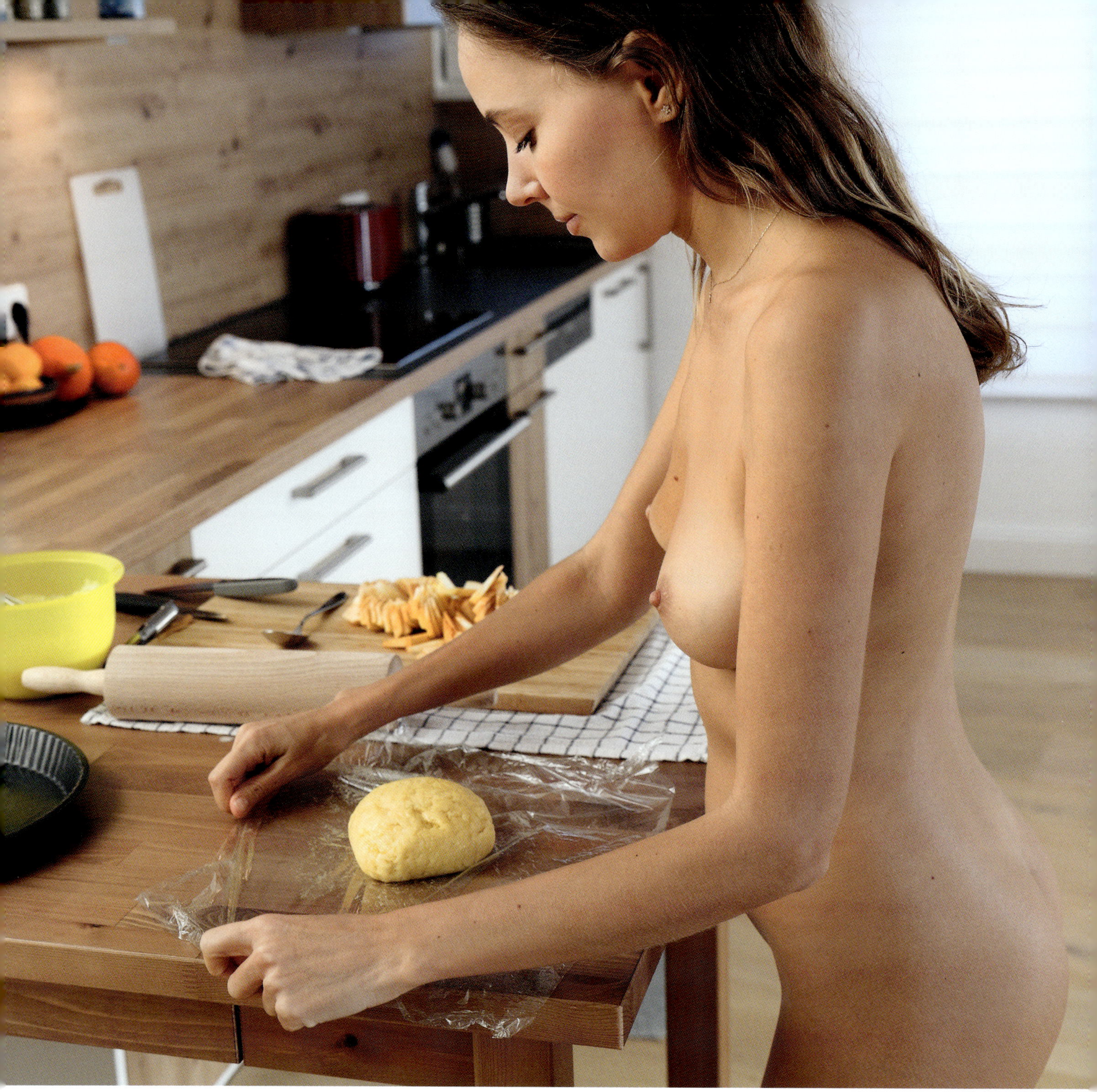

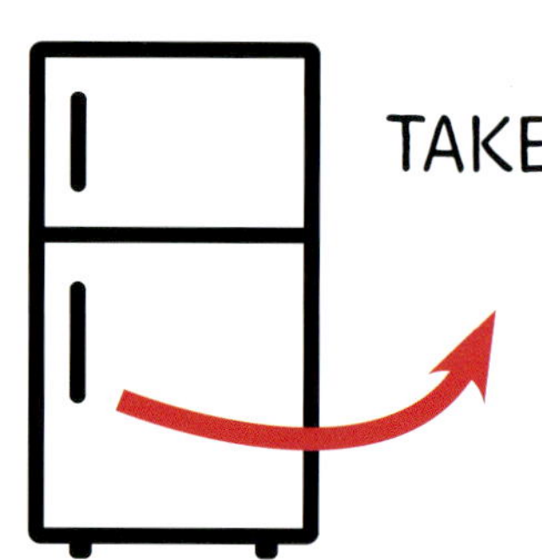

TAKE THE COOLED DOUGH
OUT OF THE FRIDGE

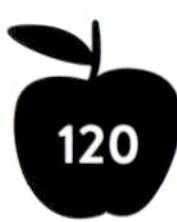

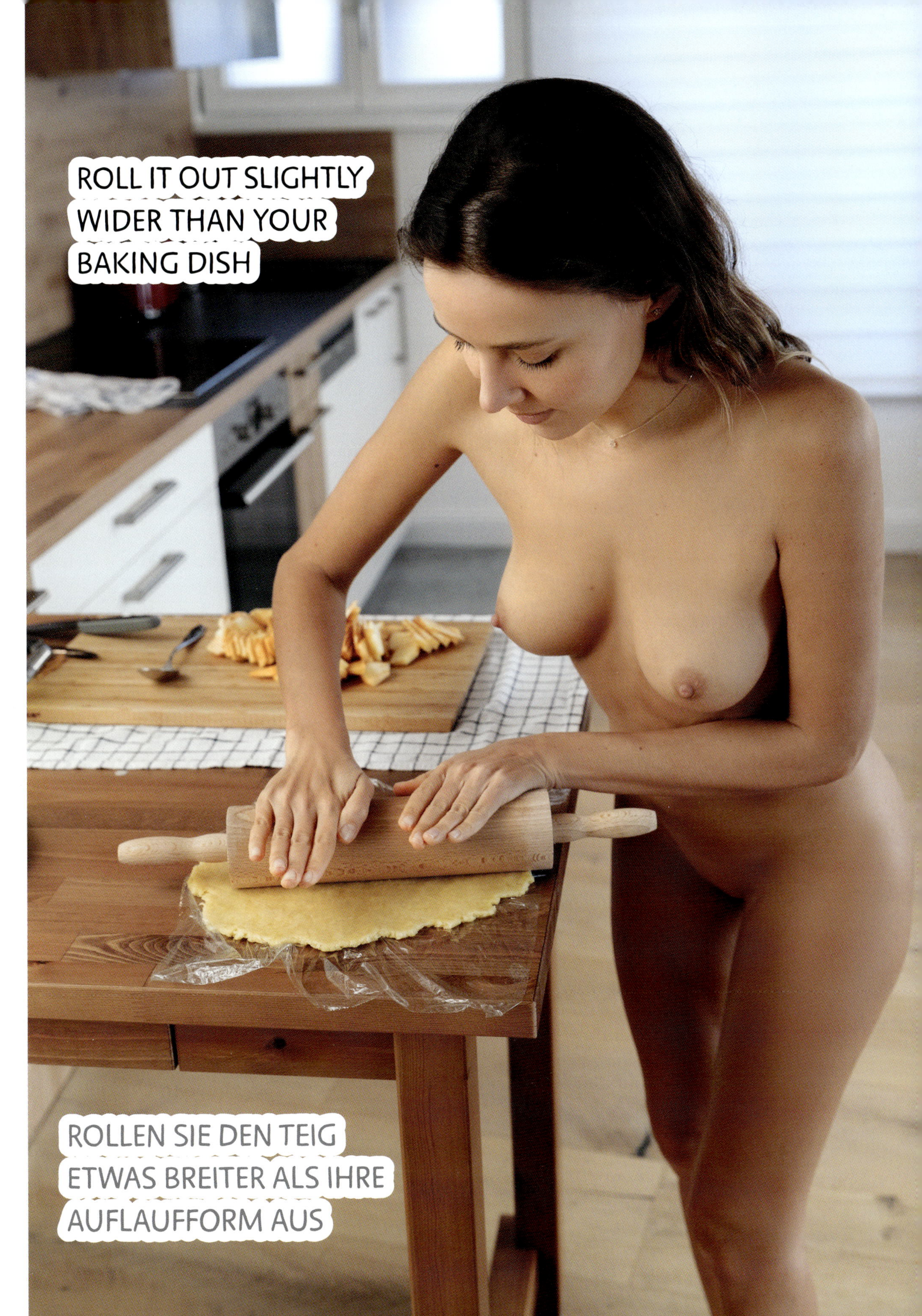
ROLL IT OUT SLIGHTLY
WIDER THAN YOUR
BAKING DISH
ROLLEN SIE DEN TEIG
ETWAS BREITER ALS IHRE
AUFLAUFFORM AUS

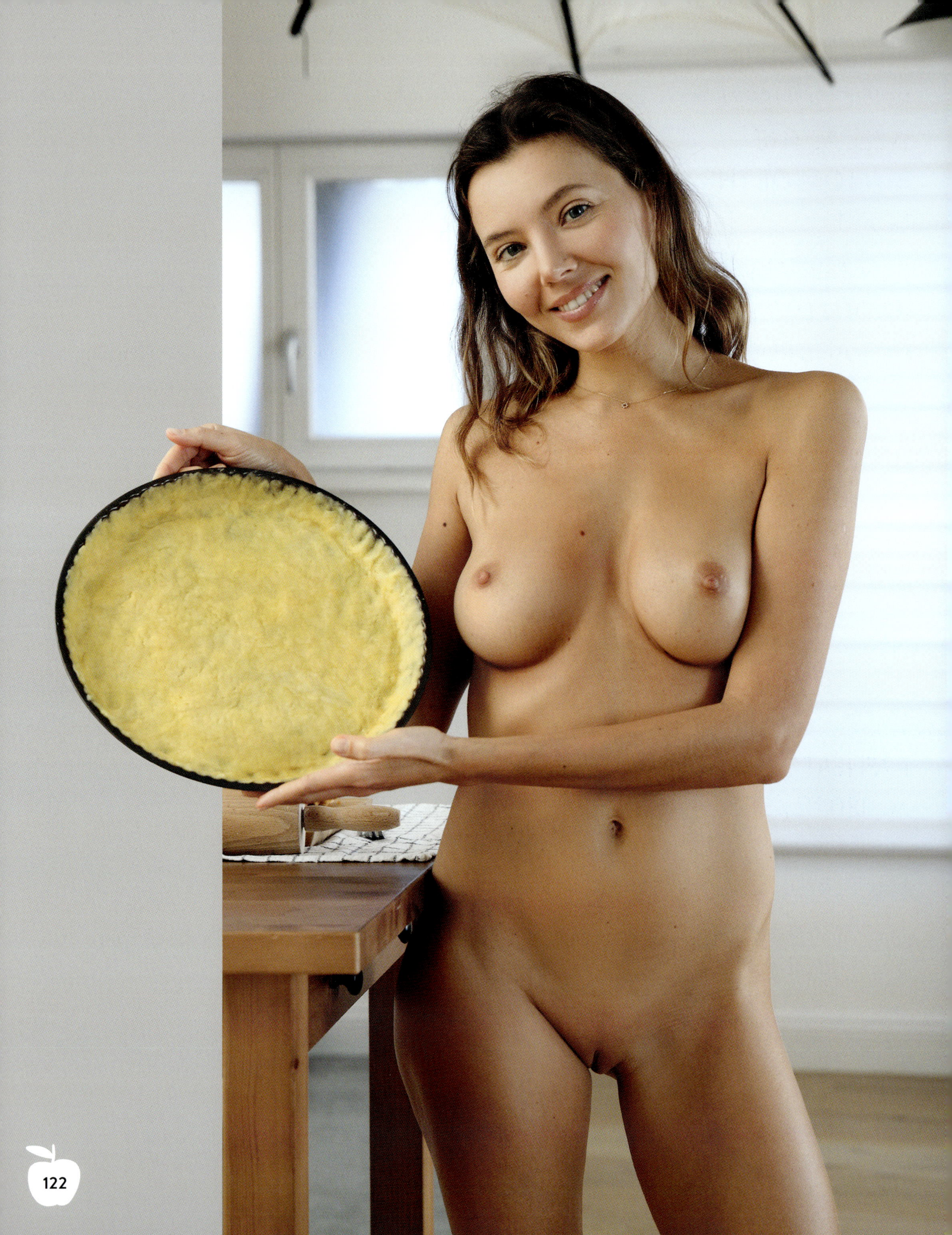

THE DOUGH IS
BEING SQUEEZED
WELL AT THE
BOTTOM OF THE
FORM

DEN TEIG AM
BODEN DER FORM
GUT ANDRÜCKEN

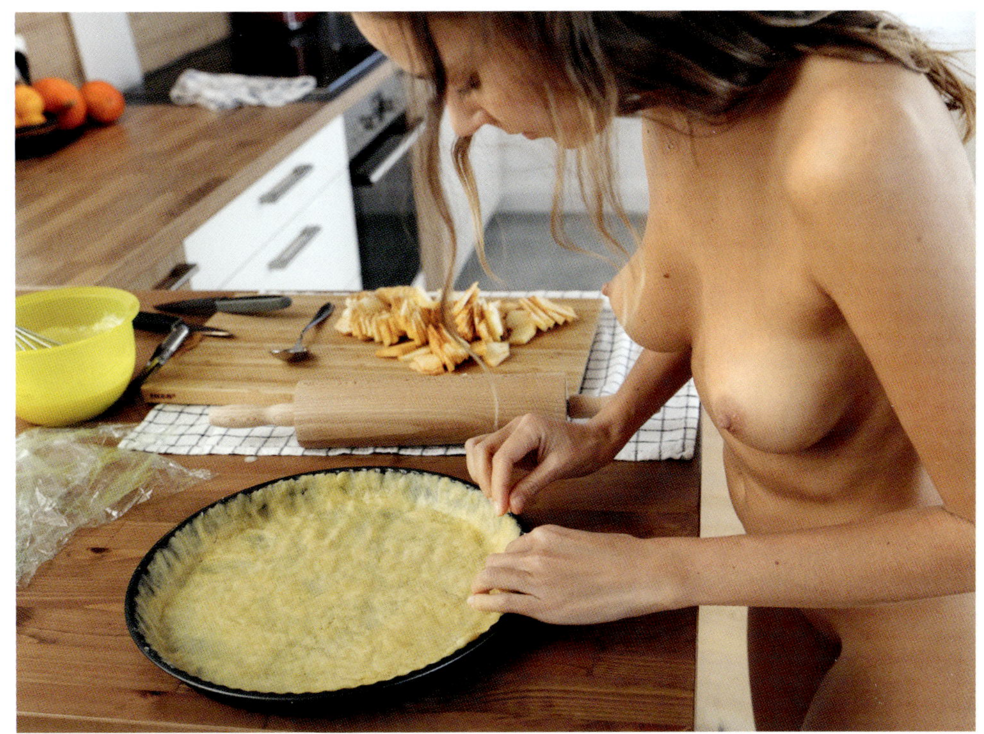

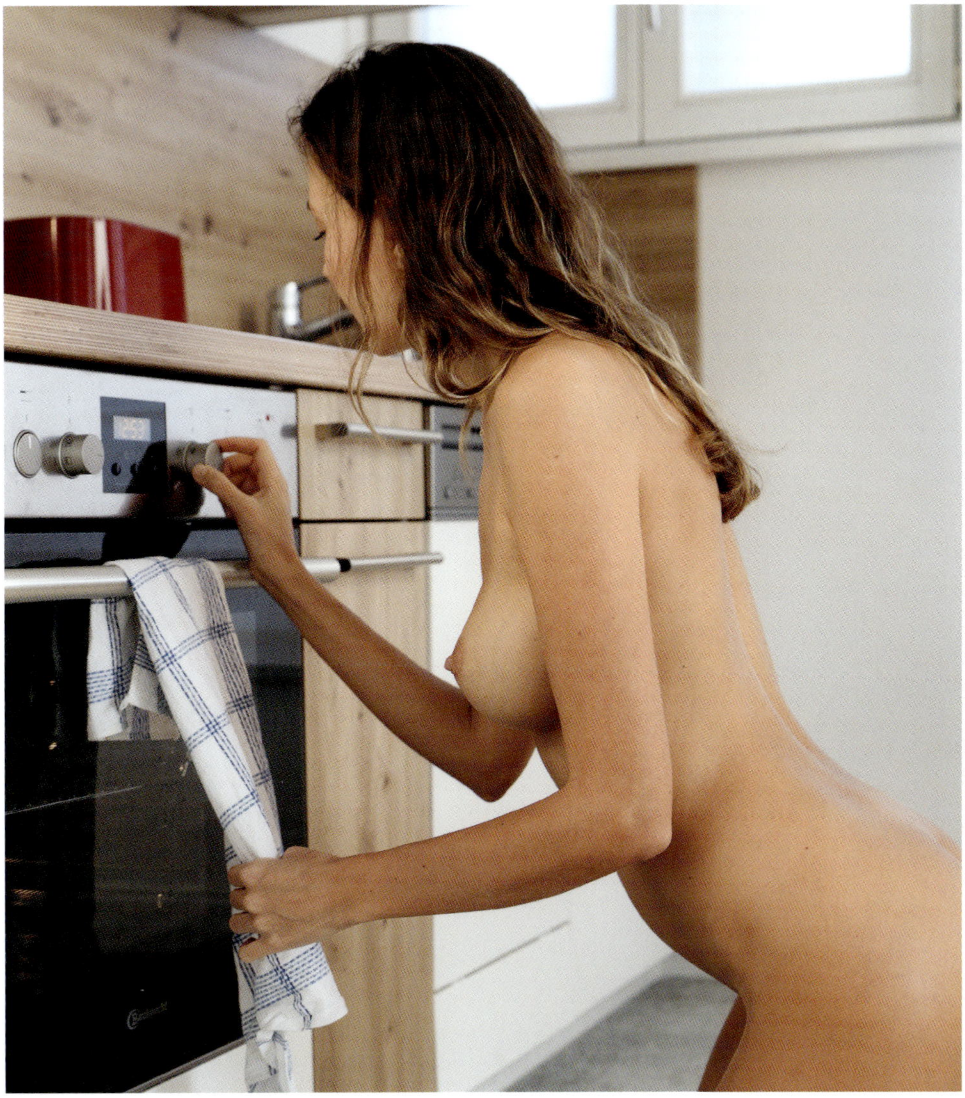

PREHEAT THE OVEN
TO 180 °C / 350 °F

DEN BACKOFEN
AUF 180 °C / 350 °F
VORHEIZEN

ARRANGE THE
APPLE SLICES
NEATLY ...

ORDNEN SIE DIE
APFELSCHEIBEN
ORDENTLICH ...

... ON TOP OF
THE DOUGH

... AUF DEM
TEIG AN

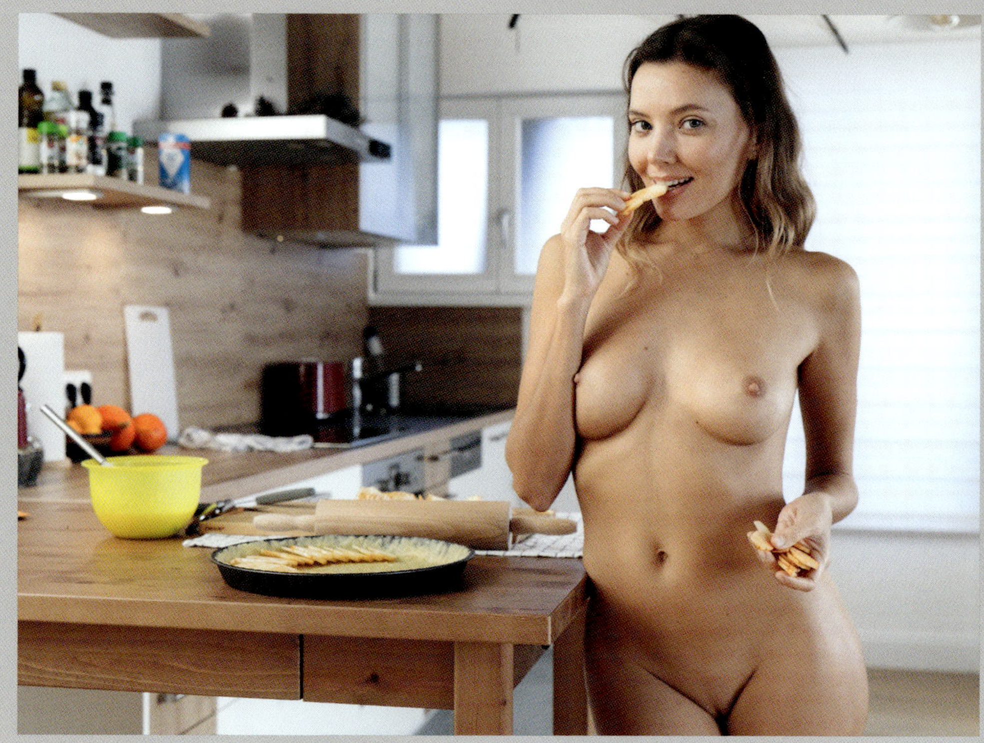

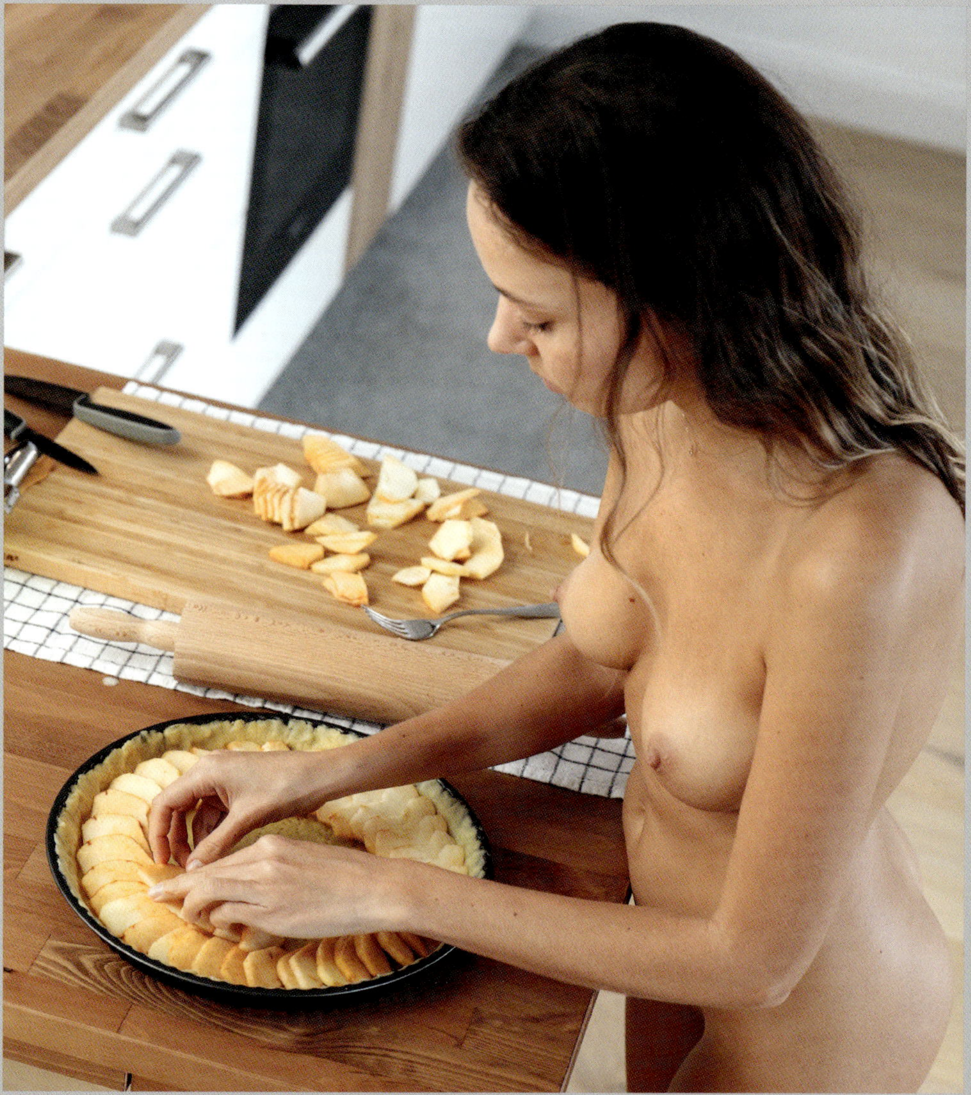

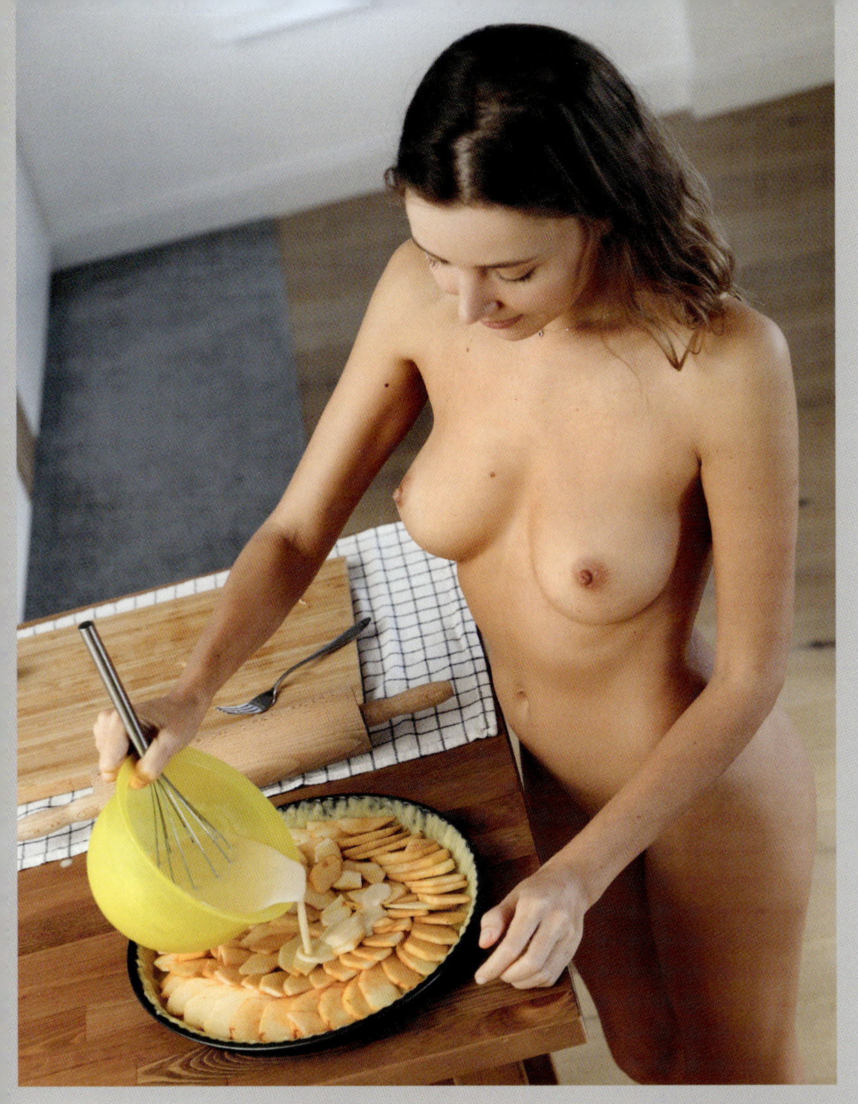

CAREFULLY POUR THE
CREAM FILLING OVER
THE DOUGH BASE

GIESSEN SIE DIE
SAHNEFÜLLUNG VORSICHTIG
ÜBER DEN TEIGBODEN

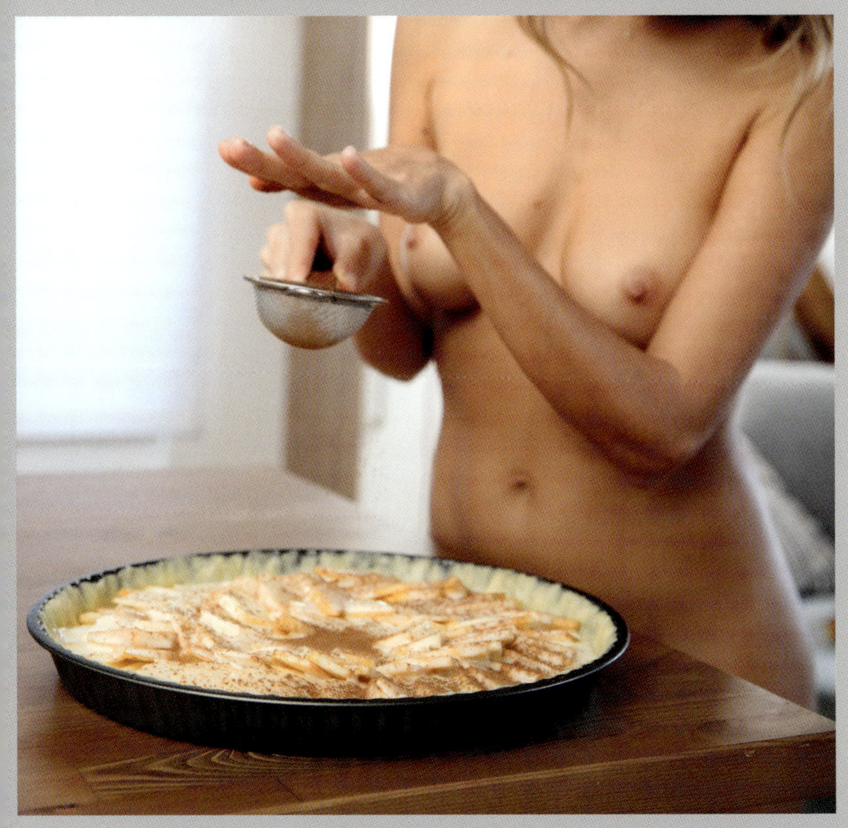

SPRINKLE SOME CINNAMON
ON TOP

STREUEN SIE ETWAS
ZIMT DARÜBER

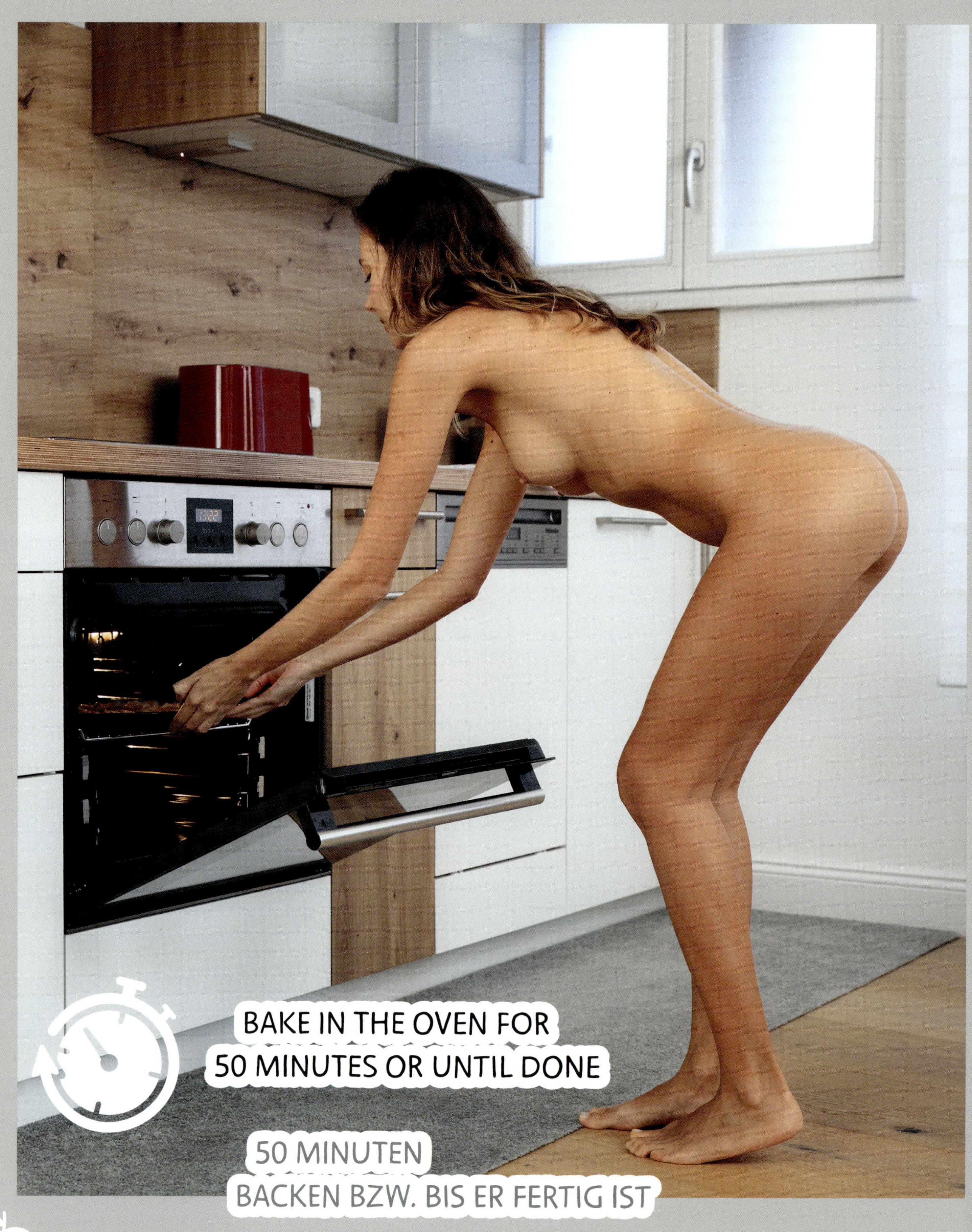

BAKE IN THE OVEN FOR
50 MINUTES OR UNTIL DONE

50 MINUTEN
BACKEN BZW. BIS ER FERTIG IST

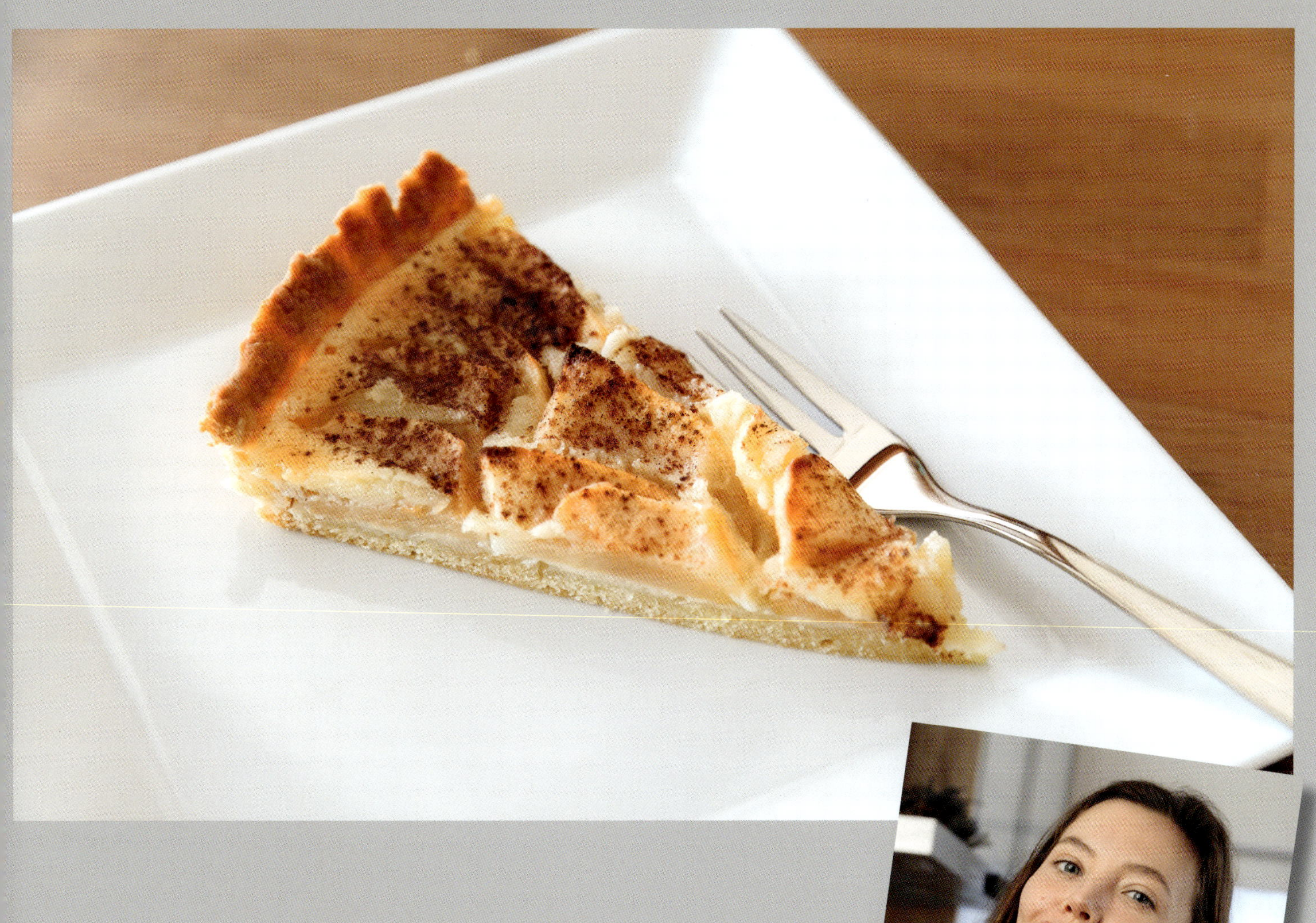

MANY THANKS TO KATYA CLOVER,
WHO BAKES THE BEST
APPLE CAKE IN THE WORLD!

VIELEN DANK AN KATYA CLOVER,
DIE DEN BESTEN
APFELKUCHEN DER WELT BACKT!